THE UNCONSCIOUS
IN SHAKESPEARE'S PLAYS

THE UNCONSCIOUS IN SHAKESPEARE'S PLAYS

Martin S. Bergmann

With an introductory essay by André Green

KARNAC

First published in 2013 by
Karnac Books Ltd
118 Finchley Road
London NW3 5HT

British Library Cataloguing in Publication Data

A C.I.P. for this book is available from the British Library

ISBN-13: 978-1-78049-156-1

Typeset by V Publishing Solutions Pvt Ltd., Chennai, India

Printed in Great Britain

www.karnacbooks.com

To my son Michael and my grandson Daniel Mercutio

CONTENTS

ACKNOWLEDGEMENTS

My first thanks go to my students, who participated in the seminar that carried the title of this book. Their readings of the plays and their willingness to speculate about the role of the unconscious in each play became its foundation. The students arrived at their own interpretations of every play and then criticised my interpretations. They convinced me that reading Shakespeare's plays contributes depth to a therapist's psychoanalytic education.

My gratitude also goes to my wife, who read every chapter and made many valuable suggestions. I also profited from discussing my findings with my son Michael. Special thanks are due to my assistant, Karen Duda, who typed and retyped these chapters and shared her interest in this book.

I owe a very different kind of thanks to the Shakespeare scholars, whose books I read and consulted. I often disagreed with their conclusions, but their work helped me to reach a wider and deeper understanding of the plays. The books I regularly consulted were *Shakespearean Tragedy* (A. C. Bradley, 1904), *Shakespeare: The Invention of the Human* (H. Bloom, 1998), *Shakespeare's Language* (F. Kermode, 2000), *Shakespeare After All* (M. Garber, 2004), *Will in the World* (S. Greenblatt,

2004), *Shakespeare's Philosophy* (C. McGinn, 2006), and *Shakespeare the Thinker* (A. D. Nuttal, 2007).

It gives me great pleasure to acknowledge the help I received from Dr. Catherine Haran (Mrs. Otto Kernberg). She was visiting her relatives in Ireland and mentioned this book, and they told her about a book published by J. C. Bucknill, M.D., FRC, written in 1861, *The Mad Folk of Shakespeare*. One of the aims of my book is to illustrate how differently psychoanalysis enables us to understand Shakespeare's plays and Bucknill's book is astonishing because it shows how deeply a psychiatrist writing before Freud understood Shakespeare.

ABOUT THE AUTHOR

Professor Martin S. Bergmann teaches a course on the history of psychoanalysis in the post-doctoral programme on psychoanalysis and psychotherapy at New York University. He is an honourary member of the American Psychoanalytic Association, an honourary fellow of the Post-Graduate Center for Mental Health, and a member of the International Psychoanalytical Association. His books include *The Evolution of Psychoanalytic Technique* (1976), *Generations of the Holocaust* (1982), *The Anatomy of Loving* (1987), *In the Shadow of Moloch* (1992), *The Hartmann Era in Psychoanalysis* (2000), and *What Silent Love Hath Writ: A Psychoanalytic Exploration of Shakespeare's Sonnets* (2008, with Michael Bergmann). He is the editor of *Understanding Dissidence and Controversy in the History of Psychoanalysis* (2004), which received the Gradiva Award from the National Association for the Advancement of Psychoanalysis. In 1997 he received the Sigourney Award for outstanding contributions to psychoanalysis, presented by the American Psychoanalytic Association, and in 1998 he received the Distinguished Psychoanalytic Educator Award from the International Federation for Psychoanalytic Education. In 2000 he delivered the Freud Anniversary Lecture to the New York Psychoanalytic Institute.

Why this book was written

The reader is entitled to know why this book was written. It was completed in my ninety-eighth year, after I had been a psychoanalyst for sixty-five years and a psychoanalytic teacher for fifty-eight years. Every day for an hour and a half I have been teaching a seminar in psychoanalytic theory and practice to younger therapists. Among my innovations is a course on "The Unconscious in Shakespeare's Plays". Every student is asked to read the same play and report what he or she thinks was the unconscious reason it was written. To my own surprise, my students reported that this course has benefited their work and deepened their understanding of their patients.

Freud and other psychoanalytic pioneers were convinced that understanding the unconscious of an author was the key to his or her work. This is not the philosophy behind this book. Not every reader of Shakespeare is necessarily interested in what was unconscious in his work. There are other interests in Shakespeare's work, for example, Frank Kermode's study of Shakespeare's language, amongst others. The psychoanalytic interest is one of many, but it has its own contribution to make. Just as concerts emerge from the interaction of many instruments, so our understanding of Shakespeare is enriched by different approaches to him. Psychoanalysis assumes that creative writers have the need to both reveal and conceal their own inner conflicts in their works. They leave residues in their works that, if we pay attention, can become building blocks that reveal aspects of the unconscious.

What about the general reader who is not interested in what psychoanalysis has to offer? Some readers may not wish to know what was unconscious in a play nor in Shakespeare's unconscious; I assume they will not proceed beyond this point, but others may find that the questions raised add to the pleasure of reading Shakespeare or that it deepens their understanding of the plays; it is for those readers that this book was written.

There are certain similarities and differences between searching for the unconscious in Shakespeare's plays and a psychoanalytic hour. Typically, analytic patients consciously want the analyst to get to know them, but unconsciously they are also resisting. Analysts then urge patients to free associate. At this point a minor miracle takes place: as patients are free-associating, listening analysts understand something more than the patient thinks they are communicating. If we listen to a play in an analogous way, we can try to read a Shakespeare play as a coded message that we can learn to understand.

At this point I should explain why the same play evokes different interpretations from different psychoanalysts. Such variations have been used to disparage the analytic process as being unscientific but this need not be true. Conversely, if a consensus about the unconscious meaning of the play has been reached it may not mean that this is the best understanding of the play. The same is true for our clinical work. The narrative of any patient, if listened to by a group of psychoanalysts, would not evoke the same reaction in everyone.

All psychoanalysts have learned from Freud to listen to their patients' narratives but at the same time they listen for more, for what patients are afraid to talk about and what they are avoiding saying. They listen to what makes patients guilty, anxious, what is repeated and much more. But above all, psychoanalysts listen to connections patients cannot make and to gaps in the narrative. When any of this is disclosed to patients it may evoke gratitude, anger, or disagreement. In many cases the result is a deepening of the analytic process.

A text, unlike a psychoanalysand, does not respond but as the text unfolds the interpretation is either confirmed or has to be given up. Psychoanalytic listening can be taught to the student only up to a point. When psychoanalysts listen they rely in part on what they have learned;

on the other, they are listening to what the patient has evoked in them and that depends on the individuality of each analyst. An analytic interpretation is usually made at the crossroad to two ideas that the patient has not seen, but some crossroads are richer in meaning than others.

There have been many psychoanalytic studies of Shakespeare's plays and some of them have been referred to in this book. However, bringing together a number of plays as I have done has an advantage, because cross-reference between plays can become a clue to the unconscious connection that an individual play alone does not reveal. To cite one example, we are justified in concluding that Shakespeare's relationship to his mother's breasts suffered a disturbance at some point, otherwise he would not have written these passages in *Coriolanus, Macbeth* and *King Lear*:

VOLUMNIA: The breasts of Hecuba,
              When she did suckle Hector, look'd not lovelier
              Than Hector's forehead when it spit forth blood
              At Grecian sword, contemning. (*Coriolanus,*
              I.iii.43–46)
LADY MACBETH: I have given suck, and know
              How tender 'tis to love the babe that milks me:
              I would, while it was smiling in my face,
              Have pluck'd my nipple from his boneless gums,
              And dash'd the brains out, had I so sworn as you
              Have done to this. (*Macbeth,* I.vii.54–59)

It is not customary to compare breasts to a bleeding forehead but it occurred to Shakespeare. We may not know why, but the comparison is striking. We are also reminded of Lear's curse of Goneril:

LEAR: Into her womb convey sterility,
       Dry up in her the organs of increase;
       And from her derogate body never spring
       A babe to honour her! If she must teem,
       Create her child of spleen, that it may live
       And be a thwart disnatur'd torment to her. (*King Lear,*
       I.iv.233–238)

We infer that some disturbance remained in Shakespeare's unconscious about his experience nursing. Volumnia expresses a disdain for nursing and that can lead us to compare her to Lady Macbeth's desire to be unsexed so that she will be unable to nurse. Goneril is cursed by her father not to have any nursing pleasure. Psychoanalysis cannot give us Shakespeare's biography but can throw light on unusual themes in his plays and their unconscious meanings.

Shakespeare wrote his plays for many reasons: to earn a living, to become known to the English aristocracy (including Queen Elizabeth and later King James) and to give his company a steady flow of new plays, amongst others. To a psychoanalyst there is still a further purpose: to resolve an intrapsychic problem that is disturbing the creative writer at the time. It is this need that this book refers to as the unconscious in Shakespeare's plays. It may be known to the author and not revealed to the audience or it may also be unconscious to the author, but will reveal itself to those who read or hear the play with interest in the unconscious.

Less creative writers are usually satisfied when they deal with one unconscious problem at a time, but truly creative authors weave together a number of unconscious conflicts in every play, making the task of the interpreter more difficult but also more of a challenge.

Creative writers also face another choice: they can create an original plot or find a plot elsewhere in literature and change it to serve their own purposes. Shakespeare employed both methods.

Freud has found that the Oedipus complex is the nucleus of every neurosis and some of Shakespeare's plays deal primarily with this complex; *Richard III*, *Julius Caesar* and *Hamlet* are examples. Freud also found that unacknowledged homosexual wishes could lead to paranoia; *Othello* and *The Winter's Tale* deal with the danger of paranoia; *The Merchant of Venice* deals with the danger of homosexual submission. The oedipal wish can also make it difficult for a father to let his daughter marry another man; this conflict appears in a number of Shakespeare's plays, including *A Midsummer Night's Dream*, *The Tempest* and *King Lear*. Of these plays, *King Lear* goes the deepest and deals with Shakespeare's wish to regress and to convert his daughters into his mother. One of Freud's achievements was the realisation of the conflict between superego and ego, or the realisation that our morality can be in conflict with our identity. *Measure for Measure* deals with this problem.

I have written this book with three audiences in mind. First, as a model for psychoanalytic societies to include a course on the unconscious in Shakespeare's plays (which is also the title of this book); second, with the hope that it will find its way to students and teachers of Shakespeare, who will find that I have added something to the understanding of Shakespeare; third, that the book will add both pleasure and interest to those readers who already love Shakespeare.

The way Freud made his initial discovery of the Oedipus complex is well documented in the exchange of letters between Freud and Fliess (Masson, 1985). In a letter written on 15 October 1897, Freud informed his friend that he had discovered in his self-analysis being in love with his mother and jealous of his father, which he considered a universal event in early childhood. He went on to draw further evidence from *Oedipus Rex* and *Hamlet*. These two tragedies acted as midwives to Freud's discovery of the Oedipus complex. Shakespeare influenced Freud but in what way remains a question.

We can see Shakespeare as an important ancestor of psychoanalysis if we acknowledge the significant role of self-knowledge in various plays. The command "Know thyself" has come down to us from Apollo's temple in Delphi but it was the contribution of psychoanalysis to transform self-knowledge into a therapy to cure emotional illnesses.

In *The Merchant of Venice* Antonio complains:

ANTONIO: In sooth I know not why I am so sad.
It wearies me, you say it wearies you;
But how I caught it, found it, or came by it,
What stuff 'tis made of, whereof it is born,
I am to learn.
And such a want-wit sadness makes of me,
That I have much ado to know myself. (*The Merchant of Venice*, I.i.1–7)

At the beginning of *King Lear* Regan assesses her father thus:

REGAN: 'Tis the infirmity of his age; yet he hath ever but slenderly known himself. (*King Lear*, I.i.285)

And of course there is Hamlet.

HAMLET: I have of late—but wherefore
I know not—lost all my mirth, forgone all custom of
exercises; and indeed it goes so heavily with my disposition
that this goodly frame, the earth, seems to me a sterile
promontory. (*Hamlet*, II.ii.280–283)

It is depression, not anxiety, that had become such a burden to Shakespeare's characters and it is the puzzle of depression that prompts them to acquire self-knowledge. We are entitled to the hypothesis that Shakespeare struggled and feared depression and his creativity represented a victory over his depression, but *The Tempest* implies that eventually this battle was lost.

The way Shakespeare understood and used the unconscious emerges as an intriguing question demanding an answer. That the search for the answer should lead very often to an unexpended understanding of the play gave me a sense of serendipity.

Bloom used Shakespeare's astonishing capacity to understand the unconscious to deprecate Freud. He accuses the discoverer of the Oedipus complex of being its victim, forced even consciously to deny that it was Shakespeare from whom he learned the nature of psychoanalysis. In this book I will show that psychoanalysis has made it possible to understand an aspect of Shakespeare not available before Freud.

It has often been argued that Shakespeare's plays cannot be submitted to psychoanalytic scrutiny because the players cannot be put on the analytic couch and asked to free associate. However, another problem, of greater significance, has not, to my knowledge, been raised: Is a great playwright like Shakespeare engaged in creating real people? Or is it the prerogative of genius to be capable of going beyond the creation of ordinary men and women and creating people larger than life?

There are great writers—Anton Chekhov comes to mind—who have a sharp eye and give us characters more extreme than those we meet, but they are recognisable personalities taken from real life. Shakespeare is not one of these writers. He creates personalities that are not only greater than life but also possess qualities not likely to be found in real people.

Psychoanalysis is a theory about real people: how they function and how they can be helped to live a better life. Is psychoanalysis applicable to the men and women Shakespeare has brought to life, even if they do not exist in real life? To my surprise and perhaps also to the surprise of my readers, the answer is a qualified yes. Shakespeare's creations are not real people but their psychic structure is modeled on that of real individuals whom Shakespeare endowed with an unconscious. He allows us to overhear their soliloquies as they confront their preconscious and at times even their unconscious.

The difference between the psychoanalytic way of looking at a play and the non-psychoanalytic way became sharply delineated in chapter thirteen on Othello. It has frequently been asked what Iago's motive was for the systematic way he proceeded to arouse Othello's jealousy and bring about not only Desdemona's death but also to orchestrate the manner in which she was killed. Scholars tend to agree with and quote Coleridge's famous statement that Iago suffered from "motiveless malignancy". By its very nature psychoanalysis cannot accept that anything is motiveless; we may not be able to find a motive but the emphasis on the unconscious demands that everything observed and particularly a sustained and most powerful drive such as that in Iago has a motive.

The next question is whether a dramatist of genius should give us access to the hero's motivation. Is a drama where the motive is withheld from the audience a greater or lesser work of art than one that ultimately supplies the answer? The value of the psychoanalytic interpretation of any play will be influenced by our answer to this question.

Freud first formulated the psychoanalytic approach to literature in 1908, eight years after the publication of his "Interpretation of Dreams". In a short essay, "Creative Writers and Day-Dreaming", Freud began by citing the question of Cardinal Ippolito D'Este to Ariosto, who wanted to know "from what sources that strange being, the creative writer, draws his material?" (Freud, 1908: p. 143). He noted that the writer typically cannot answer this question and concluded that the answer remains unconscious to the writer. Freud then made his first contribution by noting that "every child at play behaves like a creative writer" (Freud, 1908: p. 143) because children rearrange things in a way that pleases them while playing. The creative writer does the same thing as the child at play, but unlike the playing child the writing produced must evoke interest in the reader. When the child grows older fantasising replaces play with a basic difference: children are not ashamed of their play but adults are often ashamed to share their fantasies. Writers must disguise their fantasies well enough in their work or they will develop a writing inhibition. Freud concluded that a happy person does not fantasise; only unsatisfied wishes give rise to fantasies.

In a paper written in 1904 but not published in Freud's lifetime, "Psychopathic Characters on the Stage", Freud emphasised the similarity between the spectator at a play and the child at play. Freud had some harsh things to say about the spectator.

> The spectator is a person who experiences too little, who feels that he is a "poor wretch to whom nothing of importance can happen", who has long been obliged to damp down, or rather displace, his ambition to stand in his own person at the hub of world affairs; he longs to feel and to act and to arrange things according to his desires—in short, to be a hero. And the playwright and actor enable him to do this by allowing him *to identify himself* with a hero. (Freud, 1942: p. 305)

I myself am not sure that Freud's heirs did him a service by publishing a paper he did not make public himself but what matters is that Freud brought theatre going close to fantasising. I am convinced that reading *Othello*, *Macbeth* or *King Lear* did more for me than make me identify with them. The opposite feeling, dissociation, may be at least as important.

Freud's next observation, that creative writers may create their own stories or rework a version out of material created by a predecessor, is relevant to Shakespeare's work. When Shakespeare departs from his sources it indicates that the sources did not meet his requirements and had to be changed. The creative writer can "split his own ego" and transform an inner conflict into conflicts between different personalities. Up to this point Freud derived creative writing essentially from fantasy and daydreams. Without referring to Freud directly, Ernst Kris, in "Prince Hal's Conflict" (1948), had the essay by Freud in mind when he stated, "Some great writers seem to be equally close to several of their characters, and may feel many of them as parts of themselves. The artist has created a world and not indulged in a daydream" (Kris, 1948: p. 506).

On the last page of his essay Freud raised a further problem: when fantasies are communicated they cause no pleasure for the listener (unless the listener is included in them). When creative writers present their fantasies they are so disguised that we are not repelled by them and instead experience pleasure. How writers accomplish this, Freud called, their "innermost secret"—what is essential in an "ars poetica". To do so the writer "softens the character of his egoistic daydreams" and bribes us by offering us "fore-pleasure". Writers succeed if they at least temporarily help us rework our inner problems. Pertinent criticism is that Freud's view fails to differentiate between the profound works of literature that contribute the very core of Western civilisation and the popular potboilers that become best sellers for some time but are soon forgotten.

What is characteristic of the insights of Shakespeare's characters is that they are never strong enough to prevent an impending catastrophe. If a psychoanalytic patient behaved like a Shakespearean character Freud would have described it as a "negative therapeutic reaction". At this point drama and therapy part ways: what would be considered a therapeutic failure adds depth to a work of art.

If we are really successful in offering a psychoanalytic interpretation of a Shakespeare play we should arrive at a unifying theme that governs the work, and if we find it we will experience something akin to the eureka feeling and the whole play will gain new meaning. However, this is not always possible and that is the reason the same play can be interpreted differently by different analysts. In spite of the differences of psychoanalytic schools, a correct interpretation of a play carries conviction and is usually experienced as beautiful.

As I got deeper into this work I realised that I have not always sharply differentiated between two very different kinds of insight and I would like to share this differentiation with my readers. The first type of data I have collected are examples of how Shakespeare frequently endowed his characters with insight we now designate as psychoanalytic. A typical example is Angelo's insight in *Measure for Measure* Angelo, when he realises his sexual attraction to Isabella is based on aggressive wishes to "raze the sanctuary" (*Measure for Measure*, II.ii.171). This insight has no curative power to deter Angelo but it enhances our interest in his character.

The second type of insight sheds light on something Shakespeare himself did not realise. For example, I found that in the graveyard scene, Hamlet remembers a childhood homosexual love for Yorick before he can re-find his love for Ophelia. I believe this connection enriches our understanding of Hamlet, but did Shakespeare himself understand that Hamlet could re-find his love for Ophelia only after he allowed himself to remember?—that is, allowed a memory of a homosexual love to "return from repression"—how much he loved Yorick as a child? Probably not. I conclude that creative writers can transmit unconscious ideas of which even they are not aware to their audiences.

The first type of insight would be recognised by anyone familiar with psychoanalysis but the second may not, and in fact has not been realised earlier. Since we cannot summon either Hamlet or Shakespeare to answer the question, it will be the consensus of my readers that will eventually decide whether I have applied a personal, idiosyncratic interpretation to *Hamlet* or a valid additional understanding.

Shakespeare and Freud

In the third and last volume of Freud's biography, published in 1956, Ernest Jones stated, "The three great men in whose personality Freud seems to have taken the most interest, and with whom he perhaps partly identified himself, were Leonardo da Vinci, Moses and Shakespeare" (Jones, 1957: p. 428). Jones then goes on to point out that in each of these people there was a problem of identity; they all fit into what Freud called "family romance". According to Freud, Leonardo had two mothers, one biological and one adoptive; Moses was an Egyptian; and the plays of Shakespeare were actually written by Edward de Vere, the seventeenth Earl of Oxford. This conviction amounted to an obsession in Freud's case. Jones offers no explanation about Freud's need to question the identity of his heroes but one immediately thinks of the possibility that Freud questioned whether he was the biological child of his own father. There is some evidence that he wished his older and more vigorous half-brother was his father.

In the essay "The Moses of Michelangelo" Freud revealed something about himself that may throw some light on this relationship to Shakespeare.

> ... works of art do exercise a powerful effect on me, especially those of literature and sculpture, less often of painting. This has occasioned me, when I have been contemplating such things, to spend a long time before them trying to apprehend them in my own way, i.e., to explain to myself what their effect is due to. Wherever I cannot do this, as for instance with music, I am almost incapable of obtaining any pleasure. Some rationalistic, or perhaps analytic, turn of mind in me rebels against being moved by a thing without knowing why I am thus affected and what it is that affects me. (Freud, 1914a: p. 211)

Freud is telling us, that when works of art exercise a powerful effect on him, he submits this impact to free associations. The awe that the work of art evokes in him also creates an anxiety that he tries to master. By contrast to Freud, I assume most mortals experience this awe as a privilege we have been granted: the privilege of experiencing the greatness of the artistic achievement. Perhaps Freud found it difficult to bear such awe because it seemed feminine to him and evoked a fear of homosexuality, but in this case we should remember that it was Freud himself who taught us that we all have bisexual wishes that are not apparent and should not be repressed but rather subjected to sublimation. The awe before a great work of art may turn out to be an example of such sublimation. The need to understand the secret of its impact may be a competitive feeling belonging to the Oedipus complex.

In the same essay Freud also refers to Hamlet.

> Let us consider Shakespeare's masterpiece, *Hamlet*, a play now over three centuries old. I have followed the literature of psycho-analysis closely, and I accept its claim that it was not until the material of the tragedy had been traced back by psycho-analysis to the Oedipus theme that the mystery of its effect was at last explained. (Freud, 1914a: p. 212)

There is something strange about this paragraph. He says the psycho-analytic literature on *Hamlet* convinced Freud that the "Oedipus theme" solved the mystery of the play for him, while in fact it was his interpretation of Hamlet's indecision that created this literature.

Freud goes on to explain:

> Does Shakespeare claim our sympathies on behalf of a sick man, or of an ineffectual weakling, or of an idealist who is merely too good for the real world? And how many of these interpretations leave us cold!—so cold that they do nothing to explain the effect of the play and rather incline us to the view that its magical appeal rests solely upon the impressive thoughts in it and the splendour of its language. And yet, do not those very endeavours speak for the fact that we feel the need of discovering in it some source of power beyond them alone? (Freud, 1914a: p. 213)

Only after Freud unburdened himself of Shakespeare did he begin his discussion of Michelangelo's Moses. According to Freud, Shakespeare did not wish to imply that Hamlet was sick, ineffectual, a weakling or an idealist too good for this world, nor does Freud believe that the magical appeal of the play rests on the thoughts expressed and the splendor of the language. Shakespeare succeeded in evoking our sympathy for Hamlet because we unconsciously identify with both his oedipal wishes and the paralysis of action that they evoked.

Shakespeare discovered the power of the unconscious to determine our actions and even our whole destiny, but he did not name this power and differentiate the unconscious from the conscious. For one moment, in the physician's scene in *Macbeth*, Shakespeare did consider the possibility that the physician could "minister to a mind diseased" (*Macbeth*, V.iii.40) but rejected it by saying that when it comes to the mind "Therein the patient / Must minister to himself" (V.iii.45–46) or perform a self-analysis, as we would say today.

As to the relationship between Shakespeare and Freud and the finding of the Oedipus complex, the discovery could not have been made on the basis of *Hamlet* alone. Freud needed his clinical experience with neurotic patients, his self-analysis and his knowledge of both *Oedipus Rex* and *Hamlet* to make it. It was the unique combination that made the discovery possible.

As to the question of whether Shakespeare or Freud should be called the discoverer of psychoanalysis, my book leads to a new and interesting answer. If we wish to define psychoanalysis as stressing the significance of the unconscious on our lives, Shakespeare deserves a prominent place, while if we stress that psychoanalysis is a method of cure for mental illness then Shakespeare gets hardly any credit. I found the journey that led to this differentiation a very interesting one and hope my readers will share this experience.

So that the plays can speak to each other, I have divided this book into sections, but this division is not absolute. The chapter on *Hamlet* would also fit into the section on the Oedipus complex and *The Tempest* also belongs to the section dealing with the daughter as a replacement for the mother. Shakespeare seldom devoted a play to one theme. Plays not included would have added to the book but excessive bulk had to be avoided.

PART I

THE PIVOTAL POSITION OF HAMLET

HAMLET'S ENIGMAS

André Green
Translation by Catherine Lindenman

For a psychoanalyst, it can only be an additional advantage to approach Shakespeare in the twilight of life, and, indeed, how could one find fault that Shakespeare is being read through the eyes of wisdom rather than filtered through the enthusiasm of youth? To demonstrate the wisdom of Shakespeare requires lessons in life and not the fiery passions of one's younger years. Let us thank heaven that God has granted Martin Bergmann a long life, both for him to profit from his long experience as a psychoanalyst as well as to conduct this study of Shakespeare. With the eyes of the marvellous clinician that he is, Martin Bergmann lays out his analysis of the text. It is a great honour for me to have been asked by him to introduce this valuable work. In doing so, however, I must draw attention to one thing: the language of Shakespeare is not my native tongue. Even if I have taken the trouble to read the text in the original, I have found it necessary to consult translations to make the text more readily comprehensible. Even so, how can one appreciate Shakespeare without understanding his original language, his writing, his poetic thinking, and finally the magic of his prose?

I have not found it possible to write a preface to this monumental work, in which most of the chapters are devoted to the analysis of individual plays by Shakespeare. Confronted with an ensemble of

3

such magnitude I had to choose. I have therefore selected the most well-known play, one considered Shakespeare's masterpiece and the object of innumerable commentaries: *Hamlet*. I have relied in this relatively short piece on the work that I have previously done in my own book on Shakespeare: *Hamlet and Hamlet*. I will discuss here only certain themes taken up in that book, to which I refer any reader who is interested.* My contribution here should be understood as an homage to the monumental work of Martin Bergmann, which no lover of Shakespeare can from this point on ignore.

This will not be a psychoanalytic investigation of *Hamlet*. Rather, I have chosen to raise certain questions and associations that have occurred to me while reading this play. It is a tragedy, as we will see, that I can only describe as diabolical, in that its internal structure seems to me to reveal certain underlying ideas that are far from apparent at a first reading. This study will not attempt to exhaust the enigmas of this tragedy but rather will be confined to specific questions raised by features of the play's own internal structures.

To begin: As the cock crows and the ghost is about to disappear from the view of Horatio and his comrades, it seems to force this commentary from its witnesses:

BARNARDO: It was about to speak when the cock crew.
  HORATIO: And then it started like a guilty thing
              Upon a fearful summons. (*Hamlet*, I.i.147–149)

This is a surprising remark in that it presents the phantom as a guilty party. But of what exactly is the assassinated king guilty? From the first moments of his meeting with the ghost, the titular character says, "Be thou a spirit of health, or goblin damned" (I.iv.40).

Once more, suspicion is expressed. Is the ghost a heavenly envoy or a demon? The question is asked of the spectre but without any response that could explain it. As Hamlet prepares to follow the ghost to one side, Horatio invites him to use more caution.

HORATIO: What if it tempt you toward the flood my lord,
            Or to the dreadful summit of the cliff
            That beetles o'er his base into the sea,
            And there assume some other horrible form
            Which might deprive your sovereignty of reason,

> And draw you into madness? Think of it.
> The very place puts toys of desperation,
> Without more motive, into every brain
> That looks so many fathoms to the sea
> And hears it roar beneath. (I.iv.69–78)

Horatio renews the question of its demonic nature as yet another reason to mistrust the nature of the ghost. When the ghost finally does speak, it alludes to "the foul crimes done in my days of nature" (I.v.12) without giving the audience the remotest idea of what these "foul crimes" were. This nonetheless serves to reinforce the suspicion of guilt without revealing in any way the cause of it. When the ghost finally descends into hell, Hamlet is seized by a veritable frenzy, while treating the phantom in an almost flippant manner, a sign of uncontrolled jubilation. But to what can we attribute this? A remark by Hamlet sheds some light: "Touching this vision here, / It is an honest ghost, that let me tell you". (I.v.137–138).

This is proof that up to the moment of the ghost's revelation, Hamlet is still asking himself the question: angel or demon?

When Hamlet later sees the actors arrive, he rejoices and plays with them, improvising as if one of them. At this point, a comparison arises between the prince, who is charged by his dead father with a vengeance that he defers, and the actor, who is capable of feigning passion. Hamlet says, "And all for nothing? / For Hecuba!" (II.ii.509–510). After having compared himself unfavourably to the actor, Hamlet sees his character as that of a whore:

HAMLET: That I, the son of the dear murderèd,
          Prompted to my revenge by heaven and hell,
          Must like a whore unpack my heart with words. (II.ii.536–538)

Throughout the tragedy, the following triptich is repeated: cowardly son, actor, whore. Hamlet later decides that the play will be the trap in which he will catch the conscience of the king. Having despaired of getting Claudius to confess, Hamlet will use the play to reveal the truth. Can one imagine that the tragedy of Hamlet could reveal some truth?

In the celebrated monologue in Act III, an alternative is presented: "To die, to sleep" (III.i.60) or "To sleep, perchance to dream" (III.i.65).

The choice, therefore, is as follows: either the definitive sleep of death or the dream of life after death. It is the revelation of the dream that frightens Hamlet. Somewhat later a new puzzle arises as Hamlet explains death as, "The undiscovered country, from whose bourn / No traveller returns, puzzles the will" (III.1.79–80). A new hesitation arises: if no voyager can return to life, then the ghost can only be an illusion that denies his nothingness. Otherwise he could have said: "Die, sleep, nothing more—or sleep, perhaps dream".

Then Claudius, in turn, compares himself to a whore, as had Hamlet.

CLAUDIUS: The harlot's cheek, beautied with plastering art,
             Is not more ugly to the thing that helps it
             Than is my deed to my most painted word. (III.i.51–53)

For his part, Hamlet cannot stop himself from blaming Ophelia, who is completely innocent, of course. For Hamlet, Ophelia is already Gertrude, and Gertrude is the unfaithful queen. The reader, incidentally, may well ask if the queen has indeed participated in the murder of the king. For Hamlet that is not the question. The fact that she has let herself be seduced by Claudius is sufficient to prove her guilt. So Hamlet can only wait to be betrayed by Ophelia as he was by his mother: "I'll no more on't, it hath made me mad". (III.1.140–141). This avowal is not pretended. Hamlet is not playing at being mad. He is mad.

Meantime, while preparing the actors for their play, Hamlet recommends the natural approach, that is to say, truth in their interpretation. Thus life makes real-life people of actors, and in the theatre, they are true-to-life beings, a meaningful reversal. Amid all this playing and dissembling, the only character worthy of trust is Horatio. Horatio is not one to be influenced by passions that could alter his perceptions; this is why Hamlet charges him with observing the king and says to him, "And after we will both our judgments join / In censure of his seeming." (III.ii.76–77). This precaution is designed as a protection against the scheming ghost from hell, of whom Hamlet now says, "It is a damnèd ghost that we have seen". (III.ii.72). One sees it; however, suspicion does not fade.

In all the speculations about Hamlet's hesitations, I believe that one minimises the following idea: he could be the object of a demonic curse while at the same time becoming the plaything of the ghost. So, prior to the player's performance, Hamlet banters while first playing the innocent and then the rogue. He then speaks to Ophelia, all the while making explicit sexual jokes, treating her as if she were a whore. Polonius, for his part, forecasts his own fate: he acted in plays at the university, and this included the role of Cesar, whom Brutus killed. In other words, he will once more be assassinated by the very man who would be his son-in-law. As for Hamlet, he continues to play out the ambiguities. In the scene where he sends Ophelia to the convent/brothel, he oscillates between the love that he must deny and the hate that dwells within him. We see him waver between tender, loving feelings and obscene ones.

The theatrical performance is naturally made up of two parts: a very explicit pantomime followed by a spoken play. However, during the pantomime, Claudius and Gertrude seem to understand nothing of what it clearly represents. Is it that the words of the play alone can provide the meaning of its message—to the point that Claudius is forced to interrupt the performance? At this moment, when the trap has worked, Hamlet inexplicably withdraws into himself; and, at the same time he reveals his plan to kill Claudius, something the king without any doubt understands. Next, when Lucianus enters on stage, Hamlet comments: "This is one Lucianus, nephew to the king". (III.ii.221). This comment underscores Hamlet's relationship to the king. In other words, two crimes are condensed: the murder of the king by his brother and the murder of Claudius by Hamlet, his nephew. But Hamlet still needs Horatio's help to interpret the reactions of Claudius. Likewise, Polonius judges his spying necessary in order to interpret the words of Hamlet, whose intentions he now understands.

As soon as Claudius no longer doubts Hamlet's intentions, he accuses himself of hesitating—as had Hamlet while watching Claudius pray in the chapel scene. "I stand in pause where I shall first begin / And both neglect". (III.iii.42–43). Claudius cannot know what position to adopt: Ask for pardon? But what if he can't repent? He says, "Try what repentance can. What can it not? / Yet was can it when one cannot repent?" (III.iii.65–66). Transference of hesitation. Hamlet has the opportunity to execute his vengeance, when he finds Claudius at prayer. He rejects it, out of the fear that by killing Claudius he would send his soul immediately to heaven. A new excuse to postpone his vengeance.

In the famous bedroom scene (perhaps the most moving of the tragedy), we witness not only the direct conflict between Gertrude and Hamlet but also, through their exchange, the contrast between the murdered king and his brother, the murderer. First, Hamlet denounces the duplicity of his mother.

GERTRUDE: Have you forgot me?

HAMLET: No, by the rood, not so,

You are the queen, your husband's brother's wife,

And, would it were not so, you are my mother. (III.iv.14–16)

It is at this moment that Hamlet dashes towards his mother, simultaneously brandishing and contrasting the portraits of his father and Claudius. Frightened by his agitation, Gertrude cries out; Polonius, alarmed, tries to come to her aid but in doing so betrays his presence behind the curtain. Hamlet kills him.

Thus Hamlet kills Polonius, believing him to be Claudius at the very moment he is attacking his mother, reproaching her for having become the wife of Claudius. Mother and son mutually accuse each other.

The Queen blames her son for this bloody deed:

GERTRUDE: Oh what a rash and bloody deed is this!

HAMLET: A bloody deed? Almost as bad, good mother,

As kill a king, and marry with his brother. (III.iv.27–29)

So why does Hamlet kill Polonius? The obvious answer would be as follows: he takes him for Claudius. At the same time, let us remember the frenzy that comes upon him in the Queen's bedchamber, the very place of her nocturnal revels with his father and now his uncle. However, in killing Polonius, Hamlet does not for a moment dream that it could be him and could not suspect he has killed the father of Ophelia. In addition, one can only be struck by his attitude for having killed the very one who was destined to become his father-in-law. This is an act that makes Ophelia forever forbidden to him; this is a truth of which he will never speak. Moreover, in what follows, never will he have the slightest compassion for the one whose father he has killed. But if the act is an unconscious displacement, it reveals his intentions to kill his uncle, something which makes Claudius determined to assassinate him to avoid being killed himself. The tragedy moves, then, from a project for avenging the death of King Hamlet to a project involving the prince in purely murderous goals. Claudius has understood this (Act III.iii.63) and plans to poison him, as he has already done to the father.

Meanwhile, to return to the bedchamber, Hamlet passes from threats to injunctions. He forbids his mother to welcome Claudius into her bed. Everything contrasts his father with Claudius. The father carries features of the highest nobility while his brother presents the polar opposite. In all of this, Hamlet believes his mother to be the victim of a demon and says to her, "What devil was't / That thus hath cozened you at hoodman-blind?" (III.iv.76–77). This entire scene plays on duplicity and deception. Hamlet at this point is compelled to call upon the ghost to intervene and remind him of his filial duties—that is, his task is to avenge his father without touching his mother. It is worth emphasising that the ghost appears only to Hamlet in this scene: this strongly suggests that the ghost is a hallucination of the prince. The prince at this point is deterred from touching his mother, so his murderous urges next move to Rosenccrantz and Guildenstern, themselves commanded by Claudius to kill him. Hamlet's own vengeance is still being deferred.

To add to this already complicated mix, Fortinbras enters the drama in Act IV, scene four. By means of a ruse, he claims the territorial right of his king to cross Denmark in order to reach Poland, presumably with the aim of attacking a territory there. In fact, Fortinbras will try to take advantage of this pretext to replace Hamlet and install himself on the Danish throne. A few remarks are necessary to explain this character. It turns out that Hamlet, then, has two doubles: Laertes and Fortinbras. The first, who burns to avenge the death of his father, is prepared to rid himself of Hamlet. He accepts the rigged duel that Claudius proposes and that will end in the final catastrophe: the death of Gertrude and, as a consequence, that of Claudius. By contrast, Fortinbras presents as an irreproachable prince. At the same time, he intends to assert his rights on Denmark, although Shakespeare fails to clarify the reasons invoked to justify his forcibly reclaiming territories lost by his father and then annexing the kingdom of Denmark. We will return to this.

Fortinbras is the other double of Hamlet, a double who seems deserving of admiration and whose character seems the opposite of Hamlet's. He is steadfast in his aims, does not let himself get detoured from them, but rather acts to fulfill them without delay. He seems (to the degree that Shakespeare makes him known to us) devoid of any hesitation caused by useless scruple and seems, therefore, like the hero of the tragedy who will be confirmed in his goals of reclaiming the lands lost by his father. Besides this, he is the nephew of the present king of Norway and is named after his late father, the former king, just as Hamlet carries the same name as his father and is the nephew of Claudius. The symmetry of the two characters is not accidental: Shakespeare constructs one as the foil for the other. Fortinbras is a straightforward character, with no romantic intrigue to disturb him and with no reason to doubt the faithfulness of his mother or that of a young woman who he would love. On all these points, I believe that Shakespeare has sketched a character designed to place him in relief to Hamlet. Finally, Fortinbras appears at the very moment Hamlet is exiled.

In truth, as the tragedy unfolds, the spectator never ceases to wonder about the text he is hearing—a text teeming with ambiguities. For example, could the spectator have already forgotten the recounting of the past, detailed with such clarity by Horatio about the present dangers weighing on Denmark? Horatio did not fail to relate the circumstances governing the duel between Hamlet senior and Fortinbras senior.

HORATIO: Our last king,
Whose image even but now appeared to us,
Was as you know, by Fortinbras of Norway
Thereto pricked on by a most emulate pride,
Dared to the combat; in which our valiant Hamlet—
For so this side of our known world esteemed him—
Did slay this Fortinbras; who by a sealed compact,
Well ratified by law and heraldy,
Did forfeit (with his life) all those his lands
Which he stood seized of, to the conqueror;
Against the which a moiety competent
Was gagèd by our king, which had returned
To the inheritance of Fortinbras
Had he been vanquisher; as, by the same comart
And carriage of the article designed
His fell to Hamlet. (I.i.80–95)

Everything here seems to have happened according to clear rules that bear no special discussion or interpretation. Of all the characters of the tragedy, Horatio is the last to suspect of misrepresenting the truth. However, the remainder of the play suggests a more ambiguous situation. On the one hand, the young Fortinbras, son of the former king, seems bent on warlike plans in order to reconquer the lands lost by his father and, in doing so, appears to contest the legitimacy of the original pact. The young prince of Norway, after being lectured by the present king, then seems to return to a more peaceful behaviour after the intervention of Claudius. This attitude only seems to be peaceful. We soon witness him returning to his original mission on the pretext again of proceeding to Poland. This ploy will allow him to seek Claudius' permission to cross Denmark, an obvious stratagem allowing him to set foot in the country. We are now nearing the end of the tragedy, where the same dilemma raised at the beginning of the play arises once more.

Next, in the dialogue with the gravedigger, certain key dates are revealed. We learn that the day when Hamlet senior triumphed over Fortinbras is the very same day on which Prince Hamlet was born. Thus Yorick is evoked along with special emphasis on his tender care of the baby Hamlet. We understand a close, paternal affection on the part of Yorick. Then, suddenly, at the graveyard, we learn of the arrival of Ophelia, followed by a royal cortege in charge of burying her. Almost simultaneously, Laertes and Hamlet arrive and soon begin arguing over who can be said to have loved Ophelia—all this carried out in the grave itself. They act as if mad; they are separated; Claudius ponders his misdeeds. Meanwhile, Hamlet informs Horatio of his regret for having gotten carried away against Laertes. Claudius then proposes a rigged joust, to which Hamlet agrees, seemingly without suspicion. Hamlet, in conversation with Horatio, tells him of his friendship for Laertes, who is also his double. Claudius sets the trap into which Hamlet will fall.

At the beginning of the play, we have heard several allusions concerning the ghost, whose guilt was mentioned but without any possibility of our knowing to whom it is associated. Now we are presented with a rigged joust where the foils have been dipped in poison. A suspicion begins to rise in us. The duel between the elder Fortinbras and the elder Hamlet, was it completely in order? The elder Fortinbras having been vanquished, his son is not prevented from trying to claim rights on Denmark, a fact which seems to imply that he doesn't consider the outcome of his father's duel as absolutely definitive. Pure speculation, but it is a contrast that may well arise in the mind of the spectator, more or less unconsciously. In the end, the elder Fortinbras was declared defeated, while today Hamlet will die by treachery.

The hour of the duel arrives and Hamlet presents himself, telling Horatio "the readiness is all" (V.ii.194–195). This final scene is one containing all possible confusions. First, concerning sincerity, here Hamlet's repentance in regard to Laertes becomes mixed with appearances. The duplicity of the king is obvious since he has poisoned both swords, as well as the cup from which Hamlet is intended to drink during the fight. It is Osric, the very image of the conventional style of the court, whose refereeing is therefore irreproachable, who remains unaware of Claudius' deceit.

As the duel begins, Hamlet is the first to take the advantage. Gertrude drinks to the health of her son and poisons herself, this as a result of the drink destined for Hamlet, who instead has offered it to his mother. As the combat proceeds, Hamlet suspects some irregularity and switches the foils. Meanwhile, the queen faints and the duelists become heated in their duel. Hamlet wounds Laertes, who confesses all. Blood flows everywhere; Hamlet cannot escape death, and the queen realises that the cup has been poisoned.

At last, Hamlet decides to kill Claudius, whom he sends to join his mother. Hamlet charges Horatio to live in order to reveal his insights and to relate the truth. He supports the cause of Fortinbras before breathing his last breath.

At the end, Fortinbras arrives to record the carnage. He doesn't fail to recall, "I have some right of memory in this kingdom / Which now to claim my vantage doth invite me". (V.ii.368–369). Thus, the beginning and the end are connected in that Horatio's speech at the beginning of the tragedy leads up to the final commentary of Fortinbras. The contradiction is clearly exposed here: the two visions cannot coexist. It is to the spectator alone to resolve this fundamental enigma. One thing is certain: the innocence of Hamlet, who dies sacrificed even though he was the legitimate successor to his father.

I will end with some remarks that underscore the richness of the paradoxes of ambiguity, the machinations of lies, the infinite complexity of betrayal, the mysteries of enigmas. Frank Kermode has underscored the role of hendiadys, a rhetorical device "where the meaning of everything hangs on a kind of abnormal doubling brought about by a pathological intensification of the proceedings" (Kermode, 2000: p. 32). Everything is double in *Hamlet*, beginning with the double meanings of words, the double structure of the plot, the general duplicity between appearances and truth. This is an important key for a reading of *Hamlet*. A reader as well-trained as Kermode could not have been deceived. With this process in mind, much is clarified and the mysteries of this tragedy can be better understood.

As is apparent, my reading is rather different from that of Martin Bergmann. It does not contradict his. It suggests another way of dealing with what I have called "the enigmas of Hamlet"; not with the character of the prince, but with the tragedy of which he is the hero. This reading, then, completes that of Martin Bergmann, who, it is hoped, will consent to consider it a complement to his.

* * *

The late André Green was regarded by many as the most original psychoanalytic thinker of our generation. He has also written about Shakespeare, so when I asked him to write an introduction to this book I did not know he was already gravely ill. Several months before he passed away he sent me this chapter, which I am very happy to include as a memorial to him.—Martin S. Bergmann.

CHAPTER ONE

Hamlet: the inability to mourn and the inability to love

This chapter on *Hamlet* carries a special responsibility in this book. It is Shakespeare's deepest and psychologically most complex play as well as the longest running at nearly 4000 words. It is one of the greatest works of world literature. *Hamlet* contains more than 600 words not found in previous works by Shakespeare and new to the English language (Greenblatt, 2004: p. 308). Shakespeare needed new words, mostly to express psychological concepts not put into words before. Previous tragedies had already established Shakespeare as an eminent playwright but *Hamlet* is a milestone in the exploration of human interiority. A psychological study of the new words Shakespeare created could be an enriching experience.

We compare Hamlet to an earlier Shakespeare character, Richard III. There is nothing ultimately mysterious about Richard, whereas we never fully understand Hamlet. Shakespeare made the discovery that characters are more interesting and lead richer inner lives when they do not fully know themselves.

Hamlet is also the first work of literature to receive a special psychoanalytic interpretation, establishing the first bridge between psychoanalysis, a method of cure for mental illness, and world literature. In this book it will also be used to establish the difference between the psychoanalytic interpretation and other interpretations.

Freud made his famous interpretation of Hamlet's inability to carry out the command of his father's ghost in a letter to his friend Wilhelm Fliess on 15 October 1897 (Masson, 1985) and published it in his book *The Interpretation of Dreams* in 1900. Hamlet's paralysis of action was unconsciously based on the fact that he himself harboured the same wishes as his uncle: to kill his father and sexually possess his mother.

The play has been of special interest to psychoanalysts. First, while any significant work of literature can be interpreted from a psycho-analytic point of view, *Hamlet* seems to demand such an interpreta-tion because Hamlet's inability to carry out the ghost's command to kill his uncle points to an unconscious conflict that psychoanalysis can explain.

The second reason is historical: when Freud first communicated his great discovery of the Oedipus complex to Fliess on 15 October 1897 he included the following observation:

> I have found, in my own case too, [the phenomenon of] being in love with my mother and jealous of my father, and I now consider it a universal event in early childhood. If this is so, we can under-stand the gripping power of Oedipus Rex. ... the Greek legend seizes upon a compulsion which everyone recognizes because he senses its existence within himself. Everyone in the audience was once a budding Oedipus in fantasy and each recoils in horror from the dream fulfillment here transplanted into reality, with the full quantity of repression which separates his infantile state from his present one. (Masson, 1985: p. 272)

Since the discovery of the Oedipus complex ranks as Freud's single greatest discovery, this letter can claim to represent the birthday of psy-choanalysis. It clearly shows that in his self-analysis Freud did not reach the full oedipal wish, only a mild derivative of it. What enabled Freud to discover the raw Oedipus complex was his familiarity with *Oedipus Rex*. In the same letter, Freud goes on to include *Hamlet*.

> Fleetingly the thought passed through my head that the same thing might be at the bottom of Hamlet as well. I am not think-ing of Shakespeare's conscious intention, but believe, rather, that

a real event stimulated the poet to his representation, in that his unconscious understood the unconscious of his hero. How does Hamlet the hysteric justify his words, 'Thus conscience does make cowards of us all'? How does he explain his irresolution in avenging his father by the murder of his uncle—the same man who sends his courtiers to their death without a scruple and who is positively precipitate in murdering Laertes? [This was a slip on Freud's part. Hamlet actually murders Polonius; Laertes later challenges Hamlet to the duel in which both are killed.] How better than through the torment he suffers from the obscure memory that he himself had contemplated the same deed against his father out of passion for his mother, and—'use every man after his desert, and who should 'scape whipping?' His conscience is his unconscious sense of guilt. And is not his sexual alienation in his conversation with Ophelia typically hysterical? And his rejection of the instinct that seeks to beget children? And, finally, his transferral of the deed from his own father to Ophelia's? And does he not in the end, in the same marvelous way as my hysterical patients, bring down punishment on himself by suffering the same fate as his father of being poisoned by the same rival? (ibid. pp. 272–273)

In this letter Freud interprets the Oedipus complex of Hamlet before he made any such interpretation of a living patient. The two plays discussed in this letter, *Oedipus Rex* and *Hamlet*, thus acted as midwives to Freud's discovery.

The idea that *Oedipus Rex* and *Hamlet* are expressions of the Oedipus complex was an insight by Freud. Either play alone may not have created the insight; it was the combination of what is common to both of them that make the insight possible. The dictionary defines insight as internal sight with eyes of the mind, which is only subsequently subjected to logical analysis. To psychoanalysis, insight is the result of something unconscious becoming conscious. It is the main tool of the analytic investigation.

In *The Interpretation of Dreams* Freud made an interesting differentiation between the two books that made it possible for him to formulate the Oedipus complex.

Another of the great creations of tragic poetry, Shakespeare's *Hamlet*, has its roots in the same soil as *Oedipus Rex*. But the changed treatment of the same material reveals the whole difference in the mental life of these two widely separated epochs of civilization: the secular advance of repression in the emotional life of mankind. In the *Oedipus* the child's wishful phantasy that underlies it is brought into the open and realized as it would be in a dream. In *Hamlet* it remains repressed; and—just as in the case of a neurosis— we only learn of its existence from its inhibiting consequences. (Freud, 1900: p. 264)

My own formulation of the differences between the two sources of inspiration is that in *Oedipus Rex* the Oedipus complex has become conscious but only as the fate of one man. It remained for Freud to generalise that oedipus is every man and woman. In *Hamlet* the Oedipus complex appears as a symptom, the inability to act, which Freud interpreted as due to guilt. There is no logical connection between *Oedipus Rex* and *Hamlet*; connecting the two is itself an example of psychoanalytic insight.

In the letter to Fliess, Freud makes two direct quotations from *Hamlet*; both pertain to what Freud will come to call the superego after 1923: "Thus conscience does make cowards of us all" (which appears in Act III, scene 1, line 83) and "use every man after his desert, and who should 'scape whipping?'" (Act II, scene 2, lines 485–486) It would take over twenty years for Freud, in writing *The Ego and the Id* (1923), to understand all this on a theoretical level: namely that it is the psychic structure Freud called the ego that brings about repression and then the ego no longer knows what has been repressed. At the same time, another psychic structure that Freud called the superego has its own connections to the repressed and demands punishment for these unconscious wishes; the superego is so structured that it does not recognise that repression has taken place and demands punishment even for repressed wishes.

In *The Interpretation of Dreams* Freud observed:

Hamlet is able to do anything—except take vengeance on the man who did away with his father and took that father's place with his mother, the man who shows him the repressed wishes of his own childhood realized. Thus the loathing which should drive him on to revenge is replaced in him by self-reproaches, by scruples of conscience, which remind him that he himself is literally no better than the sinner whom he is to punish. Here I have translated into conscious terms what was bound to remain unconscious in Hamlet's mind; and if anyone is inclined to call him a hysteric, I can only accept the fact as one that is implied by my interpretation. (Freud, 1900: p. 265)

This paragraph summarises Freud's interpretation of Hamlet's indecision. Immediately following this passage, Freud goes on to throw light on another aspect of Hamlet's behavior.

The distaste of sexuality expressed by Hamlet in his conversation with Ophelia fits in very well with this: the same distaste which was destined to take possession of the poet's mind more and more during the years that followed, and which reached its extreme expression in *Timon of Athens*. (Freud, 1900: p. 265)

When Freud wrote the short paper "On Psychotherapy" in 1905, he quoted with approval Hamlet's reproach of Rosencrantz and Guildenstern.

HAMLET: Why, look you now, how unworthy a thing you make of me! You would play upon me. You would seem to know my stops. You would pluck out the heart of my mystery. You would sound me from my lowest note to the top of my compass. And there is much music, excellent voice, in this little organ, yet cannot you make it speak? 'Sblood, do you think I am easier to be played on than a pipe? (*Hamlet*, III.ii.329–334, quoted in Freud, 1905b: p. 262)

In the same year, 1905, in the article "Psychopathic Characters on the Stage", which was not published in Freud's lifetime, he added important observations about Hamlet.

(1) The hero is not psychopathic, but only becomes psychopathic in the course of the action of the play. (2) The repressed impulse is one of those which are similarly repressed in all of us, and the repression of which is part and parcel of the foundations of our personal evolution. It is this repression which is shaken up by the situation in the play. As a result of these two characteristics it is easy for us to recognize ourselves in the hero. (Freud, 1905c: p. 309)

Freud is suggesting that Hamlet was not psychopathic or, as we would be instructed to say, that he was free from neurosis, but became neurotic in the course of the play, when he was confronted with a task beyond his capacity to fulfill. However, there are two difficulties with this formulation. First, it is not so unusual for an intrapsychic conflict to remain dormant and emerge only later. Freud himself coined a German word for it, Nachträglichkeit. The second difficulty is that it asks us to believe in ghosts because without the ghost we cannot be sure that Claudius committed the murder and that what precipitated the outbreak of his symptom was the mother's remarriage, which he is trying to undo. A depressed Hamlet is clinically possible without the message of the ghost but his inability to act is not. The ghost is essential to the drama and to Freud's interpretation.

Implicit in Freud's remark is a theory of why works of literature arouse our interest. The poet's repression speaks to our own repression; as a result, when the two repressions are in contact it shakes us up and we recognise ourselves in the hero. It is likely that the poet found a way to create an intermediate area in which the Oedipus complex is not openly stated as in a psychoanalytic reconstruction, and yet is explicit enough to evoke our interest without adversely affecting intrapsychic balance in the audience.

Freud concluded, not without personal pride, "After all, the conflict in *Hamlet* is so effectively concealed that it was left to me to unearth it" (Freud, 1905c: p. 310).

On the basis of the data presented we can assume Freud's attitude towards Shakespeare. He remained grateful to him for having put on the stage a veiled story representing the Oedipus complex but he was not without pride over the fact that it remained for him to solve the Hamlet enigma. Shakespeare was truly astonishing in the depth of his capacity to portray the working of the Oedipus complex but without psychoanalysis the meaning of Hamlet's indecision would not have found an explanation.

Freud and his pupil Ernest Jones interpreted Hamlet as a "quasi-patient", a real person to whom the psychoanalyst interprets the unconscious wishes that do not permit Hamlet to avenge his father's murder.

It is of interest how *Hamlet* was understood before Freud. An interesting way to look back is to read the Hamlet chapter in

J. C. Bucknill's *The Mad Folk of Shakespeare* published in 1867. Bucknill's opening sentence reads:

> All critical study of Hamlet must be psychological; and as there are few subjects which have been more closely studied, and more copiously written upon, than this magnificent drama, criticism upon it might seem to be exhausted. (Bucknill, 1867: p. 48)

This exhaustion was already experienced a generation before Freud offered his new interpretation.

Hamlet has suicidal wishes that are in conflict with his religious beliefs. Bucknill finds the key to Hamlet's temper in "soul-crushing grief in close alliance with an ironical, often a broad humor" (Bucknill, 1867: p. 57). "All cheerfulness fled, all motive for action lost, he becomes listless and inert" (Bucknill, 1867: p. 77).

> How it is that the resolution of Hamlet to put on the guise of madness follows so quick upon the appearance of the Ghost to him (indeed, while the spirit is yet present, though unseen, for the resolution is expressed before the final unearthly adjuration to swear,) we are unable to explain. (Bucknill, 1867: p. 62)

Hamlet is pretending to be mad because he is afraid that what the ghost told him could easily drive him to real madness. According to Bucknill, "Hamlet's indecision to act, and his overreadiness to reflect, are placed beyond the reach of critical discovery" (Bucknill, 1867: p. 82). Bucknill describes Hamlet as "so active to think, so inert to act, so keen to appreciate the evils of life, so averse to take any active part against them" (Bucknill, 1867: p. 86). "The true melancholy and the counterfeit madness are strangely commingled" in him (Bucknill, 1867: p. 90).

Being a psychoanalyst, Freud tried to understand Hamlet without passing judgment on him. Bucknill did not differentiate the two:

> Shall we think the less nobly of him because his hand is not ready to shed kindred blood; because, gifted with God-like discourse of reason, he does look before and after; because he does not take the law in his own hands upon his oppressor until he has obtained

conclusive evidence of his guilt; that he seeks to make sure he is the natural justiciar of his murdered father, and not an assassin instigated by hatred and selfish revenge? (Bucknill, 1867: p. 83)

Bucknill's Hamlet, who suspects that his wish to kill his uncle is "instigated by hatred and selfish revenge", is already very close to Freud's Hamlet.

From Bucknill we will go to A. C. Bradley's *Shakespearean Tragedy*, published in 1904; the first chapter in the book deals with *Hamlet*. Although Bradley's book appeared four years after *The Interpretation of Dreams*, it is clear that Bradley is unfamiliar with Freud, and he therefore offers us insight into one way the play was understood before Freud's ideas became well-known.

Bradley begins with the question of why Hamlet did not obey the ghost at once and thus save seven of the eight lives lost in the play? (Bradley, 1904: p. 89). By killing Claudius immediately, he would almost certainly have prevented the deaths of Rosencrantz, Guildenstern, Ophelia, Polonius, Gertrude, Laertes, and himself. His answer is that Shakespeare intended Hamlet to represent what a mystery life is and how impossible it is for us to understand it (Bradley, 1904: p. 93). Bradley argued that this is the core of every tragedy, not because the hero is an enigma but because strength and weakness should be mingled in one soul. Hamlet never cites external difficulties; his entire difficulty is internal.

Bradley then cites the reason given by Goethe: that Hamlet, like Brutus, had a great anxiety to be right. Hamlet was repelled by the idea of falling suddenly upon a man who could not defend himself. In Bradley's words Goethe viewed Hamlet as "a lovely, pure and most moral nature, *without the strength of nerve which forms a hero*, sinks beneath a burden which it cannot bear and must not cast away" (Bradley, 1904: p. 101). A fourth view, attributed to Schlegel and Coleridge, is that Hamlet is a tragedy of reflection. This irresolution is due to excessive reflection. As Shakespeare expresses it in the play, "And thus the native hue of resolution / Is sicklied o'er with the pale cast of thought (*Hamlet*, III.i.84–85).

We have reached the point where we can state the difference between the non-Freudian interpretation and those of Freud. The other interpreters seek to understand Hamlet as a unique person while Freud sees him as embodying the typical and usually repressed wish.

Non-Freudian interpretations of *Hamlet* continued. In *Hamlet and His Problem*, published in 1919, T. S. Eliot wrote:

> Far from Shakespeare's masterpiece, the play is most certainly an artistic failure.... *Hamlet*, like the sonnets, is full of some stuff that the writer could not drag to light, contemplate, or manipulate into art.... The artistic 'inevitability' lies in the complete adequacy of the external to the emotion; and this precisely what is deficient in Hamlet. (Eliot, 1932: pp. 123–125)

The phrase "drag to light" expresses Eliot's disdain for making the unconscious conscious. What Eliot demands is that a great play leave nothing unresolved, no puzzling gaps, and therefore no indication of an unconscious conflict in the author.

Shakespeare knew that when one is conveying a message that is difficult to accept it is better to say it with a metaphor.

GHOST: ...but know, thou noble youth,
        The serpent that did sting thy father's life
        Now wears his crown. (*Hamlet*, I.v.38–40)

To which Hamlet responds with "O my prophetic soul!" (I.v.40), indicating that, preconsciously, he suspected, but refused to acknowledge, that his father was murdered by Claudius to obtain both throne and wife. The ghost, like the "weird sisters" in *Macbeth*, is the instrument making the unconscious conscious. Freud's oedipal rivalry takes place between son and father; Shakespeare shifted it towards sibling rivalry, thus combining these two important childhood events.

Hamlet has returned to Denmark about a month or so after his father's funeral. In the soliloquy "O, that this too too solid flesh would melt" (I.ii.129), Hamlet laments:

HAMLET: within a month—
        Let me not think on't—Frailty, thy name is woman!—
        A little month, or ere those shoes were old
        With which she follow'd my poor father's body,
        Like Niobe, all tears, why she, even she—
        O God, a beast that wants discourse of reason
        Would have mourned longer—married with my uncle.
        (I.ii.145–151)

Hamlet cannot forgive his mother for her "hasty marriage" and all-too-short mourning. The marriage reactivated Hamlet's oedipal feelings independently of the ghost's message. There would have been jealousy and fury at the mother and uncle due to the reactivation of the oedipal wishes even had the father died a natural death. Today, when divorces and second marriages are common, we often have the opportunity to observe how oedipal rivalry is reawakened when parents remarry. In psychoanalytic thinking the reawakening of the oedipal feelings in Hamlet could have awakened either castration anxiety (a fear that something would happen to him) or depression (the feeling that he deserves punishment).

Freud's interpretation of *Hamlet* was written shortly before the turn of the century; at that time he did not as yet formulate a distinction between mourning and melancholia, which he did in 1917. In Hamlet's soliloquies we recognise that he suffers from melancholia rather than mourning. Nuttal's statement that *Hamlet* is "a prolonged meditation on self-destruction" (Nuttall, 2007: p. 4) describes melancholia rather than mourning.

Mourning or its absence in Hamlet

In Act one, scene two Claudius the king tries to justify to Hamlet the absence of mourning for Hamlet's father; contradictory emotions take place at the same time. We should note that this speech takes place before Hamlet's encounter with the ghost.

CLAUDIUS: Yet so far hath discretion fought with nature
That we with wisest sorrow think on him,
Together with remembrance of ourselves.
Therefore our sometime sister, now our queen,
The imperial jointress to this warlike state,
Have we, as 'twere with a defeated joy,
With an auspicious and a dropping eye,
With mirth in funeral and with dirge in marriage,
In equal scale weighing delight and dole,
Taken to wife. (I.ii.4–14)

In Kermode's interpretation (2000), "our sometimes sister, now our queen" opens the question of incest. The language, full of compressed paradoxes and oxymorons, echoes the action of marrying one's brother's wife.

In the king's view, the "remembrance of ourselves", or narcissism, sets limits to mourning. The king advocates a judicious mixture of "wisest sorrow" and "remembrance of ourselves", a balance between mourning and self-regard.

Both queen and king find Hamlet's emphasis on mourning a burden. His mother uses religion as her argument.

> GERTRUDE: Good Hamlet, cast thy nighted colour off,
> And let thine eye look like a friend on Denmark.
> Do not for ever with thy vailèd lids
> Seek for thy noble father in the dust:
> Thou know'st 'tis common; all that lives must die,
> Passing through nature to eternity. (I.ii.68–73)

The king reinforces what the queen is saying but emphasises that grief is unmanly.

> CLAUDIUS: 'Tis sweet and commendable in your nature, Hamlet,
> To give these mourning duties to your father:
> But, you must know, your father lost a father;
> That father lost, lost his, and the survivor bound
> In filial obligation for some term
> To do obsequious sorrow: but to persever
> In obstinate condolement is a course
> Of impious stubbornness; 'tis unmanly grief;
> It shows a will most incorrect to heaven,
> A heart unfortified, a mind impatient,
> An understanding simple and unschool'd. (I.ii.87–97)

The king is harsher than the queen. He accuses Hamlet of "impious stubbornness", "unmanly grief", being "incorrect to heaven", and having "a heart unfortified, a mind impatient" and "an understanding simple and unschool'd". Hamlet's "vailèd lids" arouse guilt in the king and queen, spoiling their nuptials. Hamlet's "nighted colour" is guilt-evoking to the king and queen, a reminder that Hamlet's father's death has not been mourned due to their hasty marriage. The latent issue is about incest but the talk is about mourning. To have sexual intercourse with one's sister-in-law is incest but marriage to his brother's widow it is not; a hasty remarriage is disputed territory. This is the first contribution to the ambiguity of the play. I will now deal with the next one: Is Hamlet mourning or suffering from melancholia?

Hamlet's melancholia

We have just seen Hamlet reprimanded for mourning too deeply for his father but in two soliloquies—"O, that this too too solid flesh would melt" (Act I, scene 2) and the more famous "To be, or not to be" (Act 3, scene 1)—Shakespeare introduces the audience to Hamlet's melancholia. Mourning was a subject for discussion but Hamlet's lonely soliloquies introduced melancholia to the audience. The first one opens with the wish "that the Everlasting had not fix'd / His canon 'gainst self-slaughter!" (I.ii.131–132). The world is experienced as "an unweeded garden, / That grows to seed" (I.ii.135–136).

> HAMLET: O, that this too too solid flesh would melt,
>   Thaw and resolve itself into a dew!
>   Or that the Everlasting had not fix'd
>   His canon 'gainst self-slaughter! O God! God!
>   How weary, stale, flat and unprofitable,
>   Seem to me all the uses of this world!
>   Fie on't! ah fie! 'tis an unweeded garden,
>   That grows to seed; things rank and gross in nature
>   Possess it merely. (I.ii.129–137)

The rest of the soliloquy is an accusation on the mother.

> HAMLET: She married. O, most wicked speed, to post
>   With such dexterity to incestuous sheets!
>   It is not nor it cannot come to good:
>   But break, my heart; for I must hold my tongue. (I.ii.156–159)

The soliloquy adds complexity to this play. Hamlet's melancholia and his suicidal wishes have gained the upper hand even before he knows the message of the ghost, but the ghost's message activated the murderous side of the Oedipus complex.

In the next act, when Hamlet is confiding his situation to Rosencrantz and Guildenstern, we learn that he himself does not fully understand his melancholia.

HAMLET: O God, I could be bounded in a nutshell and count
myself a king of infinite space, were it not that I
have bad dreams. (II.ii.249–251)

    …

I have of late—but wherefore
I know not—lost all my mirth, forgone all custom of
exercises; and indeed it goes so heavily with my
disposition that this goodly frame, the earth, seems to
me a sterile promontory, this most excellent canopy,
the air, look you, this brave o'erhanging firmament,
this majestical roof fretted with golden fire, why,
it appears no other thing to me than a foul and pestilent
congregation of vapors. What a piece of work is a man!
How noble in reason, how infinite in faculties,
in form and moving how express and admirable,
in action how like an angel, in apprehension how like
a god! The beauty of the world, the paragon of animals!
And yet, to me, what is this quintessence of dust? Man
delights not me—no, nor woman neither, though by
your smiling you seem to say so. (II.ii.288–301)

An analyst would ask what the bad dreams were and subject them to analysis.

These lines, like the previously cited soliloquy, have become one of the treasures of the English language and justly famous. Hamlet may be depressed or even suicidal but the very words he chooses to describe what no longer matters to him are so full of the deepest appreciation that they convey the opposite feeling to the audience. The description of "What a piece of work is man!" ranks among the most ideal descriptions of the essence of humankind. Hamlet feels very depressed but at the same time aware of the beauty of the world and the wonder of humanity. He is a melancholic but one who is at the very same time aware of how rich life can be beyond the confines of melancholia. What Shakespeare gives us is "poetic melancholia".

The next soliloquy is "To be, or not to be". By far the most famous one, it takes place after the encounter with the ghost. Once more Hamlet is overwhelmed by suicidal wishes. This time religious scruples are not the main force opposing them: it is the fear that even after death bad dreams will continue to haunt him.

HAMLET: To sleep: perchance to dream: ay, there's the rub;
        For in that sleep of death what dreams may come
        When we have shuffled off this mortal coil,
        Must give us pause. (III.i.65–68)
        …
        For who would bear the whips and scorns of time,
        The oppressor's wrong, the proud man's contumely,
        The pangs of despised love, the law's delay,
        The insolence of office and the spurns
        That patient merit of the unworthy takes,
        When he himself might his quietus make. (III.i.70–75)
        …
        But that the dread of something after death,
        The undiscover'd country from whose bourn
        No traveller returns, puzzles the will,
        And makes us rather bear those ills we have
        Than fly to others that we know not of?
        Thus conscience does make cowards of us all. (III.i.78–83)

Hamlet was the heir to the throne of Denmark, studying at a famous university in Germany. Was he likely to endure "the pangs of despised love, the law's delay", or "the insolence of office"? These misfortunes may well belong to Shakespeare's biography, but not to what we know of Prince Hamlet's biography. We meet a lonelier and more desperate Hamlet in the second soliloquy.

"The undiscover'd country from whose bourn [boundary] / No traveler returns puzzles the will" (III.i.79–80) is in stark contradiction with the fact that Hamlet just talked to one of these travelers (his father's spirit), and one suspects this famous monologue may have been uttered earlier in the play—before the first encounter with the ghost—and only later moved to its current place.

Hamlet's fear of possible nightmares after death will not sound strange to psychoanalytic clinicians, for in our practice we encounter patients with a tormenting fear of death. These patients do not accept the finality of death. To them a corpse is still the person and the thought of burial and disintegration of the body is a tormenting one. We can say Hamlet's worry about postmortem nightmares implies that he has not accepted the finality of death but this non-acceptance offers no comfort because what psychoanalysis calls the bad internalised object is persecuting him, even after death.

Almost at the end of this soliloquy comes the profound line "And thus the native hue of resolution / Is sicklied o'er with the pale cast of thought" (III.i.84–85). Shakespeare gave Hamlet the insight that thought not only delays rash action, but can become an illness of its own, when thinking—or more correctly brooding—replaces action.

Without reference to *Hamlet*, Freud dealt with such suicidal wishes in his book *The Ego and the Id* (1923): "What is now holding sway in the super-ego is, as it were, a culture of the death instinct, and in fact it often enough succeeds in driving the ego into death" (Freud, 1923: p. 53). Following this model, Hamlet's superego demands his suicide, but another component of his superego, experienced as God's command, prohibits this suicidal wish.

If we read Hamlet's long soliloquy keeping in mind Freud's dual instinct theory as expressed in *Beyond the Pleasure Principle* we will see Hamlet as a dramatic personification of Freud's dual instinct theory. Hamlet exemplifies the struggle between libido as a life force and the death instinct. Freud has pointed out the profound hostility towards sexuality that Hamlet expressed in his encounter with Ophelia. What remains to be noted is that this enmity towards the sexual realm increases the force of the death instinct.

Love in Hamlet

How rich is the play in expressions of love? Hamlet attributes a great deal of love on his father's part towards his mother.

HAMLET: why, she would hang on him,
              As if increase of appetite had grown
              By what it fed on. (I.ii.143–145)

We have no evidence that this love in fact existed. When the ghost appears to Hamlet no love for Gertrude is expressed, only the admonition to "leave her to heaven" (I.v.86) rather than punish her.

One of Shakespeare's fears about love must have been satiety. He expressed this fear in a number of plays, including *Venus and Adonis* and in Enobarbus' praise of Cleopatra in *Antony and Cleopatra*.

ENOBARBUS: Age cannot wither her, nor custom stale
              Her infinite variety. Other women cloy
              The appetites they feed, but she makes hungry
              Where most she satisfies .... (*Antony and Cleopatra*, II.ii.240–243)

Claudius attributes a deep love for Hamlet to the queen when he confides to Laertes, "The queen his mother / Lives almost by his looks" (*Hamlet*, IV.vii.11–12), but there is no evidence of such love in the play. If anything, one can say that Gertrude did not consider the impact of her quick remarriage on her son. Only after she sees his strange behaviour does she recognise that her marriage to Claudius might be the cause.

It may come as a shock that the only person in the play capable of loving is the murderer, Claudius, for he confesses to Laertes:

CLAUDIUS: My virtue or my plague, be it either which,—
             She's so conjunctive to my life and soul,
             That, as the star moves not but in his sphere,
             I could not but by her. (IV.vii.13–16)

In Shakespeare's view a man who murdered his brother could also feel conjunctive to his widow.

As to the word conjunctive, this is the only place in Shakespeare's work where it is used in reference to a loving relationship. In *Othello* (1603) we find a line spoken by Iago: "Let us be conjunctive in our revenge". (*Othello*, I.iii.367). We can read this line to mean that Iago sees the joint revenge as an expression of love between himself and Roderigo. Spivack (1973) tells us that Shakespeare decided to give to Claudius a new word to describe his relationship to Gertrude, a word he did not use anywhere else in his work.

It can hardly be an accident that the very same man who is the only character in the play to express love is also the one who is convinced that love cannot endure. We recall the king's lecture to Laertes: "There lives within the very flame of love / A kind of wick or snuff that will abate it" (IV.vii.115–116). There is considerable evidence that this statement represented Shakespeare's own view of love. *Antony and Cleopatra* is an example.

When Shakespeare created Claudius, he had already created two dramatic characters whom we can designate villains: Richard III and Iago. But a real villain is too narcissistic to be able to be "conjunctive" to any woman. We have already surmised from the prayer scene that Shakespeare did not consider Claudius a genuine villain. In Claudius, Shakespeare created a complex character, a villain with a sense of guilt as well as the capacity to be "conjunctive".

CLAUDIUS: But oh, what form of prayer
               Can serve my turn? "Forgive me my foul murder?"
               That cannot be, since I am still possess'd
               Of those effects for which I did the murder,
               My crown, mine own ambition and my queen. (III.iii.51–55)

These are the thoughts of a moral person, not a villain.

Did Hamlet love Ophelia?

We first hear about Hamlet's relationship with Ophelia from a letter Hamlet wrote to her before the death of his father, which Polonius reads.

POLONIUS: "To the celestial and my soul's idol, the most beautified
               Ophelia",—
               That's an ill phrase, a vile phrase; "beautified" is
               a vile phrase: but you shall hear. Thus:
               [*Reads.*]
               "In her excellent white bosom, these, etc".
GERTRUDE: Came this from Hamlet to her?
POLONIUS: Good madam, stay awhile; I will be faithful.
               [*Reads the letter.*]
               "Doubt thou the stars are fire;
               Doubt that the sun doth move;
               Doubt truth to be a liar;
               But never doubt I love.
               O dear Ophelia, I am ill at these numbers;
               I have not art to reckon my groans: but that

> I love thee best, O most best, believe it. Adieu.
> Thine evermore, most dear lady,
> whilst this machine is to him, Hamlet". (II.ii.109–122)

Shakespeare wrote magnificent love poems, but to Hamlet he gave only an undistinguished poem. Ophelia must mistrust everything but only trust him. His love, offering Ophelia an island of trust in an ocean of mistrust, is a love with paranoid connotations.

The next encounter takes place after the soliloquy "To be, or not to be". Ophelia is trying to return remembrances she had received from Hamlet.

OPHELIA: My lord, I have remembrances of yours,
            That I have longed long to re-deliver;
            I pray you, now receive them.
HAMLET: No, not I;
            I never gave you aught.
OPHELIA: My honour'd lord, you know right well you did;
            And with them, words of so sweet breath compos'd
            As made the things more rich: their perfume lost,
            Take these again; for to the noble mind
            Rich gifts wax poor when givers prove unkind. (III.i.93–101)
            …
HAMLET: You should not have believed me; for virtue cannot so
            inoculate our old stock but we shall relish of it; I loved you
            not.
OPHELIA: I was the more deceived. (III.i.116–118)

Hamlet ends their conversation with the well-known line "Get thee to a nunnery: why wouldst thou be a breeder of sinners?" (III.i.121–122) and the equally famous "What should such fellows as I do / crawling between earth and heaven?" (III.i.127–128). If Hamlet ever loved Ophelia, his "antique disposition" has driven this love out of his mind.

The next encounter is portrayed in sexualised banter between Hamlet and Ophelia.

GERTRUDE: Come hither, my dear Hamlet, sit by me.
HAMLET: No, good mother, here's metal more attractive.
POLONIUS: [To the King.] O, ho! do you mark that?
HAMLET: Lady, shall I lie in your lap?

OPHELIA: No, my lord.

HAMLET: I mean, my head upon your lap?

OPHELIA: Ay, my lord.

HAMLET: Do you think I meant country matters?

OPHELIA: I think nothing, my lord.

HAMLET: That's a fair thought to lie between maids' legs.

OPHELIA: What is, my lord?

HAMLET: Nothing. (III.ii.102–113)

A psychoanalytically informed reader will note the reference to "nothing" is "a fair thought to lie between maids' legs" and be reminded of Bertram Lewin's paper of 1948, "The Nature of Reality, the Meaning of Nothing", where "nothing", in the unconscious, stands for the vagina.

In Hamlet's unconscious Ophelia must have been closely identified with his mother, and when his mother disappointed him his love for Ophelia waned. Hamlet may also have suffered disappointment in Ophelia when she betrayed him and chose obedience to her father over loyalty to him. Hamlet's label of Polonius as a "fishmonger" may also refer to the fact that he used his daughter as bait to trap Hamlet.

The strongest argument supporting the conclusion that Hamlet does not love Ophelia comes from the scene in which Hamlet murders Polonius. We are in Act III, scene four. Hamlet is determined to "set you up a glass / Where you may see the inmost part of you" (III.iv.19–20). The queen misunderstands and fears he intends to murder her and calls for help. Polonius, behind the arras, repeats her cry for help and is stabbed by Hamlet. Hamlet lifts the arras and discovers he did not kill Claudius but Polonius, and exclaims, "Thou wretched, rash, intruding fool, farewell! / I took thee for thy better" (III.iv.31–32). After Hamlet kills Polonius the queen laments, "Oh, what a rash and bloody deed is this?" (III.iv.27) and Hamlet answers: "A bloody deed! almost as bad, good mother, / As kill a king, and marry with his brother" (III.iv.28–29). The queen is incredulous. "As kill a king?" Hamlet answers, "Ay, lady, 'twas my word" (III.iv.30). Beyond this remark both mother and son forget Polonius and Hamlet attempts to show his mother how in every way his father was superior to his brother.

In psychoanalytic terms, a father figure spying on the mother-child scene is killed for his voyeuristic interest. Instead of the child becoming traumatised by coming unexpectedly upon a scene of parental sexual intercourse, the poet is able to transform a probable memory of his own childhood experience into a scene where the former child is now in control, killing the father figure and forcing the mother to abstain from sexual relations. The Oedipal structure of this scene demands that the father be killed but if it had been Claudius who was spying and being killed the play would have been closer to an obvious revenge play such as the ghost demanded. Shakespeare is far too subtle to give us such an obvious ending. Polonius, Ophelia's father, is killed instead and the play can continue to a more complex finale.

After the murder, mother and son continue their quarrel, and Polonius is left lying there until they finish. Only at the very end of the act is Polonius remembered.

HAMLET: Indeed this counselor
          Is now most still, most secret and most grave,
          Who was in life a foolish prating knave. (III.iv.213–215)

Not once in the scene does Hamlet remember that Polonius is Ophelia's father and that he has therefore killed the father of the woman he supposedly loves (or loved). The omission of any thought of Ophelia in this drawn out and powerful scene would alone be proof that Hamlet does not love Ophelia, and yet Shakespeare has another surprise for us.

Hamlet's love for Yorick

Act V opens with the graveyard scene. Two gravediggers discuss Ophelia's suicide as they dig her grave. Hamlet and Horatio approach; we are given no clue why they are in the churchyard. Skulls are dug out, eventually Yorick's skull. As a child, Hamlet loved Yorick.

HAMLET: Alas, poor Yorick! I knew him, Horatio: a fellow
          of infinite jest, of most excellent fancy: he hath
          borne me on his back a thousand times; and now, how
          abhorred in my imagination it is! my gorge rises at
          it. Here hung those lips that I have kissed I know
          not how oft. Where be your gibes now? your
          gambols? your songs? your flashes of merriment,
          that were wont to set the table on a roar? (V.i.156–162)

What we have just heard is a childhood memory emerging from repression. It is only after a repressed homosexual love has emerged that the heterosexual love for Ophelia has a chance to be acknowledged. As long as Hamlet was repressing his infantile homosexual love, his adult heterosexual love had no chance to develop. After the kisses to Yorick have been remembered Hamlet can express his love for Ophelia, and can now exclaim, upon seeing her body:

HAMLET: I loved Ophelia. Forty thousand brothers
            Could not, with all their quantity of love,
            Make up my sum. (IV.i.257–259)

The graveyard scene contains a psychoanalytic insight: a repressed childhood homosexual memory inhibits both mourning and the capacity to love a woman. When the memory of the childhood homosexual love returns from repression and is remembered and re-experienced, energy is liberated and Ophelia can be loved. Yorick may well be the prototype upon which "the master mistress of my passion" in Sonnet twenty was created. As a compromise solution in that sonnet, Shakespeare suggested that love go to the man and "loves use", meaning sexual intercourse, go to women. In psychoanalytic terms such an outcome represents an unconscious compromise formation between homosexual and heterosexual wishes, a division of the kingdom, as it were, without a conscious awareness of it.

That Ophelia is to be buried in Yorick's grave is another way in which Shakespeare symbolically connected the two. Had Ophelia been alive, this recall could have meant that Hamlet would make the transition from infantile homosexual love to adult heterosexual love. Since Ophelia is dead the insight has no curative effect but only confirms Hamlet's depression.

The function of the ghost

In the first appearance of the ghost at the beginning of the play Shakespeare made sure the audience believed the ghost was real by making all those present see him; in the ghost's second appearance it is an hallucination. It appears only to Hamlet, not to the queen, and this time it conveys no information but has come to spur Hamlet to avenge his murder. Being a man of the Renaissance, Shakespeare could use the ghost in two ways: as a real possibility, or as a product of the imagination. Skillfully, Shakespeare ensures that we understand the hallucination was brought about by Hamlet's superego. The ghost says only a few words: "Do not forget: this visitation / Is but to whet thy almost blunted purpose" (III.iv.109–110). The queen responds to Hamlet's insistence on the ghost's presence with "This the very coinage of your brain: / This bodiless creation ecstasy" (III.iv.138–139). The term 'coinage of your brain' implies the queen's understanding that the hallucination is created by the brain, while the expression "bodiless creation of ecstasy" conveys that Hamlet's ecstasy created a body (the ghost) that was not actually there. In this hour of stress Shakespeare gives the queen an astonishing capacity for insight.

Gertrude may well be the most enigmatic character in the play. Both Eissler (1971) and Oremland (2005) have devoted a chapter to her and her relationship to the three men who matter most: King Hamlet, Claudius and Prince Hamlet. There has been much speculation as to whether she had a sexual liaison with Claudius before her husband's murder and her possible involvement in the murder itself. Oremland sees Gertrude as an "as-if" personality.

Horatio and Hamlet

The complex relationship between Horatio and Hamlet is among the most interesting features of this play. Without the split between the two characters the play could not be what it is. Hamlet is always dependent on Horatio, who introduces Hamlet to the ghost. It is to him that Hamlet turns to justify his actions.

At the end of the play Horatio challenges Hamlet, telling him not to agree to fight Laertes. Hamlet's response to him has become famous.

HAMLET: Not a whit; we defy augury; there's a special
           providence in the fall of a sparrow. If it be now, I 'tis not
           to come; if it be not to come, it will be now; if it be not now,
           yet it will come; the readiness is all. (V.ii.192–195)

There is a new maturity in Hamlet, a greater acceptance of his destiny, and it is to Horatio that this new maturity is conveyed. Horatio can be understood as that part of Hamlet that absorbs and reveals what is happening to him. At the end of the play, Hamlet has regained the capacity to love as well as mourn. Dying, he asks Horatio to mourn for him.

HAMLET: If thou didst ever hold me in thy heart,
Absent thee from felicity awhile,
And in this harsh world draw thy breath in pain,
To tell my story. (V.ii.325–328)

Horatio has to survive to transmit the memory of Hamlet to the audience. Hamlet, a man who earlier could not mourn, asks Horatio to mourn his passing.

Hamlet's wish to be remembered has been fulfilled, but since Shakespeare did not tell us *how* Hamlet should be remembered. Is he to be remembered as an enigma? Even in this book, André Green's introduction recalls him in a different way than I do.

Discussion

There is ample documentary evidence that *Hamlet* was crucial to Freud in the discovery of the Oedipus complex, but does that mean that the Oedipus complex was in *Hamlet* waiting for Freud to come and make it explicit? Or did Freud understand something implicit in *Hamlet* that no one before him ever surmised? In one case Freud will be seen as the discoverer of the Oedipus complex; in the other view he is the creator of the concept. Psychoanalysts will tend to see Freud as the discoverer, while those who doubt the general validity of the Oedipus complex will see Freud as the creator.

There is yet another reason why Shakespeare's *Hamlet* is of special interest to psychoanalysis. In Western culture, interest in exploring the unconscious had its beginning in the plays of the three Greek tragedians Aeschylus, Sophocles, and Euripides; with few exceptions this interest became dormant for 2,000 years, until it erupted again in Shakespeare's work. Shakespeare reawakened the Western world's interest in the unconscious. Among Freud's predecessors we can count Richard Wagner, Flaubert, Stendhal, Ibsen, Dostoevsky, Nietzsche and others. Shakespeare's exact impact on Freud beyond what he said about Hamlet is explained in this book. Shakespeare may have influenced Freud's thinking more than Freud realised, but then this influence was not conscious to Freud.

PART II

THE POET AND HIS CALLING

CHAPTER TWO

A Midsummer Night's Dream: how Shakespeare won the right to write plays

A Midsummer Night's Dream was selected as the first chapter of part three, because in it Shakespeare dealt with the relationship of the poet to his unconscious. It was an achievement of a kind he would not reach again.

Two soliloquies, one by Theseus and the other by Puck, are the keys to the unconscious meaning of this play.

THESEUS: I never may believe
These antique fables, nor these fairy toys.
Lovers and madmen have such seething brains,
Such shaping fantasies, that apprehend
More than cool reason ever comprehends.
The lunatic, the lover, and the poet
Are of imagination all compact:
One sees more devils than vast hell can hold;
That is the madman. The lover, all as frantic,
Sees Helen's beauty in a brow of Egypt.
The poet's eye, in a fine frenzy rolling,
Doth glance from heaven to earth, from earth to heaven.
And as imagination bodies forth

41

> The forms of things unknown, the poet's pen
> Turns them to shapes, and gives to airy nothing
> A local habitation and a name.
> Such tricks hath strong imagination
> That if it would but apprehend some joy,
> It comprehends some bringer of that joy;
> Or in the night, imagining some fear,
> How easy is a bush supposed a bear? (*A Midsummer Night's Dream*,
> V.i.2–22)

The wish to demonstrate that madmen, lovers, and poets have something in common draws attention to the unconscious that they have in common. Their "seething brains" emphasises the restlessness of the three categories but then, being a sober man, Theseus goes on to differentiate amongst them.

Theseus is the spokesman for the part of Shakespeare's audience that resists falling under the spell of the poet. He compares the madman, the lover, and the poet. All three "Are of imagination all compact". They show an excess of fantasy, more than "cool reason ever comprehends". The lover and the lunatic are private individuals, while the poet gives "local habitation" to "airy nothing", which is Shakespeare's original way of saying the poet verbalises what is preverbal in the rest of us. In psychoanalytic language, all three have allowed their unconscious more power over their lives than sane men allow. Theseus is neither madman nor poet and may not even be in love, but he mistrusts poets. It is of interest that Theseus does not mention the dreamer along with the madman, lover, and poet.

I am indebted to Colin McGinn's book *Shakespeare's Philosophy* for the realisation that the need to compare dreaming with lunacy was discussed by philosophers of Shakespeare's generation. Both Montaigne (1580) and Descartes (1641) treated dreaming as a temporary state of insanity that sane men awake from regularly.

It turned out that the very same skill that Shakespeare gave to poets is what psychoanalytic patients are asked to achieve. The unconscious is conceptualised as chaotic and can be described as "forms of things unknown". The act of verbalisation gives shape to "airy nothing". In beautiful language Shakespeare expresses what psychoanalysis calls the transformation of "thing representation" into "word representation".

The psychoanalytic patient, in the course of analysis, learns to put into words what could not be articulated before.

Puck's apology

PUCK: If we shadows have offended,
        Think but this, and all is mended:
        That you have but slumbered here
        While these visions did appear;
        And this weak and idle theme,
        No more yielding but a dream,
        Gentles, do not reprehend;
        If you pardon, we will mend.
        And, as I am an honest Puck,
        If we have unearnèd luck
        Now to 'scape the serpent's tongue
        We will make amends ere long,
        Else the Puck a liar call.
        So good night unto you all.
        Give me your hands, if we be friends,
        And Robin shall restore amends. (V.i.401–416)

If Theseus represents the audience's suspicion of the poet, Puck represents the guilt feelings of the creative writer. Puck is afraid that the play has evoked anxiety in the audience and he offers a striking remedy: to imagine that the play was a dream. Psychoanalysis has discovered that healthy people, when awake, immediately know that they have only dreamed, while mentally disturbed people have difficulty differentiating the two states. Puck asks the audience to treat the play as if it had been a dream, using the word "mend" twice and the word "amend" twice more. He feels that the play may have offended (or in current language has evoked anxiety) and the remedy he offers is to treat the play as if it were a dream. Puck tells us that if a play has disturbed us we should treat it as a dream.

When Shakespeare wrote this play he had not yet composed his great tragedies. In the tragedies most of those who disturbed our peace of mind have to die as expiation for troubling the sleep of the audience with something akin to distressing dreams. In comedies the same disturbing thoughts may be raised but the happy ending introduces the audience to a mechanism akin to denial.

The leading couples and their interactions

I. The remorse of Theseus

We turn now to the wooing speech of Theseus.

THESEUS: Hippolyta, I wooed thee with my sword,
And won thy love doing thee injuries;
But I will wed thee in another key,
With pomp, with triumph, and with revelling. (I.i.16–19)

At first glance there is nothing remarkable in these lines but a rich psychoanalytic chapter could be written about them. Theseus wooed and won the queen of the Amazons by doing her injuries, that is, behaving sadistically, but now he advances to remorse and repara- tions. In psychoanalytic terms, the language of Theseus is the lan- guage of the phallic phase, familiar to psychoanalysts as the phase when the child witnesses the parents having sexual intercourse and imagines that the father is injuring the mother. It is in this phase of development that the sword symbolises the penis. Theseus conveys a sense of reality to the child's view of the sadistic nature of the father's attack upon the mother. In the sadistic phase the sword is an injur- ing penis inflicted wounds on the woman and the sadism is in turn responsible for a feeling of depression, which the solemnities are called upon to repair.

Classical psychoanalytic theory postulates that if a fixation takes place in the phallic phase the man will continue to believe that sexual intercourse is a sadistic act, and woman fixed on this level will continue to fear penetration as an unconscious wound inflicted on her. It is in the next developmental phase, the genital phase, that this fear is overcome in favour of sexual orgasm for both partners and the sexual experience becomes an act of love. Theseus has been functioning on the phallic level; he could neither love nor dream and cannot linger and enjoy the moment, but now he is advancing psychologically beyond the sheer phallic = sadistic phase, offering Hippolyta "pomp, ... triumph, and ... reveling" (I.i.19) as compensation for his earlier phallic sadism.

THESEUS: Go, Philostrate,
            Stir up the Athenian youth to merriments,
            Awake the pert and nimble spirit of mirth;
            Turn melancholy forth to funerals;
            The pale companion is not for our pomp. (I.i.11–15)

Theseus has injured his bride-to-be by his sadism, resulting in depression. The task of the "manager of mirth" is to transform this threatening melancholy into mirth. Earlier I presented Theseus as speaking for the audience, which resists the impact of the poet; now we meet him as the apologist to the woman for his earlier sadism.

The term "manager of mirth" is interesting. This man, Philostrate, appears briefly in Act I, scene one; he is spoken to by Theseus but has no lines himself. At the end of the play Philostrate will appear once more; in the name of refined taste he will oppose the rude presentation of *Pyramus and Thisbe*. The title "master of revels" was not an invention of Shakespeare; there was such a position at the court of Queen Elizabeth. In this play the master of revels represents the playwright.

As the play opens, Theseus finds it difficult to wait the four days until his nuptials with Hippolyta. He accuses the moon for postponing his desires. Theseus is no Romeo; he expresses no love for Hippolyta, only sexual impatience. Hippolyta, the queen of the Amazons and therefore the epitome of the phallic woman, appears in this play as a woman capable of loving. She seems to be the model wife-to-be, who teaches her husband to overcome his impatience. Hippolyta comforts him with the idea that the days will steep themselves in the nights and dreams can offer fulfillment when the day demands postponement. Hippolyta is the advocate of the dream and through her, we too accept the healing properties of the dream.

HIPPOLYTA: Four days will quickly steep themselves in night;
              Four nights will quickly dream away the time. (I.i.7–8)

Hippolyta is not mentioned in Freud's *interpretation of Dreams* but she deserves an honourable place as one of Freud's ancestors as she stresses that dreams are the fulfillment of wishes. Skillfully, she allies herself with the night and the dream, but the impatience of Theseus goes deep and will not go away. In Act V, scene one Theseus, instead of fearing the anguish of waiting four days, fears the torture of three hours.

THESEUS: Come now: what masques, what dances shall we have
                To wear away this long age of three hours
                Between our after-supper and bedtime?
                Where is our usual manager of mirth?
                What revels are in hand? Is there no play
                To ease the anguish of a torturing hour?

                ...

                Say, what abridgement have you for this evening?
                What masque, what music? How shall we beguile
                The lazy time if not with some delight? (V.i.32–37, 39–41)

We have just met a new Theseus; he is asking for a play "To ease the
anguish of a torturing hour". We encounter the poet as a comforter
and perhaps as a healer. Theseus has difficulty in spending the time
between supper and bedtime; he waits for an "abridgement" of the
waiting time. Symbolically, Theseus represents the restless audience
that demands escape from boredom and restlessness by insisting on
entertainment. One can imagine how difficult it must have been for
Shakespeare to write his plays if Theseus was a representation of his
audience. Hippolyta and Theseus exchange roles: Theseus can enjoy
the rustics' play while Hippolyta cannot.

HIPPOLYTA: This is the silliest stuff that ever I heard.
    THESEUS: The best in this kind are but shadows; and the worst are no
                    worse, if imagination amend them.
HIPPOLYTA: It must be your imagination then, and not theirs.
    THESEUS: If we imagine no worse of them than they of themselves, they
                    may pass for excellent men. (V.i.204–209)

Theseus has learned to enjoy what the imagination offers.

II. Oberon and Titania

Oberon and Titania are not mortals but fairies. In Shakespeare's plays
fairies are not evil like witches but they are not benevolent either. In
Cymbeline Imogen prays for protection from fairies and tempters of the
night. In this play Shakespeare presents them as a temperamental and
immature couple incapable of raising a child.

Oberon and Titania personify the forces of nature. When they love each other all is well in nature and when they quarrel nature is in turmoil. Shakespeare has given Titania magnificent lines, allowing all of nature to participate in their quarrel.

TITANIA: These are the forgeries of jealousy:
            And never, since the middle summer's spring
            Met we on hill, in dale, forest, or mead,
            By pavèd fountain, or by rushy brook,
            Or in the beachèd margent of the sea
            To dance our ringlets to the whistling wind,
            But with thy brawls thou hast disturbed our sport.
            Therefore the winds, piping to us in vain,
            As in revenge, have sucked up from the sea
            Contagious fog; which falling in the land
            Have every pelting river made so proud
            That they have overborne their continents.
            The ox hath therefore stretched his yoke in vain,
            The ploughman lost his sweat, and the green corn
            Hath rotted ere his youth attained a beard. (*A Misummer Night's Dream*, II.i.81–95)

Jealousy can disturb the peace of nature. Forgeries of jealousy, what a magnificent concept! When all is well between them, Oberon and Titania "dance … ringlets to the whistling wind". The poet conceptualises the whistling winds as being made happy and content by the ringlets the couple is dancing to them, but when a brawl takes place between the two, the winds are offended because they are "piping to us in vain". Since the winds feel neglected, they "have sucked up from the sea / Contagious fogs" that have fallen on the earth and caused flooding as rivers "have overborne their continents". What we hear from Titania is that not only is all nature animated and moved by the same emotions that animate humans, but also when a disagreement disturbs their "sport" nature falls into disorder. Rivers become proud and overflow their banks; these rivers are animated creatures who need the love between Oberon and Titania to stay in place. The farmers' harvest also depends on the couple loving each other. As long as they do, the night is blessed with hymn and carol and the moon, "governess of floods", holds floods in check. Titania's speech implies that love is needed to hold the forces of nature within friendly limits.

If we apply the scene to what is called "infantile sexuality" we can read the speech as the infant sleeping securely if all is well between the parents. However, when a quarrel takes place or the child awakens during the primal scene and witnesses parental quarrels or sexual intercourse, the child, now turned poet, will describe the world as Titania just did.

The quarrel between Oberon and Titania, which has created such an upheaval in nature, is over a changeling. This is how Puck describes the crisis:

PUCK: The King doth keep his revels here tonight.
        Take heed the Queen come not within his sight,
        For Oberon is passing fell and wrath,
        Because that she as her attendant hath
        A lovely boy stol'n from an Indian king;
        She never had so sweet a changeling,
        And jealous Oberon would have the child
        Knight of his train, to trace the forests wild.
        But she perforce withholds the lovèd boy,
        Crowns him with flowers, and makes him all her joy.
        And now they never meet in grove or green,
        By fountain clear or spangled starlight sheen,
        But they do square, that all their elves for fear
        Creep into acorn cups and hide them there. (II.i.18–31)

Puck has not described an oedipal child but a child desired by both mother and father separately and not as a couple. It is the excessively desired child who separates the parents.

Being fairies, Oberon and Titania cannot have children of their own, but it is not difficult to translate Oberon's wrath as the jealousy of a husband for the love the mother gives to the child. Each one wants to be the sole possessor of this child. Some mortals have known this kind of jealousy. Examined from a psychoanalytic point of view, the changeling represents every child's unconscious desire to separate the parents, with each parent wanting the child to his or her self.

Titania gives us a different view of the changeling, whose mother was one of Titania's votaries.

TITANIA: Set your heart at rest.
The fairy land buys not the child of me.
His mother was a votaress of my order,
And in the spicèd Indian air by night,
Full often hath she gossip'd by my side,
And sat with me on Neptune's yellow sands
Marking th'embarkèd traders on the flood,
When we have laughed to see the sails conceive
And grow big-bellied with the wanton wind;
Which she, with pretty and with swimming gait
Following (her womb then rich with my young squire),
Would imitate, and sail upon the land
To fetch me trifles, and return again
As from a voyage, rich with merchandise.
But she, being mortal, of that boy did die,
And for her sake do I rear up her boy;
And for her sake I will not part with him. (II.i.121–137)

Titania and her votaress were watching the sailboats "embarked … on the flood" and they sexualised what they saw: "When we have laugh'd to see the sails conceive / And grow big-bellied with the wanton wind".

There is some disagreement between Puck's and Titania's versions of the events. In Puck's interpretation the changeling was stolen from an Indian king, while in Titania's account, his mother, a mortal, died and Titania has taken over her maternal functions. In both versions, Titania has fallen in love with the changeling and Oberon is furious and jealous. Oberon demands that Titania yield him the boy and she refuses. The quarrel between the fairy king and queen is replicated by many mortals when husband and wife cannot raise a child together, each one mistakenly believing that the child needs only one parent.

In our culture, where divorce is common, many children find themselves in this position in the custody battles of the parents. Psychoanalysis has taught us that Oberon's desire to take the changeling away from Titania and possess him all by himself is based on a bisexual wish; he imagines himself to be both father and mother. The definition of a changeling is a child surreptitiously put in the place of another. That is not the case here, but if we take the unconscious into consideration the term changeling is appropriate, for the child has usurped and therefore changed the heterosexual love of the couple.

The love juice

Oberon sends Puck to bring him the juice of "a little western flower, / Before, milk-white; now purple with love's wound" (II.i.166–167). He notes:

OBERON: The juice of it on sleeping eyelids laid
Will make or man or woman madly dote
Upon the next live creature that it sees. (II.i.170–172)

It is interesting to compare Oberon's love juice with the love potion that Tristan and Isolde drink in Wagner's opera *Tristan and Isolde*. The couple has a complex relationship before they drink the love potion. They both believe they are taking poison and then discover they have taken the love potion by mistake. Oberon's love juice performs no intrapsychic alchemy. Its power is confined to making the drinker fall in love literally at first sight. This power is not an intrapsychic change but the disappearance of old love ties in a new love. The love juice is a parody of love itself. The mischief brought about by this love juice is entertaining but not fatal.

Love and magic

Egeus, Hermia's father, accuses Lysander of bewitching his daughter, an example of a lover becoming a dangerous poet.

EGEUS: This man hath bewitched the bosom of my child.
Thou, thou, Lysander, thou hast given her rhymes,
And interchanged love-tokens with my child.
Thou hast by moonlight at her window sung
With feigning voice verses of feigning love,
And stolen the impression of her fantasy,
With bracelets of thy hair, rings, gauds, conceits,
Knacks, trifles, nosegays, sweetmeats—messengers
Of strong prevailment in unhardened youth;
With cunning hast thou filched my daughter's heart,
Turned her obedience, which is due to me,
To stubborn harshness. And, my gracious Duke,
Be it so she will not here, before your grace
Consent to marry with Demetrius,

> I beg the ancient privilege of Athens;
> As she is mine, I may dispose of her;
> Which shall be either to this gentleman
> Or to her death, according to our law. (I.i.27–44)

Lysander has "stolen the impression" of Hermia's fancy and "filched" his daughter's heart. The daughter's love has changed her father's relationship to her into murderous jealousy.

Egeus represents a familiar figure in Shakespeare's plays: the father who cannot let his daughter go. If he cannot keep her for himself at least he should be the one to choose her husband. When the lover becomes a poet he ensnares the innocent daughter.

Hermia is a familiar figure in Shakespeare's plays: she is the dutiful daughter who comes to have a personality of her own when she loves a man of her own choosing and refuses to marry the man her father has chosen for her. In this play Shakespeare has introduced a comic element because Demetrius and Lysander are so similar that the struggle between father and daughter is a quarrel over no significant differences. Shakespeare has given Hermia interesting reasons for not yielding to her father's wish.

HERMIA: So will I grow, so live, so die, my lord,
> Ere I will my virgin patent up
> Unto his lordship, whose unwishèd yoke
> My soul consents not to give sovereignty. (I.i.79–82)

The daughter who disobeys her father and insists on choosing her own man was of interest to Shakespeare not only in this play but also in Desdemona's case in *Othello* and Miranda in *The Tempest*. Seen psychoanalytically the father who insists on his right to choose his daughter's husband is expressing his oedipal wishes to retain symbolic possession of her.

EGEUS: And what is mine my love shall render him;
> And she is mine, and all my right of her
> I do estate unto Demetrius. (I.i.96–98)

The use of the word estate suggests that the daughter is the property of the father, which, if he chooses, he can give to another man.

The line "The course of true love never did run smooth" (I.i.134), spoken by Lysander, has entered our language, as well as the line "O hell, to choose love by another's eyes!" (I.i.140), spoken by Hermia. It is followed shortly afterwards by a statement that reflects Hermia's acceptance of the pain of loving.

HERMIA: If then true lovers have been ever crossed
              It stands as an edict in destiny.
              Then let us teach our trial patience,
              Because it is a customary cross,
              As due to love as thoughts, and dreams, and sighs,
              Wishes and tears—poor fancy's followers. (I.i.150–155)

Love consists of thoughts, dreams, sighs, wishes, and tears. They are followers of "poor fancy".

Later Helena, speaking of her unrequited love for Demetrius, says:

HELENA: Love looks not with the eyes but with the mind,
              And therefore is winged Cupid painted blind.
              Nor hath Love's mind of any judgment taste. (I.i.234–236)

Shakespeare offers an original interpretation of the blindness of Cupid. Not the eyes but the mind determines whom we love. The word mind stands for the then-uncoined term unconscious.

Love and masochism

The connection between love and masochism must have been important to Shakespeare because he returned to it time and again. The most important play to deal with this connection is *Antony and Cleopatra*: Antony loses an empire because of his submission to Cleopatra. In *A Midsummer Night's Dream* the connection between love and masochism is treated with humour, but all we need is to read the following passage more than once and the humour in the exchange turns into pity for Helena.

Lysander and Hermia have decided to elope when Helena, sick with love for Demetrius, enters.

HELENA: O, teach me how you look, and with what art
          You sway the motion of Demetrius' heart.
HERMIA: I frown upon him; yet he loves me still.
HELENA: O that your frowns would teach my smiles such skill!
HERMIA: I give him curses; yet he gives me love.
HELENA: O that my prayers could such affection move!
HERMIA: The more I hate, the more he follows me.
HELENA: The more I love, the more he hateth me. (I.i.192–199)
          Later Helena appeals directly to Demetrius.
HELENA: I am your spaniel; and, Demetrius,
          The more you beat me I will fawn on you.
          Use me but as your spaniel: spurn me, strike me,
          Neglect me, lose me; only give me leave,
          Unworthy as I am, to follow you.
          What worser place can I beg in your love
          (And yet a place of high respect with me)
          Than to be usèd as you use your dog?
DEMETRIUS: Tempt not too much the hatred of my spirit;
          For I am sick when I do look on thee.
HELENA: And I am sick when I look not on you. (II.i.203–213)

When the love juice does its work Helena feels mocked by the sudden declarations of love she receives. She has just realised that her very close friend has become heterosexual. Shakespeare captured this situation in these magnificent lines.

HELENA: Lo, she is one of this confederacy!
          Now I perceive they have conjoined all three
          To fashion this false sport in spite of me.
          Injurious Hermia, most ungrateful maid,
          Have you conspired, have you with these contrived
          To bait me with this foul derision? (III.ii.192–197)

Helena's masochism is turning into paranoia.

Bottom's dream

Bottom is one of the most delightful characters created by Shakespeare. He has a strong sense of his own identity even when he undergoes very extensive physical changes, acquiring the head of an ass. He, too, is struggling to separate a vision (memory) from a dream.

> I have had a most rare vision. I have had a dream, past the wit of man to say what dream it was. Man is but an ass if he go about to expound this dream. Methought I was—there is no man can tell what. Methought I was—and methought I had—but man is but a patched fool if he will offer to say what methought I had. The eye of man hath not heard, the ear of man hath not seen, man's hand is not able to taste, his tongue to conceive, nor his heart to report what my dream was! I will get Peter Quince to write a ballad of this dream; it shall be called "Bottom's Dream", because it hath no bottom; (IV.i.200–209)

Strictly speaking, what Bottom is recalling is not a dream but a memory of how Titania made love to him while he had the head of an ass, but he has no way of recording this memory except by treating it as if it had been a dream. Bottom accomplishes one of Shakespeare's unconscious aims in this play, blurring the line between memory and dreams. Such false memories are called screen memories. Memories also appear regularly hidden in dreams.

I owe this to Nuttall (2007), the realisation that Bottom's love encounter with Titania while an ass, has antecedents in Greek mythology. One example is Pasiphaë, who coupled with a bull. She fell in love with Zeus when he assumed the form of a bull and asked Daedalus to make a wooden cow and placed herself inside of it. When Zeus mounted the cow Pasiphaë became pregnant by him and gave birth to the minotaur. Apuleius tells the story of a woman who lusts for Lucius after he was metamorphosed into an ass. These myths express the fear of the Greeks that woman are drawn to animals and their larger penises.

From a psychoanalytic perspective Bottom is a reassuring figure in the play. Even when he has metamorphosed into a man with the head of an ass he is remarkably unchanged; he remains the same person throughout the play, and even the love of the powerful Titania has no visible effect on his identity. If anyone is afraid of love's power to change the personality of the lover, Bottom is a symbol of the stability of personality.

As we enter Act III, Quince and his fellow artisans are rehearsing *Pyramus and Thisbe*, to be presented at the royal wedding. Shakespeare takes the opportunity to reflect in a comic vein upon the same topic that both Theseus and Puck have dealt with in a serious way, the relationship between stage and reality. Bottom is concerned that if Pyramus draws his sword to kill himself the ladies in the audience will be frightened. He therefore suggests a prologue be written to prepare the ladies and to assure them that Pyramus will not really be killed. To further reassure them, they are told that Pyramus is not really Pyramus but Bottom. In the same way the lion should explain to them that he is not a real lion. Bottom represents the kind of audience that has difficulty separating the stage from real life. In the same play, what Puck treats as a serious problem—the relationship of the audience to the play—Bottom repeats in a comic way. To present the same problem in such different ways was Shakespeare's unique talent; what we are witnessing can be called a creative splitting.

Already in Puck's apology we were struck by Shakespeare's fear that the audience will see the play not as a fantasy of the author but will lose the necessary distance and treat the play as if it were real: hence his advice that the play should be treated like a dream. Bottom is experiencing this fear. We note an aspect of Shakespeare's genius: he can treat the same fear seriously in Puck's apology and comically in Bottom's fear that a staged drama will be taken for reality.

Bottom's fear is not as groundless as Shakespeare makes it. It requires an awareness of the "ego boundary" for an individual to enjoy a play or film and not to be drawn into it. In psychoanalysis we encounter children and even some adults who cannot see a play without thinking they are in it. It is not unusual after seeing a movie to have a dream in which one is in some part of the movie. In his own comic way Bottom tries to protect us from such an event.

Reflecting on this play, we have come closer to understanding what Freud called the poet's "Ars poetica". It is the unique balancing of many diverse themes and holding them together. The poet is first related and then differentiated from the lunatic, the lover, and the dreamer. The poet is introduced as the disturber of the audience's tranquility and then as the healer of the audience's depression. Art is introduced as an attempt to overcome man's sadism towards women. A new infantile pathology is introduced, with the child as the disturber of the couple and each parent finding the other superfluous. The nature of love is both introduced and mocked. The fear that the audience will take the stage to represent life and become frightened is presented and reassurance is provided. All these various themes are presented and woven together so the play is experienced as very interesting and a pleasure to watch. No wonder the poet sees himself as a magician!

CHAPTER THREE

The Tempest: the abdication of creativity

*T*he Tempest is an abdication and renunciation play; it is a personal play of greater interest to the author but not a topic easily welcome to the audience. Shakespeare is trying to explain to us the reasons for his abdication and unconsciously he is asking for our permission to do so. He is pursuing two not-easily-reconciled wishes: to explain his abdication and at the same time not to depress his audience.

The Tempest is believed to have been written in 1611, when Shakespeare was forty-seven years old. Shakespeare's first play, *Henry VI, Part I*, is thought to have been written in 1589, when he was twenty-five years old, a span of twenty two years of creative play writing.

The Tempest is believed to be Shakespeare's last independently written play. It describes in symbolic language the playwright's waning powers as a poet and the decision to abdicate. In my reading, it can be read as the counterpart to *A Midsummer Night's Dream* (1589), in which the poet overcame his doubts and inhibitions, gaining the inner right to be a poet.

Both plays take place outside of ordinary civilisation; *A Midsummer Night's Dream* in a forest near Athens and *The Tempest* on an uncharted island. In both, fairies and spirits are assigned crucial roles. Shakespeare himself must have been at least preconsciously aware of the similarity

57

between the two plays, for he gave lines to Prospero that belong to *A Midsummer Night's Dream* and appear to be inserted into *The Tempest*.

PROSPERO: Our revels now are ended. These our actors,
                 As I foretold you, were all spirits and
                 Are melted into air, into thin air.
                 And like the baseless fabric of this vision,
                 The cloud-capped towers, the gorgeous palaces,
                 The solemn temples, the great globe itself—
                 Yea, all which it inherit—shall dissolve,
                 And like this insubstantial pageant faded,
                 Leave not a rack behind. We are such stuff
                 As dreams are made on, and our little life
                 Is rounded with a sleep. (*The Tempest*, IV.i.138–148)

For a moment we are back in A Midsummer Night's Dream, where Puck expresses similar feelings.

Hazlitt said: "*The Tempest* is one of the most original and perfect of Shakespeare's productions, and he has shewn in it all the varieties of his powers …. The real characters and events partake of the wildness of a dream" (Hazlitt, 1817: p. 116).

Caroline Spurgeon called the play "an absolute symphony of sound" (Spurgeon, 1966: p. 300).

> We hear, as we visit different parts of the island, the singing of the winds and the roaring of the waters, the cries of the drowning men, the reverberation of the thunder; our ears are assailed by the hollow bellowing of wild beasts making "a din to fright a monster's ear" (II.i.314), chattering apes and hissing adders, the drunken shouts and catches of Caliban and his companions, the hallooing of hunters and dogs, and other "strange, hollow, confused" and nerve-shaking noises … (Spurgeon, 1966: pp. 300–01)

By contrast, Harold Bloom finds the play "fundamentally plotless" (Bloom, 1998: p. 662). "Caliban, though he speaks only a hundred lines in *The Tempest*, has now taken over the play for so many" (Bloom, 1998: p. 663). As to Ariel, Bloom considers him "more a figures of vast suggestiveness than a character possessing an inwardness available to us" (Bloom, 1998: p. 666).

To Marjorie Garber, Caliban is something like libido, sexual desire or id, basic human drives, while Ariel is imagination personified. Going back to categories current in Shakespeare's time, Caliban is a spirit of earth and water and Ariel that of fire (Garber, 2004: pp. 852–853).

Nuttall, like Bloom, was disturbed by Ariel. "We do not know what he is. He is that thing that becomes normal in science fiction, a vividly imagined being for which no covering concept is readily available". (Nuttall, 2007: p. 361). Nuttal singles out the moment where Prospero forgives his brother Antonio.

> For you, most wicked sir, whom to call brother
> Would even infect my mouth, I do forgive
> Thy rankest fault. (*The Tempest*, V.i.130–132)

Nuttall comments: "Never did forgiveness sound more like continuing, unabated hatred" (Nuttall, 2007: p. 371). Nuttal concludes, "Prospero's fear is of something that lies deeper than his own murder. It is the thought that he has never really been born at all" (Nuttall, 2007: p. 375). If Nuttall is right, and he well may be, then Shakespeare has failed to endow Prospero with the sense of personal reality that he succeeded in giving to his other creations.

Psychoanalytic studies of The Tempest

In 1923 Hanns Sachs, a member of Freud's closest circle wrote a long and erudite paper on *The Tempest*; I cite his main conclusions:

1. "If Prospero is the poet, then the island—on which he lived alone with his daughter for so long, and which he leaves upon breaking his magic wand—means poetry, to which he is bidding farewell" (Sachs, 1923: p. 70).
2. In the epilogue the poet speaks to the public through the mouth of Prospero.
3. "Ariel—who quickens the island with his music and sweet songs, who, by his master's command, bewitches everybody that sets foot on it, who entangles the senses and then frees them again—Ariel is the very embodiment of Shakespeare's art" (Sachs, 1923: p. 70).
4. Prospero induces drowsiness in Miranda. In this induced drowsiness Miranda recalls "all the blotted out and forgotten memories of her

earliest childhood" (Sachs, 1923: pp. 71–72). Sachs is struck by the similarity of this technique to psychoanalysis.

5. In *The Winter's Tale* Perdita, like Oedipus, is sent away to die. In *The Tempest* it is Miranda who makes the exiled father into a magician and without her, his life is over.

Another psychoanalytic study, written in 1946, was by the English psychoanalyst Ella Sharpe, titled "From *King Lear* to *The Tempest*". In both plays the storm plays a major role; to Sharpe the storm represents the rage before the onset of depression. Prospero represents "the re-emergence of the psyche after depression" (Sharpe, 1946: p. 215).

In his book *Discourse on Hamlet and HAMLET*, published in 1971, K. R. Eissler devoted the last section of over one hundred pages to *The Tempest*. Eissler sees *The Tempest* as Shakespeare undoing what he had written in the earlier plays (Eissler, 1971: p. 557). Eissler assumes that the human passions that were brought onto the stage by Shakespeare must have shaken their creator (Eissler, 1971: p. 558). Shakespeare may have become traumatised by what he created. Within psychoanalysis this view was revolutionary. Creative work was traditionally seen as sublimation and as the opposite of neurosis. Now Eissler is suggesting that great artists may also traumatise themselves by their own creative work. Many tragic events almost happen in *The Tempest*, like murder and rape, but the play itself remains static, without psychological development. The twelve years of Prospero's stay on the island were not a preparation for any future; they were years of fulfillment of his life's mission. Caliban has strong ties to his mother, the witch Sycorax; Prospero, the father figure, tries to drive out Caliban's pre-oedipal fixation. Eissler quotes D. G. James (1937), who noted that *The Tempest* is the ultimate destruction of the world of the imagination. Shakespeare dissolves the world he had created.

In 2001 another study of the play, by Melvin Lansky, centred on the role of forgiveness. Lansky saw forgiveness as equivalent to the psychoanalytic concept of working through. The inability or unwillingness to forgive perpetuates the state of withdrawal and precludes re-involvement. Forgiveness represents identification with the loving aspects of the good object. It represents the triumph of Eros over Thanatos. Miranda is the good object that enables Prospero to reach a state of forgiveness.

The four psychoanalytic essays cited differ in their concepts and imagery, but all four find that *The Tempest* describes an inner crisis that Shakespeare must have experienced in order to write this play. Nor is there any evidence, as we sometimes feel about certain plays, that it was in some sense helpful or even curative to the author. Nor is the language as rich; there are no quotations that stay with us after we have seen or read the play.

Prospero was the ruler of Milan but he was more interested in magic than the administration of his kingdom and left the city in the care of a brother who usurped his power. A similarity to the behaviour of the Duke of Vienna in *Measure for Measure* springs to mind: Prospero's loss of his kingdom to a greedy brother leads to the thought that a younger brother may have displaced the poet. The storm created by Prospero brought his brother and his fellow conspirators under his power. As in *Hamlet*, the temptation to make it a simple revenge play is offered but rejected.

A scene of special psychoanalytic interest now takes place between Prospero and his fifteen-year-old daughter Miranda.

We are immediately introduced to Miranda's nobility of spirit.

MIRANDA: If by your art, my dearest father, you have
            Put the wild waters in this roar, allay them.
            The sky, it seems, would pour down stinking pitch,
            But that the sea, mounting to th' welkin's cheek,
            Dashes the fire out. Oh, I have suffered
            With those that I saw suffer. A brave vessel
            Who had, no doubt, some noble creature in her
            Dashed all to pieces. Oh, the cry did knock
            Against my very heart! Poor souls, they perished. (I.ii.1–9)

Prospero tells Miranda that he magically ordered the storm but that no one was harmed. He then tells her for the first time that when she was less than three years old his usurping brother drove him out of Milan. These enemies are now on the island and are under Prospero's control. To have one's enemies at one's mercy is a common theme in daydreams, but Shakespeare uses this opportunity for an inner struggle between forgiveness and revenge.

An interesting exchange takes place between father and daughter.

PROSPERO: I have done nothing but in care of thee,
             Of thee, my dear one—thee my daughter, who
             Art ignorant of what thou art, naught knowing
             Of whence I am, nor that I am more better
             Than Prospero, master of a full poor cell
             And thy no greater father.
MIRANDA: More to know
             Did never meddle with my thoughts.
PROSPERO: 'Tis time
             I should inform thee farther. (I.ii.16–23)

To our astonishment he is probing her infantile amnesia as a psychoanalyst would.

PROSPERO: Canst thou remember
             A time before we came unto this cell?
             I do not think thou canst, for then thou wast not
             Out three years old.
MIRANDA: Certainly, sir, I can.
PROSPERO: By what? by any other house or person?
             Of any thing the image tell me that
             Hath kept with thy remembrance.
MIRANDA: 'Tis far off
             And rather like a dream than an assurance
             That my remembrance warrants. Had I not
             Four or five women once that tended me? (I.ii.38–47)

Miranda contrasts "like a dream" with "assurance". The language is
Shakespeare's but the phenomenon described is familiar. In psychoanalysis, infantile memories are experienced as dreams and often they
turn out to be "screen memories" or fantasies that were transformed
into memories. *The Tempest* must be the first investigation of infantile amnesia in world literature. We are astonished to discover that
Shakespeare was both interested in infantile amnesia and aware of
its dream-like quality. Like any psychoanalyst, Prospero is amazed to
learn why a particular detail survived the infantile amnesia. He asks,
"But how is it / That this lives in thy mind?" (I.ii.48–49). If Prospero
had been psychoanalytically trained he would not be so surprised
by the memory. Miranda is the only female on the island. She must

have struggled with the issue of gender difference and her memory assured her, however dimly, that she is not the only female in the world.

Prospero then discloses to Miranda the treachery of his brother.

PROSPERO: My brother and thy uncle, called Antonio—
I pray thee, mark me (that a brother should
Be so perfidious!)—he whom next thyself
Of all the world I loved and to him put
The manage of my state, as at that time
Through all the signories it was the first,
And Prospero the prime duke, being so reputed
In dignity, and for the liberal arts
Without a parallel. Those being all my study,
The government I cast upon my brother
And to my state grew stranger, being transported
And rapt in secret studies. Thy false uncle—
Dost thou attend me? (I.ii.66–78)

It must have been difficult for Prospero to disclose this information; we feel how out of breath he is. He transmits many more details than Miranda can assimilate and then suspects her of not paying attention. He tells her that he essentially abdicated his dukedom to a loved brother in order to devote himself to secret studies, but the brother betrayed him and forced him to seek refuge with his daughter on the enchanted island. If he suspects her of not listening, it is because of a trauma her father suffered and it is he who has difficulty recalling it.

To a psychoanalyst the scene is familiar from when a patient discovers that what was considered a happy childhood was in fact traumatic. Shakespeare, disguised as Prospero, discovers what he considered a magic island through something akin to self-analysis. His own creativity was really based on a traumatic childhood experience that now forces him to abdicate his magic, or creativity. Miranda stands for the innocent self that knows nothing of the trauma that Prospero is now disclosing to her.

PROSPERO: Twelve year since, Miranda, twelve year since,
Thy father was the Duke of Milan and
A prince of power.

MIRANDA: Sir, are not you my father?
PROSPERO: Thy mother was a piece of virtue and
               She said thou wast my daughter. (I.ii.53–57)

The logical question for Miranda to ask would have been, "Were you the Duke of Milan?" but unconsciously the new information evokes in her the anxiety that he is not her father.

This is the only time in the play the mother is mentioned. We realise that this play deals with the relationship between a father and daughter, a relationship in which the mother is eliminated. Strikingly, we recall a similar absence of the mother in *King Lear*. A mother is needed to give birth to the child, but she is denied a role in the child's upbringing. The father's belief that he can be both father and mother to the daughter can be a sign of bisexuality.

Prospero continues the tale of woe.

PROSPERO: they hurried us aboard a bark,
               Bore us some leagues to sea, where they prepared
               A rotten carcass of a butt, not rigged,
               Nor tackle, sail, nor mast. The very rats
               Instinctively had quit it. There they hoist us
               To cry to th' sea that roared to us, to sigh
               To th' winds whose pity, sighing back again,
               Did us but loving wrong.
MIRANDA: Alack, what trouble
               Was I then to you!
PROSPERO: Oh, a cherubim
               Thou wast that did preserve me. Thou didst smile
               Infusèd with a fortitude from heaven,
               When I have decked the sea with drops full salt,
               Under my burthen groaned; which raised in me
               An undergoing stomach to bear up
               Against what should ensue. (I.ii.144–158)

Prospero is disclosing the traumatic past to Miranda, but Miranda experiences only what a burden she must have been to her father. Prospero assures her that she was the inspiration that made it possible for him to "bear up / Against what should ensue". We hear feelings of inadequacy in Miranda and a declaration of love for her from Prospero.

In Act IV we learn how essential Miranda is to Prospero and that he is in love with her. He tells Ferdinand:

> If I have too austerely punished you,
> Your compensation makes amends, for I
> Have given you here a third of mine own life—
> Or that for which I live—who once again
> I tender to thy hand. All thy vexations
> Were but my trials of thy love and thou
> Hast strangely stood the test. Here, afore heaven,
> I ratify this my rich gift. O Ferdinand,
> Do not smile at me that I boast of her,
> For thou shalt find she will outstrip all praise
> And make it halt behind her. (IV.i.1–11)

The expression "a third of mine own life" has evoked much comment. It is not logical since Miranda is Prospero's only child; the statement should have been half of my life. However, Shakespeare, unlike Prospero, had two daughters, hence the slip?

If we think of the dialogue between Prospero and Miranda as an inner struggle, then Prospero represents the part of the individual that remembers the trauma and Miranda is the part that has succumbed to infantile amnesia. The constant accusation that she is not listening represents what we call resistance, which is shown by the patient who does not want to remember a trauma.

What Miranda has been told corresponds to an analytic overcoming of the infantile amnesia. In the chapter on *Hamlet* I have shown how a similar overcoming of a childhood amnesia liberated Hamlet to love Ophelia. In a similar vein the overcoming of childhood amnesia enables Miranda to leave her father and transfer her love to a heterosexual relationship with Ferdinand. Remembering the women who took care of her enables her to become a woman and fall in love.

The parting from Miranda

The love that Prospero has for Miranda has helped him to move beyond the wish for revenge against his brother. His next task is to be able to give her up and this happens when she falls in love with Ferdinand, but now an interesting compromise formation takes place. He will give her to Ferdinand provided Ferdinand can abstain sexually until the marriage ceremony has taken place. The marriage is the moment when the father relinquishes his rights over his daughter.

PROSPERO: Then as my gift and thine own acquisition
Worthily purchased, take my daughter. But
If thou dost break her virgin knot before
All sanctimonious ceremonies may
With full and holy rite be ministered,
No sweet aspersion shall the heavens let fall
To make this contract grow, but barren hate,
Sour-eyed disdain, and discord shall bestrew
The union of your bed with weeds so loathly
That you shall hate it both. Therefore take heed,
As Hymen's lamps shall light you. (IV.i.13–23)

What we hear is a father's curse. Should the two engage in premarital sex they will be denied heaven's "sweet aspersion" and will encounter "barren hate" and "sour-eyed disdain". The language is so powerful that we surmise that Shakespeare was adamantly opposed to pre-marital sexuality. Ferdinand, unlike Caliban, can have Miranda, but only if he can control his lust for her. We have become familiar with Shakespeare's fear of lust. The haunting Sonnet 129 is a monument to the poet's overwhelming fear of lust.

Th' expense of spirit in a waste of shame
Is lust in action, and till action, lust
Is perjured, murd'rous, bloody, full of blame,
Savage, extreme, rude, cruel, not to trust,
Enjoyed no sooner but despisèd straight,
Past reason hunted, and no sooner had,
Past reason hated as a swallowed bait
On purpose laid to make the taker mad;
Mad in pursuit, and in possession so,
Had, having, and in quest to have, extreme;
A bliss in proof, and proved, a very woe;
Before, a joy proposed; behind, a dream.
All this the world well knows, yet none knows well
To shun the heaven that leads men to this hell.

Another equally vehement denunciation of lust is Arianna's condemnation in *The Comedy of Errors*:

> How dearly would it touch thee to the quick,
> Shouldst thou but hear I were licentious
> And that this body, consecrate to thee,
> By ruffian lust should be contaminate!
> Wouldst thou not spit at me, and spurn at me,
> And hurl the name of husband in my face,
> And tear the stained skin off my harlot brow,
> And from my false hand cut the wedding ring,
> And break it with a deep-divorcing vow?
> I know thou canst, and therefore see thou do it.
> I am possessed with an adulterate blot;
> My blood is mingled with the crime of lust. (*The Comedy of Errors*, II.ii.132–143)

And from the ghost in *Hamlet*:

> So lust, though to a radiant angel linked,
> Will sate itself in a celestial bed
> And prey on garbage. (*Hamlet*, I.v.55–57)

The condemnation of lust is also the dominant theme in "The Rape of Lucrece":

> This momentary joy breeds months of pain
> This hot desire converts to cold disdain:
> Pure chastity is rifled of her store,
> and Lust, the thief, far poorer than before. (*The Rape of Lucrece*, 690–93)
>
> ...
>
> She says her subjects with foul insurrection
> Have battered down her consecrated wall
> And by their mortal fault brought in subjection
> Her immortality, and made her thrall
> To living death and pain perpetual. (*The Rape of Lucrece*, 722–726)
>
> ...

> She bears the load of lust he left behind,
> And he the burden of a guilty mind.
> He like a thievish dog creeps sadly thence,
> She like a wearied lamb lies panting there;
> He scowls and hates himself for his offence,
> She desperate with her nails her flesh doth tear. (*The Rape of Lucrece*, 734–39)

On the basis of this evidence we are justified in assuming that Prospero's vehement attack on sexual lust represented Shakespeare's own feelings.

Prospero can teach himself to give Miranda away provided that Ferdinand does not take her passionately. Symbolically, Ferdinand accepts the obedient son role; he will obey the "law of the father". He will receive Miranda from Prospero and not conquer her. Prospero, and behind him Shakespeare, will tolerate the transfer of the daughter to another man only if their relationship is not passionate, and Ferdinand complies.

Caliban

Prospero and Miranda are not alone on their island; they share it with Caliban and Ariel. Who is Caliban? Shakespeare scholars have speculated about the origins of the name Caliban. The most likely literary source was Montaigne's essay on the cannibals. Before Caliban met Prospero he was preverbal. Having learned language from Prospero made it possible for him to express aggression.

CALIBAN: You taught me language, and my profit on 't
            Is I know how to curse. The red plague rid you
            For learning me your language! (*The Tempest*, I.ii.369–371)

A normal child is happy to learn to speak; an unloved child may not be. Caliban is not and he tells us why. To him, speech means the capacity to express aggression. If Caliban is part of Shakespeare, then Shakespeare just discovered that his creativity has enabled him to express his aggression.

A few lines earlier we got to know another aspect of Caliban. Speaking of his attempted rape of Miranda, he says:

> Oh ho, oh ho! Would 't had been done!
> Thou didst prevent me. I had peopled else
> This isle with Calibans. (I.ii.355–357)

We now have three facts about Caliban: he is a cannibal by virtue of his name, he knows how to curse, and he sexually desires Miranda. He is Prospero before education and socialisation had done their work. In the analyst Melanie Klein's words, he is the infant in the paranoid position.

In Act III we will learn to know another redeeming aspect of Caliban. When he meets Stephano and Trinculo he is both friendly and assuring to them.

> Be not afeard. The isle is full of noises,
> Sounds, and sweet airs that give delight and hurt not.
> Sometimes a thousand twangling instruments
> Will hum about mine ears, and sometime voices
> That, if I then had waked after long sleep,
> Will make me sleep again. And then, in dreaming,
> The clouds methought would open and show riches
> Ready to drop upon me, that when I waked
> I cried to dream again. (III.ii.129–137)

In Shakespeare's work the capacity to sleep and have happy dreams is the usual sign that all is well intrapsychically. That Caliban can describe such a state of bliss to Stefano and Trinculo just after he persuades them to murder Prospero is surprising. It suggests that he is not just the embodiment of evil. The ability to hear such music makes Caliban a more complex figure.

If Caliban can hear music and if he can sleep well he has grown a great deal and has become more civilised. *The Tempest* deals with the difficulty a father has in allowing his daughter form a relationship with another man. Prospero is a stand in for the playwright. Unlike most of Shakespeare's works, the play is not built on previously known sources; he invented the whole plot.

Ariel

Who is Ariel? The name is biblical, meaning in Hebrew "the lion of God", and if we wish to go to a more primitive, pre-monotheistic time it could also mean the lion god. It was Ariel who boarded the ship and created the storm at Prospero's command. Ariel has no personality of his own. He is a representation of Prospero's omnipotent wishes and Shakespeare's daydreams. Ariel was the slave of the witch Sycorax but being "a spirit too delicate / To act her earthy and abhorred commands" (I.ii.275–276) he was confined in a rift in a cloven pine and imprisoned for a dozen years. The witch died and left Ariel imprisoned. If we think psychoanalytically, Ariel represents Prospero when he freed himself from a witch-mother and experienced himself as creative.

The shipwreck originally expressed Prospero's fury and revenge wishes, but when Ariel carries these wishes out, a transformation takes place and no one is hurt by Prospero's aggressive wishes. In the play Caliban and Ariel are often two opposing forces. We understand why Prospero had to be deposed as the duke of Milan before he could take his daughter to the magic island. If it had been Prospero's free choice to live in exile with his daughter, the aspect represented by Caliban would have been stronger and resulted in the danger of a father-daughter incestuous relationship.

Act V opens with a discussion between Ariel and Prospero. Ariel assures his master that the shipwrecked crew is safely under control but then adds,

ARIEL: Your charm so strongly works 'em
          That if you now beheld them, your affections
          Would become tender.
PROSPERO: Dost thou think so, spirit?
ARIEL: Mine would, sir, were I human.
PROSPERO: And mine shall.
          Hast thou, which art but air, a touch, a feeling
          Of their afflictions, and shall not myself,
          One of their kind, that relish all as sharply
          Passion as they, be kindlier moved than thou art?
          Though with their high wrongs I am struck to th' quick,
          Yet with my nobler reason 'gainst my fury
          Do I take part. (V.i.17–27)

Ariel, a spirit, succeeds in humanising his master.

Both Caliban and Ariel are forces within Prospero. Caliban pulls him downward into incest and Ariel upward towards forgiveness. Only after Ariel has accomplished his work is Prospero ready to relinquish Miranda.

Prospero the magician represents Shakespeare the creative writer. In a self-analysis that Shakespeare carried out while writing this play, he recognised, probably with horror, that his creativity was fuelled by two Caliban-like wishes. These were revenge wishes, expressed in the shipwreck, and incestuous wishes for his daughter, represented by Caliban's wish to rape Miranda. When these two wishes found expression in this play, however veiled, the magician had to abjure his magic and the poet to give up his creativity.

Eissler's hypothesis, discussed earlier, was that Shakespeare became traumatised by his creative activity. We can be more precise: writing a play like *The Tempest* bears a similarity to self-analysis, in which the poet becomes aware of his aggression (the shipwreck) and his incestuous wishes towards his daughter (Caliban's wish to rape Miranda). If these wishes come too close to consciousness as a result of writing the play, a creative inhibition sets in.

If the hypothesis here advanced is correct, something can be added to the psychoanalytic theory of creativity. To be creative means for the artist to convert something that belongs to oneself into something others can share; it also means that something that was deeply repressed has become less repressed and closer to consciousness. The creative process in this play, called Prospero's magic, is facing two dangers. Prospero should not know that Caliban expresses his own wishes and Prospero should not become the forgiving Ariel. Some artists have been known to be afraid of psychoanalysis because they fear the loss of their creativity; they can use Prospero to express their fears.

The strange ending of The Tempest

Prospero's epilogue at the very end of the play goes even further than the previous quote:

PROSPERO: Now my charms are all o'erthrown,
              And what strength I have's mine own,
              Which is most faint. Now, 'tis true,
              I must be here confined by you,
              Or sent to Naples. Let me not,
              Since I have my dukedom got
              And pardoned the deceiver, dwell
              In this bare island by your spell,

But release me from my bands
With the help of your good hands.
Gentle breath of yours my sails
Must fill, or else my project fails,
Which was to please. Now I want
Spirits to enforce, art to enchant,
And my ending is despair,
Unless I be relieved by prayer,
Which pierces so that it assaults
Mercy itself and frees all faults.
As you from crimes would pardoned be,
Let your indulgence set me free. (V.Epilogue.1–20)

Seen psychoanalytically, *The Tempest* is a description of a self-analysis in which Shakespeare the poet is represented by Prospero the magician. The self-analysis resulted in the recognition of two intra-psychic forces, here called Caliban and Ariel. The self-analysis was a success; the magician gave up his magic and incestuous wishes and returned to the world of reality (Milan). Shakespeare is not happy, however; Prospero the magician was much more interesting that the now "cured" former magician. Once more we understand why Shakespeare can be called the discoverer of the unconscious but not the discoverer of psychoanalysis as therapy.

Shakespeare has described Prospero as motivated by two forces: his love for Miranda and his creativity. His self-analysis leads to a double loss and leaves him bereft. It was a self-analysis that ended in abdication.

Shakespeare recognised that much of his creativity was unconsciously fed by incestuous wishes for the daughter and hostile wishes for revenge. In *The Tempest* his enemies have been defeated by his magic but he has succumbed to Ariel's forgiveness. Through Prospero, Shakespeare conveys to us that his creativity was based on what psychoanalysis calls "sublimated aggression". Once the aggression becomes conscious magician and poet have to abdicate.

We are now at an amazing moment. A thin-edged forgiveness of his brother's betrayal together with a most reluctant decision to give Miranda to Ferdinand has led Prospero to give up his magic. It is as if Shakespeare analysed the motives behind his creativity and found that they were based on neurotic foundations. Having realised this,

Shakespeare turned against his muse. Using the language of Freud's *Interpretation of Dreams*, the latent content of *The Tempest* is Shakespeare's recognition that his art was fuelled by neurotic needs for revenge and holding onto his daughter.

PROSPERO: I'll bring you to your ship and so to Naples,
            Where I have hope to see the nuptial
            Of these our dear-belovèd solemnized,
            And thence retire me to my Milan, where
            Every third thought shall be my grave. (V.i.325–329)

Prospero gives up Miranda but every third thought anticipates his death.

The two interpretations that I consider strictly psychoanalytic are the equation of the magic island with the early years of infancy and the terrible usurpation of the horrible brother with the reaction of a child to the birth of a sibling. Beyond these two items looms the strictly psychoanalytic emphasis that the play is an attempt to solve a problem that belongs to early childhood. The struggle to give up the daughter repeats the earlier struggle for the child to give up the mother.

Timon of Athens: the loss of creativity

I t is generally assumed that *Timon of Athens* was written in 1607–08, the year *Coriolanus* was written and before *The Winter's Tale* or *The Tempest*. It was never performed in Shakespeare's time and it is far more likely to be read than seen on stage. It is very simple in design but not easy to read. Anyone interested in understanding what failing inspiration in a great poet looks like, will find this play clinically interesting if not a satisfactory work of art. It also highlights the difference between a psychoanalytic approach and that of a literary study of Shakespeare's plays.

It so happens that two prominent contemporary Shakespeare scholars have given us two different evaluations of *Timon of Athens* and I will present both.

Harold Bloom suspects that with this play "Shakespeare experienced a personal revulsion at what he was finishing, and turned away from it" (Bloom, 1998: p. 588). Bloom also found that "the play stages better than it reads; it is intensely dramatic, but unevenly expressed" (Bloom, 1998: p. 588).

Timon has no family connections and without a mother, wife, or daughter it is Shakespeare's only play without women except for two prostitutes. "Timon, when he raves to Alcibiades's whores, is outrageously obsessed with venereal infection …. The play is in some crucial respects an open wound" (Bloom, 1998: p. 589). Bloom notes Timon has no inwardness and dismisses the play as unworthy of Shakespeare.

Marjorie Garber's evaluation is significantly different. She calls *Timon of Athens* "Shakespeare's remarkable play about philanthropy and misanthropy" (Garber, 2004: p. 634).

> *Timon* is a superb piece of writing, characterization, and theater, and it deserves more recognition …. In the second half of the play, once Timon has lost his money—he tries to call upon those to whom he has given gifts and support in the past, and is turned away with an amusingly diverse array of (im)plausible excuses—he flees Athens, takes up residence in a cave, digs in the earth and with bitter irony discovers gold, and flings the gold at visitors unwise enough to call upon him. (Garber, 2004: p. 635)

The radically different views of this play held by two contemporary Shakespeare scholars should heighten our interest in this play.

J. C. Bucknill's book *The Mad Folk of Shakespeare*, published in 1867, has some very interesting observations on Timon's character. He believes that an inferior artist originally wrote *Timon of Athens* and that Shakespeare remodeled it, changing Timon's character. Bucknill sees Timon as resembling Lear, "full of unreasoning confidence" and "unreasoning hate …. His prodigality is unsoiled with profligacy" (Bucknill, 1867: p. 237). He spends for the pleasure of spending, a character trait directly opposite to the hoarder, or, as Shakespeare makes Timon express it, "more welcome are ye to my fortunes / Than my fortunes to me" (*Timon of Athens*, I.ii.19–20) and "Methinks, I could deal kingdoms to my friends, / And ne'er be weary" (I.ii.209–210). To Bucknill "There is doubtless much vanity in Timon's ostentation, but there is also a magnanimous disregard of self" (Bucknill, 1867: p. 246). Shakespeare makes Timon say, "Unwisely, not ignobly, have I given" (II.ii.168). Timon develops a distempered mind dominated by his belief in the utter unworthiness of humankind. If we translate these valuable observations into psychoanalytic language then this boundless wish to give will appear as a reaction formation against the opposite wish, to accumulate. Timon is an anal character with a reaction formation against his own fixation. Timon throws away the gold he finds in his cave. Gold, in psychoanalytic thinking, is equated with faeces, and these are not accumulated but hurled at unwelcome visitors.

A psychoanalyst approaching this play will see Timon as a case of pathological generosity. He feels compelled to give to anyone who approaches him and even to those he only hears about. Timon's "reality testing" is weak, for he only notices his depletion when he has lost all his money. We also notice that when he was rich he was generous but failed to establish any meaningful relationships with the recipients of his exaggerated generosity. Timon is no longer young and it is hinted that he was once a successful general, but Shakespeare does not tell us when this trait of pathological generosity took hold.

A psychoanalyst will next be struck by Timon's need for gratitude. Why was it so important to him when he did not receive it? A psychoanalyst will attempt to establish a connection between the two characters traits of Timon: his excessive generosity, particularly towards strangers, and the vehemence of his demand for gratitude from them. If Timon had been undergoing psychoanalysis he would eventually be confronted with the problem of whether he unconsciously planned the whole sequence of events in order to demonstrate the absence of gratitude in the world. The play forces us to consider the difference between gratitude as an experience that we are capable of having, that enriches our lives and makes life worth living, and gratitude as a demand upon others. Shakespeare is telling us that Timon found life without gratitude is not worth living; its absence forced him to withdraw from society. Why has gratitude become so crucial to him? I turn to psychoanalysis to see what it has to say about gratitude.

The word gratitude appears thirty two times in Freud's published writings. In the 1910 paper "A Special Type of Choice of Object Made by Men" he noted that gratitude to the mother could be the motive for oedipal love of the mother. "His mother gave him a life—his own life—and in exchange he gives her another life, that of a child which has the greatest resemblance to himself" (Freud, 1910: p. 173). In 1918, in the paper "The Taboo of Virginity", Freud observed that it would take a considerable time after defloration for a woman to develop a sense of gratitude towards the man who deflowered her (Freud, 1918: p. 201).

More incidents could be cited but gratitude was not an emotion that was intensely studied by Freud. The psychoanalyst who recognised the central role gratitude plays in our lives was Melanie Klein in her 1935 book *Envy and Gratitude*. She regarded gratitude as a major derivative of the capacity to love and says it "underlies ... the appreciation of goodness in others and in oneself" (Klein, 1935: p. 17). "Gratitude is closely bound up with generosity. Inner wealth derives from having assimilated "the good object" so that the individual becomes able to share its gifts with others" (Klein, 1935: p. 19). The main enemy of gratitude is envy. When we are envious we feel that the world is unjust; when we are grateful we are at peace with the world and feel that we have been given enough or even more than we deserve. We feel we have been loved and nourished and all is well with the world. Envy and jealousy are the opponents of gratitude.

Klein quotes from *Othello*:

> But jealous souls will not be answer'd so;
> They are not ever jealous for the cause,
> But jealous for they are jealous; 'it's a monster
> Begot upon itself, born on itself. (Klein, 1935: p. 8)
> Oh beware my Lord of jealousy;
> It is the green-eyed monster which doth mock
> The meat it feeds on ... (Klein, 1935: p. 9)

She also quotes Spenser's *The Faerie Queene*:

> He hated all good workes and virtuous deeds
> ...
> And eke the verse of famous Poets witt
> He does backebite, and spightfull poison spues
> From leprous mouth on all that ever writt. (Klein, 1935: p. 41)

Ultimately Klein thinks that our very feeling of sanity depends on our feeling free from envy (Klein, 1935: p. 41). Ideally a personal analysis is experienced with gratitude at the point of termination.

Since Klein's work, psychoanalysts have learned to highly value the capacity for gratitude. Analytic patients who are capable of gratitude are more likely to benefit from psychoanalytic treatment than those who are not. Parents often mistakenly insist that children be grateful and that they write "thank you" letters to relatives and friends for gifts received. When gratitude becomes an obligation it is transferred from a self feeling into the realm of the superego and gratitude is transformed into a demand. Gratitude is the by-product of love and cannot be achieved upon demand.

We return to the character of Timon. We can assume that his compulsive need to collect gratitude from others is a reaction to his own inability to be grateful. Timon so desperately needs to receive the gratitude of others because he suffers from an inner emptiness. Once he discovers that he will not receive the gratitude he hoped for and expected, he withdraws to a cave from which he emerges from time to time only to find the world as bad as he thought and then withdraws from it again. The gold found in the cave will not restore gratitude and it is therefore useless and is thrown at visitors. In psychoanalytic thought the cave is a symbol of a return to the womb and gold symbolises excreta. Timon thus symbolically represents a double regression to the womb and to anal sexuality.

Othello was written in such a way as to make us believe that if Shakespeare allowed Othello to kill the innocent Desdemona, he discharged paranoid tendencies and overcame the homosexual feelings that caused the paranoia. We do not feel that the portrayal of Timon made it possible for Shakespeare to experience gratitude again but rather that Shakespeare gave Timon the upper hand and this is the reason Timon is not a play we enjoy. We do not feel that Shakespeare, the creative writer, was in control of the play and transformed Timon into a complex character who interests us, but rather that the character, representing an aspect of the author, gained the upper hand and paralysed the creative writer.

An individual who remains fixated on the anal level does not develop meaningful relationships with other people. A baby living on this level of development when feeling generous gives its faeces freely and when angry is apt either to withhold them or to throw them out. From a psychoanalytic perspective Timon has undergone a regression to the anal phase.

There is no hint of any sexual wishes from another human being in this play. Timon lacks a family, for without gratitude to compensate for his inner deficit Timon cannot find love or build a family. Without the capacity for gratitude the world is cold and indifferent. It is interesting that Bloom acknowledged Timon's beauty of language in his curses. I had failed to respond to this beauty and was curious to know if the

Penguin Dictionary of Quotations contained any lines from the play. There are six of them but I did not find any of them memorable.

Most students of this play have noticed that Timon is a lonely man. We can describe him as a case of "financial promiscuity". As long as he is rich he will use his money to buy short-term relationships. He saves a man whom he does not know who is jailed for non-payment of debts; he buys objects he does not need because he cannot disappoint the seller. However, all the spending is not conducive to the establishment of real relationships. Predictably, Timon runs out of money and asks for help from those whom he has assisted only to discover in them an alarming lack of gratitude.

Timon is a person we can diagnose and describe clinically but he has no uniqueness of his own, whereas most of Shakespeare's characters, even though some of them served Freud as "types", have a uniqueness that manifests itself in their language or in some unexpected action. This cannot be said about Timon. We have noted in this book how frequently Freud cited Shakespearean characters to illustrate clinical categories like those who are "wrecked by success" or "the exceptions", but in all these cases the character chosen was more than just a clinical example. Timon, however, has no individuality of his own and therefore lacks memorable language.

The world that Timon inhabits is not nearly as depraved as he makes it out to be. His own servant has retained his loyalty and Alcibiades is coming as a friend who remembers Timon's acts of valour. Even the two prostitutes who go with Alcibiades into exile are, by their devotion to Alcibiades, psychologically speaking, no longer harlots but mistresses. The senators wish Timon to return to the city demonstrate that he matters to them, but his traumatic disappointment is too strong to allow him to do so. Timon hates Athens.

> TIMON: Sow all th' Athenian bosoms, and their crop
> Be general leprosy! Breath infect breath,
> That their society, as their friendship, may
> Be merely poison! Nothing I'll bear from thee
> But nakedness, thou detestable town!
> (*Timon of Athens*, IV.i.29–33)

We understand that Timon expresses Shakespeare's hatred of London. Readers who feel the sentiments Timon expresses for their own societies may get some pleasure from reading the play, but while it may be clinically interesting to find that Shakespeare expressed his rage and regressed to the anal phase, in my opinion it is not dramatically gratifying.

Timon has nothing unique to communicate to us, and as a result little memorable is said in the play. The events bring no change in his character and we see no inner development. Timon has no impact on any other person. We can use *Timon of Athens* to appreciate the other plays by Shakespeare in a new way, realising how hard it must have been to create the complex characters and let them productively interact with others. If the critical observer in Shakespeare survived longer than the creative artist then Timon was no equal to any of his other creations, and he may have decided that it was time to stop writing. In this play we can see how inspiration departs and regression to the anal phase takes place.

Throughout this book I have assumed that there must be a point at which the author is identified with the character he created. With some characters like Prospero or King Lear this is almost self-evident; with others like Othello and Leontes it requires an assumption that Shakespeare had to struggle against homosexual wishes. The point of identification with Timon, however, is difficult to establish. Did he know his own genius and was he disappointed that his friends and colleagues did not recognise it? We do not know anything about pathological generosity ruining Shakespeare's financial situation. There remains the possibility that in creating Timon the playwright brought to life his father, whom we know to have been a failure not unlike Timon.

The poet anticipated Timon's fate in the magnificent language of Sonnet 73.

> That time of year thou mayst in me behold
> When yellow leaves, or none, or few, do hang
> Upon those boughs which shake against the cold,
> Bare ruin'd choirs, where late the sweet birds sang.
> In me thou seest the twilight of such day
> As after sunset fadeth in the west,
> Which by and by black night doth take away,
> Death's second self, that seals up all in rest.
> In me thou see'st the glowing of such fire
> That on the ashes of his youth doth lie,

> As the death-bed whereon it must expire
> Consumed with that which it was nourish'd by.
>   This thou perceivest, which makes thy love more strong,
>   To love that well which thou must leave ere long.

When the poet wrote this sonnet he may have been as lonely as Timon, but he was capable in identifying himself, in magnificent language, with a barren tree and to experience that tree as welcoming sweet birds singing in other seasons. The poet was alive to experiencing himself as the twilight. Finally, he is still capable of creating the splendid metaphor of the glowing fire that lies on the ashes of his youth. Timon has no comparable richness of imaging to fall back on.

PART III

THE OEDIPUS COMPLEX

CHAPTER FIVE

Richard III: the Oedipus complex and the villain

The play opens with a long soliloquy of the Duke of Gloucester, later King Richard III, explaining how he decided to become a villain. Shakespeare's interest in creating villains (and there is a whole series of them) was stimulated by the dramatic success of Marlowe's villain in *The Jew of Malta*. We are drawn into the action and feel as if he is confiding in us, as if we were given special permission to enter the mind of the chief actor. What we hear is standard Renaissance, beautifully expressed. Mars, the god of war, is lying in the arms of Venus and as a result peace prevails.

Now that England's civil war is over Richard is restless.

RICHARD: Grim-visaged war hath smoothed his wrinkled front,
 And now, instead of mounting barbèd steeds
 To fright the souls of fearful adversaries,
 He capers nimbly in a lady's chamber
 To the lascivious pleasing of a lute.
 ....
 I that am curtailed of this fair proportion,
 Cheated of feature by dissembling nature,

85

> Deformed, unfinished, sent before my time
> Into this breathing world scarce half made up,
> And that so lamely and unfashionable
> That dogs bark at me as I halt by them,
> Why, I, in this weak piping time of peace,
> Have no delight to pass away the time,
> Unless to spy my shadow in the sun
> And descant on mine own deformity.
> And therefore, since I cannot prove a lover
> To entertain these fair well-spoken days,
> I am determinèd to prove a villain. (*Richard III*, I.i.9–13, 18–30)

It takes some suspension of disbelief for us to imagine that such a deformed man was nevertheless a great warrior. Furthermore, the soliloquy implies that becoming a villain was entirely a conscious decision, which strikes those of us acquainted with Freud's work as unlikely.

A "dissembling nature" is an original metaphor that betrays paranoid tendencies, as if nature, personified as a woman, has deliberately decided to cheat him of what he was entitled to have. Most of Richard's encounters in this play are with women whose husbands or children he has killed, a symbolic revenge on dissembling nature. In today's language Richard III has an "inferiority complex" and a powerful sense of narcissistic entitlement, which will transpose him into a villain. In psychoanalytic history Richard sides with Alfred Adler in his debate with Freud. Adler put "the feeling of inferiority with the inferiority of certain organs" as causing a "passionate desire for triumph". It was in this debate, on 1 February 1911 that Freud declared, "This is not psychoanalysis" and then started the first irreconcilable division within psychoanalysis (Nunberg & Federn, 1974: p. 129). Had Adler known Shakespeare he could have quoted *Richard III* in his own defense.

Debarred from lovemaking, all that Richard can do is "spy my shadow in the sun / And descant on mine own deformity", that is, become engaged with himself. In psychoanalytic terms he becomes a narcissist.

Richard owes no obedience to civilisation because "dissembling nature" cheated him. We should linger here to admire Shakespeare's genius in making the villain a deformed man. Shakespeare made sure the audience never fully turns against the main hero until the very last scene. Richard's actions are terrible but a grain of sympathy based on his deformity remains with us until the end.

In the same scene we hear another soliloquy from which I quote only a part:

RICHARD: Clarence hath not another day to live:
            Which done, God take King Edward to his mercy
            And leave the world for me to bustle in!
            For then I'll marry Warwick's youngest daughter,
            What though I killed her husband and her father?
            The readiest way to make the wench amends
            Is to become her husband and her father. (I.i.151–157)

The next scene, Act I, scene two, will be the encounter between Richard and the Earl of Warwick's daughter Lady Anne. The audience does not find out what the other "secret" purpose in wooing and marrying Anne is, but the logic of killing her male relatives and making amends by marrying her will be repeated twice. Richard III represents a villain who kills the father and the husband and makes amends by the sexual possession of the widow.

When we meet Anne she is as a mourner in the funeral procession of King Henry VI (her father-in-law, as she is the widow of his son Edward; Richard killed both men). Gloucester blocks the path of the procession.

ANNE: What, do you tremble? Are you all afraid?
          Alas, I blame you not; for you are mortal,
          And mortal eyes cannot endure the devil.—
          Avaunt, thou dreadful minister of hell.
          Thou hadst but power over his mortal body;
          His soul thou canst not have; therefore, be gone.
RICHARD: Sweet saint, for charity, be not so curst.
ANNE: Foul devil, for God's sake hence, and trouble us not,
          For thou hast made the happy earth thy hell. (I.ii.43–51)

A long and wonderfully written dialogue takes place between the cursing Anne and the supposedly wooing Gloucester. It culminates Gloucester's assertion that it was due to Anne's beauty that her husband was slain.

RICHARD: Is not the causer of the timeless deaths
          Of these Plantagenets, Henry and Edward,

As blameful as the executioner?

ANNE: Thou wast the cause and most accursed effect.

RICHARD: Your beauty was the cause of that effect.
Your beauty, which did haunt me in my sleep
To undertake the death of all the world,
So I might live one hour in your sweet bosom. (I.ii.122–129)

Richard may be a villain but he gains our admiration by his courage. He offers Anne his sword, inviting her to kill him if she wishes, and when she cannot do so, he even offers to stab himself if she orders him to, and once more she refuses. We have encountered Shakespeare the dramatic psychologist at his best; it is after her aggressive drive has failed to carry out Richard's murder that Anne succumbs to him sexually. The very many who told us he cannot caper "nimbly in a lady's chamber" now shows he can win the widow of the man he killed.

Left alone, Richard denies that the motive for killing Anne's husband Edward was an expression of the oedipal wish by saying he "will not keep her long". We now see that the wish was narcissistic and aggressive but not oedipal. The villain uses the oedipal wish to conquer the woman but does not really desire her.

RICHARD: Was ever woman in this humour wooed?
Was ever woman in this humour won?
I'll have her, but I will not keep her long.
...
Hath she forgot already that brave prince,
Edward, her lord, whom I some three months since
Stabbed in my angry mood at Tewkesbury?
A sweeter and a lovelier gentleman,
Framed in the prodigality of nature,
Young, valiant, wise, and (no doubt) right royal,
The spacious world cannot again afford.
And will she yet abase her eyes on me,
That cropped the golden prime of this sweet prince
And made her widow to a woeful bed? (I.ii.231–233, 243–252)

In my 2010 paper "The Oedipus complex and psychoanalytic technique" I pointed out that in clinical practice we never encounter the two sides of the oedipal wish expressed by one patient. We either hear aggression towards one parent or sexual wishes for the other, but the two wishes are not expressed together at the same time. I concluded that the oedipal wish as such is never experienced and therefore is only a reconstruction by the analyst. I now add that a literary figure, Richard III, did experience both sides of the oedipal wish. What is particularly striking is that Shakespeare must have been capable of this experience as well.

In Act IV, scene one, Lady Anne is explaining her behaviour to Queen Elizabeth, widow of King Edward IV.

> ANNE: Oh, when, I say, I looked on Richard's face,
>   This was my wish: 'Be thou,' quoth I, 'accursed
>   For making me, so young, so old a widow.
>   And, when thou wed'st, let sorrow haunt thy bed;
>   And be thy wife, if any be so mad,
>   More miserable by the life of thee
>   Than thou hast made me by my dear lord's death'.
>   ...
>   Within so small a time, my woman's heart
>   Grossly grew captive to his honey words. (IV.i.71–77, 79–80)

Lady Anne confesses that at first she cursed Richard and her curse took the form of an unhappy marital scene, but then what started as a hate fantasy was transformed into a sexual fantasy in which she put herself into the accursed bed, but she is not conscious of this transformation.

Anne's explanation of why she succumbed to Gloucester's request is a psychological masterpiece. Thinking about Richard's bed sexualised her fury at him; instead of merely wishing that sorrow should haunt his bed, she herself will succumb to this sorrow. Today we know that sexual wishes can express not only love but also aggression. Shakespeare knew it and expressed it here as well as in Angelo's attraction to Isabella in *Measure for Measure*. It is interesting to note that what we designate as the unconscious today (after Freud), Anne calls her "woman's heart".

To conquer Anne, Richard used his supposed Oedipus complex as an excuse. He knows its power, but only to conquer. In clinical psychoanalysis we may find that a deformed and angry narcissist has become a villain, but this decision was reached unconsciously and has to be discovered in the course of an analysis. Shakespeare presents it to us as a conscious decision.

The villain has knowledge of the Oedipus complex but is not under its power and can use it to obtain narcissistic gratification. Clinically Richard III probably does not exist but as an argument between the Oedipus complex and narcissism the play is an amazing document.

We recall that in his second soliloquy in the first act Richard emphasised that he killed Lady Anne's husband and father-in-law out of love for her. In psychoanalytic language he denied that he acted out his Oedipal wishes but there is another possibility: in a narcissistic person the Oedipal wish is not the primary wish; it is the double victory that matters, the murder and the possession. Together they offer the greatest narcissistic satisfaction.

One of the puzzles of this play is that Shakespeare in essence repeated the scene between Anne and Richard; in the second case Richard did not win over the woman he sought to wed but the woman's mother. It may well have been Shakespeare's admission that it was the mother he was trying to obtain. We are in Act IV and Richard is talking to the former Queen Elizabeth.

RICHARD:	Stay, madam. I must talk a word with you.
QUEEN ELIZABETH:	I have no more sons of the royal blood
	For thee to slaughter. For my daughters, Richard,
	They shall be praying nuns, not weeping queens,
	And therefore level not to hit their lives.
RICHARD:	You have a daughter called Elizabeth,
	Virtuous and fair, royal and gracious.
QUEEN ELIZABETH:	And must she die for this? O, let her live. (IV.iv.199–206)

Richard tells Queen Elizabeth that he loves her young daughter and asks her to intercede on his behalf. There follows a dialogue similar to the one he had with Lady Anne. We hear once more the kind of thinking that had become typical of Richard.

RICHARD:	Say that I did all this for love of her.
QUEEN ELIZABETH:	Nay, then indeed she cannot choose but hate thee,
	Having bought love with such a bloody spoil.
	Richard: Look what is done, cannot be now amended.
	Men shall deal unadvisedly sometimes,
	Which after-hours give leisure to repent.
	If I did take the kingdom from your sons,

To make amends I'll give it to your daughter.
If I have killed the issue of your womb,
To quicken your increase I will beget
Mine   issue   of   your   blood   upon   your   daughter.
(IV.iv.292–302)

Richard attempts to comfort Queen Elizabeth:

RICHARD: Your children were vexation to your youth,
But mine shall be a comfort to your age.
The loss you have is but a son being king,
And by that loss your daughter is made queen.
I cannot make you what amends I would;
Therefore accept such kindness as I can.

...

The liquid drops of tears that you have shed
Shall come again, transformed to orient pearl,
Advantaging their loan with interest
Of ten times double gain of happiness. (IV.iv.309–314, 325–328)

Richard killed two of Elizabeth's sons and now has the temerity to say that through her daughter he will restore her lost children. This is basically the same kind of logic he employed with Lady Anne and once more Shakespeare makes him successful. While Richard did not marry this daughter he appealed to and won her mother's approval and this is what mattered psychologically.

QUEEN ELIZABETH: Yet thou didst kill my children.
RICHARD: But in your daughter's womb I bury them,
Where in that nest of spicery they will breed
Selves of themselves, to your recomforture.
ELIZABETH: Shall I go win my daughter to thy will?
RICHARD: And be a happy mother by the deed.
ELIZABETH: I go. Write to me very shortly,
And you shall understand from me her mind.
RICHARD: Bear her my true love's kiss, and so farewell. (IV.iv.427–435)

We come now to the appreciation of another skill with which Shakespeare endowed his characters: a capacity to express their hatred in a highly original way.

In Act IV, scene four, three widows meet: Queen Margaret, the widow of King Henry VI; Queen Elizabeth, the widow of King Edward IV, and the Duchess of York, mother to Edward IV, George (the Duke of Clarence), and Richard III (the Duke of Gloucester). There was enmity among them in their days of glory but now they are closer to each other because they all share the grief of having a husband killed.

Queen Margaret is speaking to Richard's mother, the Duchess of York.

MARGARET: Thou hadst a Clarence too,
             And Richard killed him.
             From forth the kennel of thy womb hath crept
             A hell-hound that doth hunt us all to death:
             That dog, that had his teeth before his eyes
             To worry lambs and lap their gentle blood,
             That foul defacer of God's handiwork,
             That reigns in gallèd eyes of weeping souls,
             That excellent grand tyrant of the earth
             Thy womb let loose to chase us to our graves.
             O upright, just, and true-disposing God,
             How do I thank thee, that this carnal cur
             Preys on the issue of his mother's body
             And makes her pew-fellow with others' moan! (IV.iv.45–58)

Queen Margaret hates the Duchess of York for bringing Richard into the world, expressed as "From forth the kennel of thy womb hath crept / A hell-hound that doth hunt us all to death". She then creates an original metaphor of a dog that had his teeth before his eyes and causes worry to lambs. Shakespeare's characters know how to curse, that is, they can find words to express their anger, which in turn appeals to the audience's repressed aggression. "That foul defacer of God's handiwork" is a good example of such an original expression. Margaret recognises that "this carnal cur / Preys on the issue of his mother's body".

The Duke of Gloucester has become King Richard III and is facing a dangerous rebellion against his rule. Richard enters the scene and Shakespeare lets us see a scene of hatred between mother and son. Consciously we are horrified at a mother's capacity to curse her son but it also awakens our admiration.

RICHARD: Who intercepts my expedition?

DUCHESS OF YORK: Oh, she that might have intercepted thee,
By strangling thee in her accursèd womb,
From all the slaughters, wretch, that thou hast done.

…

Thou toad, thou toad, where is thy brother Clarence.
And little Ned Plantagenet, his son?

…

Either thou wilt die by God's just ordinance
Ere from this war thou turn a conqueror,
Or I with grief and extreme age shall perish
And nevermore behold thy face again.
Therefore take with thee my most grievous curse,
Which in the day of battle tire thee more
Than all the còmplete armour that thou wear'st.
My prayers on the adverse party fight,
And there the little souls of Edward's children
Whisper the spirits of thine enemies
And promise them success and victory.
Bloody thou art, bloody will be thy end;
Shame serves thy life and doth thy death attend. (IV.iv.136–
139, 145–146, 184–196)

A maternal death wish is unendurable. We respond to the curse of Richard's mother with a shudder.

Queen Margaret joins in attacking Richard:

MARGARET: Stay, dog, for thou shalt hear me.
If heaven have any grievous plague in store
Exceeding those that I can wish upon thee,
Oh, let them keep it till thy sins be ripe
And then hurl down their indignation
On thee, the troubler of the poor world's peace.
The worm of conscience still begnaw thy soul.
Thy friends suspect for traitors while thou liv'st,
And take deep traitors for thy dearest friends.
No sleep close up that deadly eye of thine,
Unless it be while some tormenting dream
Affrights thee with a hell of ugly devils.

> Thou elvish-marked, abortive, rooting hog,
> Thou that wast sealed in thy nativity
> The slave of nature and the son of hell.
> Thou slander of thy mother's heavy womb,
> Thou loathèd issue of thy father's loins,
> Thou rag of honour! thou detested—(I.iii.214–231).

The hatred expressed between the mother and son in this play gains interest when we consider the relationship to the mother in Shakespeare's other plays. We note that in many plays she is notably absent, including *King Lear*, *The Tempest*, and *The Merchant of Venice*. In *Hamlet* the relationship is tense and in *Coriolanus* the ambivalence of the mother brings death to her son.

In all Shakespeare's work there is no parallel to a mother hating her son and wishing him dead, while also attacking her own womb for bringing him to life. The impact of the expression of this hatred on the audience is to prepare us for Richard's coming death.

Did Richard III acquire conscience?

In Act V, scene three the play shifts to Bosworth Fields. The king's camp is facing the camp of Henry, Earl of Richmond, the future King Henry VII. We hear Richmond's prayer the night before the battle.

RICHMOND: O Thou, whose captain I account myself,
> Look on my forces with a gracious eye.
> Put in their hands thy bruising irons of wrath,
> That they may crush down with a heavy fall
> The usurping helmets of our adversaries!
> Make us thy ministers of chastisement,
> That we may praise thee in the victory!
> To thee I do commend my watchful soul,
> Ere I let fall the windows of mine eyes.
> Sleeping and waking, O, defend me still! (V.iii.112–121)

Psychologically this prayer is the very opposite of the curses; the aggression that found expression in them shifts the aggression to God. It is God who will punish Richard.

Richard's challenger, the Earl of Richmond, trusts God and can sleep well before battle, while Richard is haunted by his deeds and cannot sleep. In psychoanalytic terms Richard's enemy is at peace with his inner objects and therefore can sleep while Richard's inner objects demand punishment.

The ghosts of those whom Richard III killed arise one after the other, all wishing Richmond victory, each one recalling Richard's crimes and saying to him, "Let me sit heavy on thy soul, despair and die". I will quote Anne's ghost:

LADY ANNE'S GHOST: Richard, thy wife, that wretched Anne thy wife,
That never slept a quiet hour with thee,
Now fills thy sleep with perturbations
To-morrow in the battle think on me,
And fall thy edgeless sword: despair, and die!
(V.iii.159–163)

On the night before the battle, Richard wakes up from a nightmare and reflects,

RICHARD: Have mercy, Jesu!—Soft! I did but dream.
O coward conscience, how dost thou afflict me!
The lights burn blue. It is now dead midnight.
Cold fearful drops stand on my trembling flesh.
What do I fear? myself? there's none else by:
Richard loves Richard; that is, I am I.
Is there a murderer here? No. Yes, I am:
Then fly. What, from myself? Great reason why:
Lest I revenge. What, myself upon myself?
Alack. I love myself. Wherefore? for any good
That I myself have done unto myself?
O, no! alas, I rather hate myself
For hateful deeds committed by myself!
I am a villain: yet I lie. I am not.
Fool, of thyself speak well: fool, do not flatter. ...
My conscience hath a thousand several tongues,
And every tongue brings in a several tale,
And every tale condemns me for a villain.

> Perjury, perjury, in the high'st degree
> Murder, stem murder, in the direst degree;
> All several sins, all used in each degree,
> Throng to the bar, crying all, Guilty! guilty!
> I shall despair. (V.iii.178–199)

In its psychological depth this soliloquy is extraordinary. Like anyone awakening from a nightmare, it takes Richard some time to remember that what he just experienced was a dream, not reality. "O coward conscience" is another variant on Hamlet's attitude towards conscience, but what we hear next is not so much remorse as a new capacity for self reflection. Richard is reflecting upon Richard. If he is the murderer, how can he fly away from himself? He also realises the impossibility of revenging himself upon himself and now goes on to reflect upon his narcissism and finds no justification for loving himself. In the third part of the soliloquy conscience, pushed aside for a time, returns in full force. Richard is self condemned.

If we ask ourselves if Shakespeare created in Richard III a man likely to exist in real life, a clinically plausible man, our answer is likely to be negative: a man capable of these two soliloquies is not likely to have existed. But is it the function of great literature to be true to life? Or is it the function of literature to give us characters that are larger than life? The play deserves the fame it has enjoyed.

We notice another characteristic of Shakespeare: he often endows his characters with insights but never, to my knowledge, did these insights help achieve a different outcome. Shakespeare was not a therapeutically oriented writer.

With Richard's death the play ends but Shakespeare's plays always contain more than the main topic. Two subplots imply that the question of guilt was very much in Shakespeare's mind when he wrote *Richard III*.

Questions of guilt in other characters

Just before the murderers enter his cell in the tower, Clarence (Richard's brother, whose death was ordered by Richard) tells a nightmare he had to his jailer. The intimacy between jailer and prisoner is striking.

KEEPER: Why looks your grace so heavily today?
CLARENCE: Oh, I have passed a miserable night,

So full of fearful dreams, of ugly sights,
That, as I am a Christian faithful man,
I would not spend another such a night
Though 'twere to buy a world of happy days,
So full of dismal terror was the time.

KEEPER: What was your dream, my lord? I pray you tell me.

CLARENCE: Methoughts that I had broken from the Tower
And was embarked to cross to Burgundy,
And in my company my brother Gloucester,
Who from my cabin tempted me to walk
Upon the hatches. Thence we looked toward England
And cited up a thousand heavy times
During the wars of York and Lancaster
That had befall'n us. As we paced along
Upon the giddy footing of the hatches,
Methought that Gloucester stumbled, and in falling
Struck me, that thought to stay him, overboard
Into the tumbling billows of the main.
O Lord, methought what pain it was to drown,
What dreadful noise of waters in my ears,
What sights of ugly death within my eyes.
Methoughts I saw a thousand fearful wracks,
A thousand men that fishes gnawed upon,
Wedges of gold, great anchors, heaps of pearl,
Inestimable stones, unvalued jewels,
All scattered in the bottom of the sea.
Some lay in dead men's skulls, and in the holes
Where eyes did once inhabit, there were crept,
As 'twere in scorn of eyes, reflecting gems,
That wooed the slimy bottom of the deep
And mocked the dead bones that lay scattered by.

KEEPER: Had you such leisure in the time of death
To gaze upon the secrets of the deep?

CLARENCE: Methought I had, and often did I strive
To yield the ghost; but still the envious flood
Stopped in my soul and would not let it forth
To find the empty, vast, and wandering air,
But smothered it within my panting bulk,
Who almost burst to belch it in the sea.

KEEPER: Awaked you not in this sore agony?
CLARENCE: No, no, my dream was lengthened after life.
    Oh, then began the tempest to my soul.
    I passed, methought, the melancholy flood,
    With that sour ferryman which poets write of,
    Unto the kingdom of perpetual night.
    The first that there did greet my stranger-soul
    Was my great father-in-law, renownèd Warwick,
    Who spake aloud, 'What scourge for perjury
    Can this dark monarchy afford false Clarence?'
    And so he vanished. Then came wandering by
    A shadow like an angel, with bright hair
    Dabbled in blood, and he shrieked out aloud
    'Clarence is come, false, fleeting, perjured Clarence,
    That stabbed me in the field by Tewkesbury.
    Seize on him, furies, take him unto torment.'
    With that, methought, a legion of foul fiends
    Environed me, and howlèd in mine ears
    Such hideous cries that with the very noise
    I trembling waked, and for a season after
    Could not believe but that I was in hell,
    Such terrible impression made my dream.
KEEPER: No marvel, lord, though it affrighted you.
    I am afraid, methinks, to hear you tell it. (I.iv.1–65)

We can learn from this dream report how Shakespeare understood dreams. The reality is that the brother is actually conspiring to have Clarence killed. Consciously Clarence does not know this but in the dream both brothers are in danger. Gloucester stumbles first and now Clarence himself is in danger of being devoured and at the same time he is aware of a world of riches. The paradox surprises the jail keeper. Dreams seem to know things we do not acknowledge but they also offer us riches to lure us to our death. Clarence has all the guilt that was lacking in Richard.

We note that the jail keeper is interested in the dream and has sympathy for the agony of the dreamer but is also a skillful listener. He notices the contradiction in the dream: the dreamer is in great peril but he has the leisure to examine the treasures of the deep in spite of this danger. Had he persisted in exploring the contradiction he would have been a psychoanalytic dream interpreter. Once more we note how Shakespeare comes close to becoming a dream interpreter. The empathy with which the jailer listens to the nightmare and the way he hardly interrupts but tactfully asks a few questions that keep the narrative going, is a model for any psychoanalyst listening to an anxiety dream or nightmare in a psychoanalytic hour.

The dream opens as a typical rescue dream that any prisoner is likely to have—he has broken out of the tower—but soon it turns into a nightmare.

In the last part of the dream Greek mythology is recalled. Charon, the Greek ferryman who led the dead to Hades, takes Clarence to the isle of the dead and once there guilt feelings overtake him; he is to be punished by the Furies for murders committed and denied the wish to refind a loving mother in the form of a peaceful death.

The murderer's feelings of guilt

I come now to another powerful scene in the play. *Richard III*, together with *Hamlet* and *Measure for Measure*, is a play in which Shakespeare dealt with the problems of conscience. In Act I, scene three, Richard, the Duke of Gloucester, has hired murderers to kill his brother George, the Duke of Clarence. We listen to an interesting discussion about the nature of guilt feelings between the two murderers.

SECOND MURDERER: What, shall we stab him as he sleeps?

FIRST MURDERER: No. He'll say 'twas done cowardly, when he wakes.

SECOND MURDERER: Why, he shall never wake until the great judgment day.

FIRST MURDERER: Why, then he will say we stabbed him sleeping.

SECOND MURDERER: The urging of that word 'judgment' hath bred a kind of remorse in me.

FIRST MURDERER: What, art thou afraid?

SECOND MURDERER: Not to kill him, having a warrant for it; but to be damned for killing him, from which no warrant can defend us.

FIRST MURDERER: I thought thou hadst been resolute.

SECOND MURDERER: So I am, to let him live.

FIRST MURDERER: Back to the Duke of Gloucester, tell him so.

SECOND MURDERER: I pray thee, stay a while: I hope my holy humour will change; 'twas wont to hold me but while one would tell twenty.

FIRST MURDERER: How dost thou feel thyself now?

SECOND MURDERER: 'Faith, some certain dregs of conscience are yet within me.

FIRST MURDERER: Remember our reward, when the deed is done.

SECOND MURDERER: 'Zounds, he dies: I had forgot the reward.

FIRST MURDERER: Where is thy conscience now?

SECOND MURDERER: In the Duke of Gloucester's purse.

FIRST MURDERER: So when he opens his purse to give us our reward, thy conscience flies out.

SECOND MURDERER: Let it go; there's few or none will entertain it.

FIRST MURDERER: How if it come to thee again?

SECOND MURDERER: I'll not meddle with it: it is a dangerous thing: it makes a man a coward: a man cannot steal, but it accuseth him; he cannot swear, but it cheques him; he cannot lie with his neighbour's wife, but it detects him: 'tis a blushing shamefast spirit that mutinies in a man's bosom; it fills one full of obstacles: it made me once restore a purse of gold that I found; it beggars any man that keeps it: it is turned out of all towns and cities for a dangerous thing; and every man that means to live well endeavours to trust to himself and to live without it. (I.iv.101–148)

Shakespeare gives us his unique combination of entertainment and meditation on the value and nature of conscience.

From a psychoanalytic point of view there is something amazing about this play because Richard III not only articulates the two sides of the Oedipus complex but also uses this superior knowledge to win a widow whose husband and father-in-law he has just murdered. His freedom from ordinary guilt feelings enables him to win over a mother to give him her daughter in marriage even after he killed the girl's brothers. We hear the villain cursed by his mother and surviving victims and observe the ultimate collapse of the villain's inner world before the punishment is meted out. The play also contains an almost psychoanalytic interpretation of a nightmare and a lively discussion on the usefulness of conscience. If we were at the Globe, our time was well spent.

CHAPTER SIX

Julius Caesar and Freud's *Totem and Taboo*

From a psychoanalytic perspective, *Julius Caesar* is an oedipal play. Its central theme consists of a band of brothers uniting to kill a father figure. What is astonishing is that the leader of this band, Brutus, is a highly moral person. What is further surprising is that, contrary to what clinical experience has taught us, Brutus' superego not only does not forbid this murder but actually demands it.

As the play unfolds it turns out that this murder was not a success. The conspirators succeed in killing Caesar but psychologically the victory goes to Caesar. The playwright is not a republican; his heart is not with the rebels. This attitude was also the wise one politically, as Shakespeare lived under a strict monarchy and siding with the rebels would have prohibited this play from being performed. *Julius Caesar* can be contrasted with another play *Don Carlos* by Friedrich Schiller, written a century later and made into an opera by Verdi, who clearly sided with the son rather than the father.

Skillfully interwoven with the oedipal theme is the sibling-like relationship between Brutus and his brother-in-law Cassius, with Brutus the high minded one who spares the life of Mark Antony and is later defeated by him. Brutus loves Caesar and is loved by him, whereas Cassius shows no inner conflict about the slaying.

101

Brutus' relationship is ambivalent; he both loves and fears Caesar. After Caesar's assassination Brutus spends his whole life attempting to justify the murder and deal with his guilt feelings.

It is likely that everyone who has seen or read *Julius Caesar* will remember the contrast in the funeral speeches of Brutus and Mark Antony. The oration of Brutus culminates thus:

BRUTUS: … not that I loved Caesar less, but that I loved Rome more. Had
            you rather Caesar were living and die all slaves, than that Caesar
            were dead, to live all free men? As Caesar loved me, I weep
            for him. As he was fortunate, I rejoice at it. As he was valiant,
            I honour him. But, as he was ambitious, I slew him. (*Julius Caesar*,
            III.ii.22–28)

Brutus, a real intellectual, enjoys the complexity of his relationship to Caesar, but the fact that he imagined the Roman populace would comprehend and sympathise with such a complex attitude shows that he was not meant to be a political leader. Shakespeare sees clearly that this complexity is beyond the understanding of the Roman plebeians. Brutus and his fellow conspirators stabbed Caesar to death. As if in a religious ceremony everyone had to participate in the collective murder. Brutus is a unique creation of Shakespeare because his moral sense (superego) does not oppose the murder of a father figure but demands it. It was a murder not out of hatred or momentary passion but a moral resolve of the whole group to commit murder of a father figure collectively, for the good of Rome and its citizens. But now something strange happens.

Brutus stands before the crowd, asking it to side with him and agree that Caesar had to be killed so that all could be free. At this point psychoanalysis makes a contribution: Brutus needs the crowd's approval because the murder of Caesar left him with an unconscious sense of guilt and inner conflict. By contrast, for Mark Antony the crowd is there to be manipulated and he does so successfully. To show the difference between the two approaches so clearly evokes admiration. The oration that Shakespeare gives to Mark Antony has always been admired as one of the treasures of English literature.

The speech of Brutus is greeted with applause but then the "third plebian", as enthusiastic as the others, asks Brutus to become Caesar, thus undermining the rationale for the assassination.

In his death scene Caesar utters only three words and Shakespeare gives them in Latin: "Et tu, Bruté?" (III.i.85), "You too, Brutus?" Caesar is not surprised at his murder; he seems to have anticipated it. The only thing that pains him and was unexpected is that Brutus, whom he loved and upon whose love he depended, is among the conspirators. The position of Brutus among the conspirators is unique: it is that of the true son who kills his father not because hate was stronger than love, but because of devotion to an ideal. The murder takes place because his sense of duty demands it. In Brutus, Shakespeare created a figure unique in cultural history: a son figure killing a father figure not out of jealousy but out of a sense of moral obligation.

No hatred, no jealousy, no base feelings of any kind enter Brutus' mind. The murder is to be performed as a sacrifice to the gods. Brutus demands such purity not only from himself but also his fellow conspirators and even the Roman plebeians must understand and accept it as a noble murder.

BRUTUS: Let us be sacrificers but not butchers,

      ...

      Oh, that we then could come by Caesar's spirit
      And not dismember Caesar! But, alas,
      Caesar must bleed for it. And, gentle friends,
      Let's kill him boldly but not wrathfully.
      Let's carve him as a dish fit for the gods,
      Not hew him as a carcass fit for hounds. (II.i.173, 176–181)

Despite these powerful words of high nobility, we note that in this case the gods still feast on human sacrifice.

To kill boldly but not wrathfully is probably beyond human capacity. The idea of killing as a sacrifice sounds strange because at that time in Rome human sacrifices had been overcome long ago. Caesar could only be sacrificed to the gods because in Brutus' view his wish to rule was experienced as directed against the gods being the only rulers, a biblical rather than Roman idea.

The play is a purely masculine affair. With the notable exception of two scenes, women play no role in it. When, in the Victorian era, sexual repression overcame the English-speaking world, *Julius Caesar* could still be taught in schools without fear of awakening sexually dangerous wishes in adolescent boys and girls, as no sexual passion is expressed and not a bawdy word is uttered. *Julius Caesar* is an amazing creation: its central theme is the oedipal wish but it takes place without any expression of sexual or aggressive wishes. The collective father dies but his image does not.

CAESAR: Cowards die many times before their deaths.
            The valiant never taste of death but once.
            Of all the wonders that I yet have heard,
            It seems to me most strange that men should fear,
            Seeing that death, a necessary end,
            Will come when it will come. (II.ii.32–37)
            Caesar compares himself to the North Star.

CAESAR: But I am constant as the northern star,
            Of whose true-fixed and resting quality
            There is no fellow in the firmament.
            The skies are painted with unnumbered sparks.
            They are all fire and every one doth shine,
            But there's but one in all doth hold his place. (III.i.66–71)

Lines such as these are calculated to turn the audience against the conspirators but not against Brutus.

Earlier, we heard Brutus' thoughts on death.

BRUTUS: Set honour in one eye and death i' th' other,
            And I will look on both indifferently,
            For let the gods so speed me as I love
            The name of honour more than I fear death. (I.ii.88–91)

Both Caesar and Brutus share this confidence in their own place in the world. Both are admirable and yet Brutus has to kill Caesar.

If we turn to psychoanalysis it helps us understand Shakespeare as a playwright. We should note that it is an oedipal play, but with both aggression and sexuality removed, the writer achieved more. In everyday clinical practice it is the superego that replaces the oedipal wish, while in this play the superego brings about the murder.

Women appear only in two short scenes and in both they play a positive role. We are in Act II, scene one; it is late at night and both Brutus and Portia have left their bed.

PORTIA: Is Brutus sick? And is it physical
    To walk unbracèd and suck up the humors
    Of the dank morning? What, is Brutus sick,
    And will he steal out of his wholesome bed,
    To dare the vile contagion of the night
    And tempt the rheumy and unpurgèd air
    To add unto his sickness? No, my Brutus.
    You have some sick offense within your mind,
    Which by the right and virtue of my place
    I ought to know of.
    (kneels) And upon my knees
    I charm you, by my once-commended beauty,
    By all your vows of love and that great vow
    Which did incorporate and make us one
    That you unfold to me, your self, your half,
    Why you are heavy. (II.i.269–284)
    …
    Within the bond of marriage, tell me, Brutus,
    Is it excepted I should know no secrets
    That appertain to you? Am I yourself
    But, as it were, in sort or limitation,
    To keep with you at meals, comfort your bed,
    And talk to you sometimes? Dwell I but in the suburbs
    Of your good pleasure? If it be no more,
    Portia is Brutus' harlot, not his wife. (II.i.289–296)

The speech is memorable by itself and has the added significance of establishing that Caesar's murderer is a happily married man. In psychoanalytic practice when oedipal wishes are strong they prevent a man from finding a wife like Portia, but for dramatic purposes the image of Brutus is enhanced by being married to a woman like Portia.

  Shakespeare took the plot of the play from the Roman historian Plutarch's "Lives". Even the encounter between Brutus and his wife is contained in that source. We can learn something important about the nature of creativity by comparing the two versions. Plutarch relates (as found in the Scott-Kilvert translation):

  Porcia [sic], who loved her husband deeply and was not only of an
  affectionate nature but full of spirit and good sense, did not press

her husband to reveal his secrets until she had put herself to a test. She dismissed her attendants from her room, and then taking a little knife such as barbers use to cut finger-nails, she gave herself a deep gash in the thigh. She lost a great quantity of blood, after which the wound became intensely painful and brought on fits of shivering and a high fever. When she was in great pain and saw that Brutus was deeply distressed for her, she said to him: "Brutus, I am Cato's daughter, and I was given to you in marriage not just to share your bed and board like a concubine, but to be a true partner in your joys and sorrows. I have no reproach to make to you, but what proof can I give you of my love, if you forbid me to share the kind of trouble that demands a loyal friend to confide in, and keep your suffering to yourself? I know that men think women's natures too weak to be entrusted with secrets, but surely a good upbringing and the company of honourable men can do much to strengthen us, and at least Porcia can claim that she is the daughter of Cato and the wife of Brutus. I did not know before this show either of these blessings could help me, but now I have put myself to the test and find that I can conquer pain". At this she showed him her wound and explained what she had done. Brutus was amazed and lifting up his hands to heaven he prayed to the gods to help him to succeed in his enterprise and show that he was a worthy husband of such a wife. Then he did all that he could to bring his wife to health. (Scott-Kilvert, 1965: p. 234)

Following Plutarch's lead, Shakespeare has written the following exchange.

PORTIA: I grant I am a woman, but withal
           A woman that Lord Brutus took to wife.
           I grant I am a woman, but withal
           A woman well-reputed, Cato's daughter.
           Think you I am no stronger than my sex,
           Being so fathered and so husbanded?
           Tell me your counsels. I will not disclose 'em.
           I have made strong proof of my constancy,
           Giving myself a voluntary wound
           Here in the thigh. Can I bear that with patience,
           And not my husband's secrets?

BRUTUS: O ye gods,
                   Render me worthy of this noble wife! (*Julius Caesar*, II.i.301–312)

Portia expresses the feeling many women still harbour in spite of the work of the Women's Liberation Movement: her feelings about herself are enhanced by being both the daughter and the wife of two prominent men. She then wounds herself to prove that she is equal to men in courage.

Did Shakespeare believe that dreams were prophetic? Caesar reports to Decius Brutus:

CAESAR: Calpurnia here, my wife, stays me at home.
                   She dreamt tonight she saw my statue,
                   Which, like a fountain with an hundred spouts,
                   Did run pure blood. And many lusty Romans
                   Came smiling and did bathe their hands in it. (II.ii.75–79)

Calpurnia sees the dream as a warning that Caesar should not go to the Senate but Decius Brutus offers a different interpretation.

DECIUS: This dream is all amiss interpreted.
                   It was a vision fair and fortunate.
                   Your statue spouting blood in many pipes,
                   In which so many smiling Romans bathed,
                   Signifies that from you great Rome shall suck
                   Reviving blood, and that great men shall press
                   For tinctures, stains, relics, and cognisance.
                   This by Calpurnia's dream is signified. (II.ii.83–90)

Since the dream came true we conclude that Shakespeare did believe that dreams can be prophetic but he also showed his mistrust in the symbolic meaning of dreams.

So far I have stressed Shakespeare's conservatism but there must have been other ideas active in him that found expression in the portrayal of Cassius.

CASSIUS: I was born free as Caesar. So were you.
                   We both have fed as well, and we can both
                   Endure the winter's cold as well as he.

> For once upon a raw and gusty day,
> The troubled Tiber chafing with her shores,
> Caesar said to me, "Darest thou, Cassius, now
> Leap in with me into this angry flood
> And swim to yonder point?" Upon the word,
> Accoutred as I was, I plungèd in
> And bade him follow. So indeed he did.
> The torrent roared, and we did buffet it
> With lusty sinews, throwing it aside
> And stemming it with hearts of controversy.
> But ere we could arrive the point proposed,
> Caesar cried, "Help me, Cassius, or I sink!"
> I, as Aeneas, our great ancestor,
> Did from the flames of Troy upon his shoulder
> The old Anchises bear, so from the waves of Tiber
> Did I the tired Caesar. And this man
> Is now become a god, and Cassius is
> A wretched creature and must bend his body
> If Caesar carelessly but nod on him. (I.ii.97–118)

If Cassius saved Caesar from drowning it is not surprising that he will not allow him the superiority he now claims. What is surprising is that he compares himself to Aeneas, the son who rescued his aging father even while he is plotting to conspire against Caesar (the father whom he saved). Did Shakespeare allow him to make what we call today a Freudian slip and acknowledge Caesar as a father? The question has further implications, as Aeneas is the founder of Rome. Did the Romans take pride in their mythology as being founded by an anti-oedipal ancestor?

As Cassius is trying to win Brutus to the conspiracy, Shakespeare shows us why he is in conflict with Caesar. When Brutus and Cassius together with the conspirators kill Julius Caesar, the two are in very different relationships to him. For Brutus, Caesar is still the idealised father figure, while for Cassius he is the debased father clinging to a position he no longer deserves.

CASSIUS: Why, man, he doth bestride the narrow world
           Like a Colossus, and we petty men
           Walk under his huge legs and peep about

> To find ourselves dishonourable graves.
> Men at some time are masters of their fates.
> The fault, dear Brutus, is not in our stars
> But in ourselves, that we are underlings.
> Brutus and Caesar—what should be in that "Caesar"?
> Why should that name be sounded more than yours?
> Write them together, yours is as fair a name.
> Sound them, it doth become the mouth as well.
> Weigh them, it is as heavy. Conjure with 'em,
> "Brutus" will start a spirit as soon as "Caesar".
> Now in the names of all the gods at once,
> Upon what meat doth this our Caesar feed
> That he is grown so great? Age, thou art shamed!
> Rome, thou hast lost the breed of noble bloods! (I.ii.136–152)

If we listen to Cassius the way psychoanalysts listen to their patients we hear that he sees Caesar as a colossus and sees himself under his huge legs. The image contains a child's memory of looking up at the father's legs, and what does the child see but the father's much bigger penis. We can see the position as a painful one for him and we can say that it injures his narcissism and has a depressive effect, hence the reference to "dishonourable graves". Cassius tries to evoke the jealousy of the oedipal complex in Brutus. What we see is the extension of the term from the private sector of the child to the Roman Forum. Cassius' words are effective but they also evoke a powerful intrapsychic conflict in Brutus.

BRUTUS: Since Cassius first did whet me against Caesar,
         I have not slept.
         Between the acting of a dreadful thing
         And the first motion, all the interim is
         Like a phantasma or a hideous dream. (II.i.63–67)

Today psychoanalysis has given us the vocabulary to understand the inner conflict that Cassius evoked in Brutus but Shakespeare had to create the language he needed. We note the use of "whet me" where we would say "arouse in me". We also note that it evoked insomnia in Brutus and that life was a nightmare to him until the assassination. The murder was experienced as a relief from the inner conflict. In psychoanalytic terms it is the reliving of the violence and guilt feelings of the Oedipus complex. Brutus calls himself "poor Brutus, with himself at war", (I.ii.48) and later notes:

BRUTUS: the state of man,
          Like to a little kingdom, suffers then
          The nature of an insurrection. (II.i.69–71)

For us today, civil insurrection has become a common metaphor for intrapsychic conflict, but in Shakespeare's time this was a surprising metaphor.

We turn once more to compare Shakespeare with Plutarch. In Plutarch's version Brutus and Cassius are brothers-in-law and also competitors for the most coveted praetorship of the capital. The deep love of Cassius for Brutus is Shakespeare's creation. In Plutarch the relationship of the two men is more ambivalent.

> When he [Caesar] heard that Mark Antony and Dolabella were plotting a revolution, he remarked, "It is not these sleek, long-haired fellows who frighten me, but the pale, thin ones", by whom he meant Brutus and Cassius. (Scott-Kilvert, 1965: p. 229)

The murder itself takes place in a state of manic intoxication. The conspirators dip their hands and swords in Caesar's blood as if they are performing a religious ceremony.

BRUTUS: Stoop, Romans, stoop,
          And let us bathe our hands in Caesar's blood
          Up to the elbows, and besmear our swords.
          Then walk we forth, even to the marketplace,
          And waving our red weapons o'er our heads
          Let's all cry, "Peace, freedom, and liberty!"
CASSIUS: Stoop, then, and wash. (*Julius Caesar*, III.i.105–111)

The relationship between Cassius and Brutus opens up a rich psychoanalytic chapter. Brutus is a man with a very powerful superego, which is why he insists that the killing of Caesar should be seen as a "sacrifice to the gods" and be free from any murderous lust. For

Cassius it was revenge for an injury to his own self-esteem and therefore foremost a narcissistic injury. Cassius is in need of Brutus' love while Brutus, with his powerful superego, does not need Cassius' approval. Rather, he needs the assurance that after the assassination the conspirators will behave like priests and be free from personal shortcomings. The difference between them guarantees that the two men will not be able to work together, which contributes to their defeat. Again, I stress that Shakespeare found a way to describe this complex relationship at a time when the language and concepts to describe it were not yet available. Because Freud gave us the needed vocabulary we are in a position to appreciate Shakespeare's achievement all the better.

A further interesting exchange takes place between Brutus and Cassius.

CASSIUS: You love me not.
BRUTUS: I do not like your faults.
CASSIUS: A friendly eye could never see such faults.
BRUTUS: A flatterer's would not, though they do appear
                As huge as high Olympus.
CASSIUS: Come, Antony, and young Octavius, come,
                Revenge yourselves alone on Cassius,
                For Cassius is aweary of the world;

                ...

                Strike, as thou didst at Caesar; for, I know,
                When thou didst hate him worst, thou lovedst him better
                Than ever thou lovedst Cassius. (IV.iii.92–98, 109–111)

                ...

                Fill, Lucius, till the wine o'erswell the cup.
                I cannot drink too much of Brutus' love. (IV.iii.167–168)

We stop once more to admire Shakespeare's genius, for he has combined murderous oedipal wishes towards Caesar and desexualised homosexual love towards Brutus in the same character, Cassius.

Act V, the last act in the play, can be described as the triumph of Caesar's ghost over the conspirators. On the plains of Philippi, Brutus and Cassius meet their enemies, Octavius and Antony, face to face. This is an unrealistic but highly dramatic encounter.

ANTONY: In your bad strokes, Brutus, you give good words.
                Witness the hole you made in Caesar's heart,
                Crying "Long live, hail, Caesar!"
CASSIUS: Antony,
                The posture of your blows are yet unknown.
                But for your words, they rob the Hybla bees
                And leave them honeyless.
ANTONY: Not stingless too?
BRUTUS: Oh, yes, and soundless too.
                For you have stol'n their buzzing, Antony,
                And very wisely threat before you sting.
ANTONY: Villains, you did not so when your vile daggers
                Hacked one another in the sides of Caesar. (V.i.30–41)

The combatants are taunting each other more like schoolboys than generals.

Caesar is omnipresent when Cassius dies. Cassius asks Pindarus to kill him.

CASSIUS: Now be a free man, and with this good sword
                That ran through Caesar's bowels, search this bosom.
                Stand not to answer. Here take thou the hilts
                And, when my face is covered, as 'tis now,
                Guide thou the sword.
                (*Pindarus stabs Cassius.*)
                Caesar, thou art revenged,
                Even with the sword that killed thee. (*dies*). (V.iii.44–49)

In a similar vein, upon learning of the deaths of Cassius and Tintinius, Brutus exclaims:

BRUTUS: O Julius Caesar, thou art mighty yet!
                Thy spirit walks abroad and turns our swords
                In our own proper entrails. (V.iii.100–102)
                Mark Antony pays homage to Brutus.
ANTONY: This was the noblest Roman of them all.
                All the conspirators save only he
                Did that they did in envy of great Caesar.
                He only in a general honest thought
                And common good to all, made one of them.
                His life was gentle, and the elements

So mixed in him that Nature might stand up
And say to all the world, "This was a man". (V.v.74–81)

Even his enemies pay homage to Brutus.

Discussion

Julius Caesar has a unique place in Shakespeare's work. It deals with a group that can be described, psychologically, as a group of brothers deciding to kill a father figure together. Caesar is not a tyrant yet he is killed because to the conspirators it seems certain he will become one once he is crowned. Shakespeare himself was living under an absolute monarch, but Queen Elizabeth was not a father figure, and the "virgin Queen" was perhaps not even a mother figure. The play does not end on a republican note, and the last scene leaves no doubt that Caesar, in the minds of the two main conspirators, had his revenge. We may assume that the play could be performed during Shakespeare's day because it took place in a far away and long ago civilisation and it did not end in a republican victory. It was an act of genius on Shakespeare's part to balance the defeat of the conspirators with a description of their leader as such a noble man. It is also of psychological interest that the murder of the father figure is associated with a special love of Cassius for Brutus, as if the father figure can be killed if the conspirators, or at least one of them, transfer the love from the father to a sibling. It is no less striking that Shakespeare understood what psychoanalysis took many years to understand. Brutus' powerful superego makes him less in need of being loved.

A psychoanalyst reading *Julius Caesar* will inevitably compare this play with Freud's *Totem and Taboo* (1912–13), in which Freud formulated his theory about the beginning of culture:

> The most ancient and important taboo prohibitions are the two basic laws of totemism: not to kill the totem animal and to avoid sexual intercourse with members of the totem clan of the opposite sex. (Freud, 1913: p. 32)

The theory was dear to Freud and he repeated it in his last book, *Moses and Monotheism*:

> …in primaeval times, primitive man lived in small hordes, each under the domination of a powerful male. … The strong man was

> lord and father of the entire horde and unrestricted in his power,
> which he exercised with violence. All the females were his prop-
> erty ... The lot of the sons was a hard one: if they roused their
> father's jealousy they were killed or castrated or driven out. Their
> only resource was to collect together in small communities, to get
> themselves wives by robbery, and ... raise themselves to a position
> similar to their father's. (*Freud*, 1939: p. 81)

What *Totem and Taboo* did for Freud was to anchor his basic discovery
of the Oedipus complex in an early historical event, which gave to psychoanalysis a hypothetical social psychology.

Harold Bloom (1998, p. 108), noted the affinity between Julius Caesar
and Freud's *Totem and Taboo* but regarded *Totem and Taboo* as a rewriting of *Julius Caesar*. However, try as I may I see no way in which *Totem
and Taboo* can be derived from the play. In my view, it is the other way
around: knowing *Totem and Taboo* allows for a deeper understanding of
Julius Caesar. Shakespeare transplanted Freud's "primal horde" into a
highly civilised world. According to Freud, civilisation began after the
murder of the primal father; according to Shakespeare highly civilised
men committed the murder.

While Freud was writing *Totem and Taboo* he was in active correspondence
with Jung, Abraham, Jones, and Ferenczi, but I did not find any reference
to *Julius Caesar* in these correspondences. There is, however, a famous reference to the play in *The Interpretation of Dreams* (Freud, 1900: p. 425); it takes
place in the discussion of Freud's "non vixit" dream about his deceased
friend Joseph Paneth and Brutus' funeral oration for Caesar is quoted in
full. The same quote is repeated in *A Case of Obsessional Neurosis* (Freud,
1909: p. 180). The words of Brutus that meant so much to Freud were:

BRUTUS: As Caesar loved me, I weep for him. As he was fortunate, I rejoice at
           it. As he was valiant, I honour him. But, as he was ambitious, I slew
           him. (*Julius Caesar*, III.ii.22–28)

Freud was fascinated by Shakespeare's capacity to portray conflicting
feelings that give rise to ambivalence.

We should pause once more to admire how Shakespeare was able to
use contradictory behaviour in his play. Any logical person would have
noted the contradiction and refrained from the murder, but Shakespeare
made Brutus capable of overriding the contradiction and committing

murder. Later, instead of the remorse assumed by Freud in *Totem and Taboo*, the effect on Brutus was to increase the severity of the superego.

Today we know that Freud's analysis of the "non vixit" dream did not go deeply enough, for Freud had a younger brother named Julius who died when he was six months old, when Freud was less than two. It must have seemed to the infant Freud that his death wishes towards his younger sibling came true, so he had a deeper reason to identify himself with Brutus.

Julius Caesar is one of Shakespeare's best-known plays. It is generally read in secondary education. We can assume that it stirs up universal oedipal feelings and helps transfer them from a personal to a historical context. It therefore has a social function. At the same time it does not support any revolutionary feelings that may have been aroused. Shakespeare showed us that to carry out the oedipal wish does not bring about the happiness expected but rather a lifelong sense of guilt culminating in a death sentence upon the rebellious sons.

CHAPTER SEVEN

Macbeth: an audacious variant on the oedipal theme

In this chapter the reader will find a radically new interpretation of the joint murder of King Duncan.

The witches have just delivered their prophecy to Macbeth. Banquo turns to Macbeth and says, "Good sir, why do you start, and seem to fear / Things that do sound so fair?" (*Macbeth*, I.iii.51–52). Banquo then, without fear, invites the "weird sisters" to tell him what is in store for him. The differences in how the two men react to the prophecies is Shakespeare's way of telling us that for Macbeth the prophecy suddenly made conscious wishes that had already been active but repressed; to hear them expressed made him "start", but the prophecy had no similar effect on Banquo because he had no unconscious oedipal wishes to replace the king.

Had the witches reversed their prophecies, would Banquo have killed the king? Most likely not: he would have assumed that the prophecy would be fulfilled if he simply waited. Macbeth assumes that he himself must bring about the fulfillment of the prophecy and do it immediately. For a moment Macbeth hesitates and considers adopting Banquo's attitude, and says in an aside, "If chance will have me king, why, chance may crown me, / Without my stir" (I.iii.143–144). However, once the wish was aroused he is not capable of inaction, nor can Macbeth wait until he arrives home to let his wife know what has happened; she must be informed immediately. Scene five of act I opens with Lady Macbeth reading his letter. What impressed Macbeth is that the first part of the prophecy, that he would become Thane of Cawdor, was immediately fulfilled when a messenger sent by the king announced his new honour. The letter states:

> Whiles I stood rapt in the wonder of it, came missives from the king, who all-hailed me 'Thane of Cawdor;' by which title, before, these weird sisters saluted me, and referred me to the coming on of time, with 'Hail, king that shalt be!' This have I thought good to deliver thee, my dearest partner of greatness, that thou mightst not lose the dues of rejoicing, by being ignorant of what greatness is promised thee. Lay it to thy heart, and farewell'. (I.v.i)

At first Macbeth is merely reporting events but the end of the letter reveals the psychological relationship between the two. By this urgency to share the news Shakespeare conveys to us Macbeth's great dependency on his wife. In psychoanalytic thinking the country has replaced the family, the king has replaced the father and regicide has replaced patricide.

I realised the unique way Shakespeare used the witches after I read Greenblatt's (2004) description of how prevalent and all-powerful the belief in witches was at the time Shakespeare wrote the play. Shakespeare followed the popular image of the witches, but only as facilitators of psychological forces within the individual. The witches in *Macbeth* draw out what was already in Macbeth's unconscious.

In psychoanalytic terms witches are phallic women. They are feared because they castrate men. These witches also have a feminine aspect; as E. Jones portrayed in *On the Nightmare* they have sexual relations with the devil and inflict impotence on men and devour the newborn (Jones, 1931). To Freud, the fear of witches in Shakespeare's time was an example of a mass neurosis (Freud, 1923).

The persecution of so-called witches is one of the most horrible chapters in the history of Western culture. Freud's own interest in the devil and in witches can be read in the letters to Fliess (Masson, 1985). On 24 June 1897, he reported to Fliess that his interest in witches was gaining strength: "The broomstick they ride is the great Lord penis!" (Masson, 1985: p. 227). In his 1923 study "A Seventeenth Century Demonological Neurosis" Freud equated the fear of witches with current neuroses.

Chapter seven of Ernest Jones' book *On the Nightmare,* is devoted to witches. It was published in 1931 but based on studies conducted in 1909–1910, at the very beginning of psychoanalytic history. What emerges in this history is the close relationship between sexuality and witchcraft. Witches have sexual relationships with the devil; at the same time they inflict impotence on men and devour newborns. They are personifications of the hated and feared phallic mother. Shakespeare endowed them with a capacity, not mentioned in Jones' chapter, to predict the future, and their fortune telling makes conscious what was repressed. Neither Freud nor Jones explains why the witches, as phallic women, are so dreaded. It must be that they have acquired their phallic power by castrating men.

In Act I, scene five, in Macbeth's castle in Inverness. Lady Macbeth is reading her husband's letter telling her the prophecy, when a messenger arrives to inform her the king will be visiting that night. The news elicits the following soliloquy:

LADY MACBETH: The raven himself is hoarse
That croaks the fatal entrance of Duncan
Under my battlements. Come, you spirits
That tend on mortal thoughts, unsex me here,
And fill me from the crown to the toe top-full
Of direst cruelty! make thick my blood;
Stop up the access and passage to remorse.
(*Macbeth,* I.v.39–45)

The feminine Oedipus complex culminates in desiring the father sexually while the masculine oedipus urges the death of the father. In psychoanalytic language what Lady Macbeth is asking is to exchange her feminine Oedipus complex for a masculine one.

The passage combines two different ideas not usually brought together. Lady Macbeth asks to be "unsexed" because she feels that women are naturally compassionate, but then she also asks, in psychoanalytic language, to silence her superego and "Stop up the access ... to remorse". These two very different "operations" seem one and the same to this remarkable woman. At the same time, Lady Macbeth is aware of the fact that her husband may not be able to commit the necessary murder.

LADY MACBETH: Yet do I fear thy nature;
It is too full o' th' milk of human kindness
To catch the nearest way: thou wouldst be great,
Art not without ambition, but without
The illness should attend it. What thou wouldst highly,
That wouldst thou holily; wouldst not play false,
And yet wouldst wrongly win. (I.v.3–10)

What we just heard from Lady Macbeth is an excellent formulation of intrapsychic conflict. She grants that her husband is not without ambition but lacks the "illness should attend it". This is Shakespeare's way of saying Macbeth is not neurotic enough to carry out his ambition because he is "full o' th' milk of human kindness", or, in our language, has too much libido to commit the murder of the king. Shakespeare endowed Lady Macbeth with remarkable insight.

Psychoanalysis has familiarised us with the prevalent penis envy in women, but it has not dealt extensively with a woman's fear of losing her femininity. However, analyses of women in menopause and of women who cannot conceive show how very difficult this experience, symbolising a loss of femininity can be. Lady Macbeth feels that she can only be steadfast in the murder with her husband if she sacrifices her femininity. Shakespeare introduces this theme twice. The first time is when Lady Macbeth reads the letter in which Macbeth tells her of the prophecy that he will be king. The next reference to the castration of Lady Macbeth's femininity takes place in scene seven. Macbeth has decided not to commit the murder and says, "We will proceed no further in this business" (I.vii.31). Lady Macbeth now belittles her husband and threatens him with castration anxiety:

LADY MACBETH: Art thou afeard
To be the same in thine own act and valour
As thou art in desire? Wouldst thou have that
Which thou esteem'st the ornament of life,
And live a coward in thine own esteem,
Letting "I dare not" wait upon "I would". (I.vii.39–44)

Shakespeare makes clear that this belittling of her husband's masculinity is not nearly as effective as her willingness to sacrifice her maternal feelings.

LADY MACBETH: I have given suck, and know
                 How tender 'tis to love the babe that milks me:
                 I would, while it was smiling in my face,
                 Have pluck'd my nipple from his boneless gums,
                 And dash'd the brains out, had I so sworn as you
                 Have done to this. (I.vii.54–59)

The words are so powerful that we shudder to hear them. The logic is not easy to follow. Lady Macbeth is saying that had she committed herself to the act of murder she claims her husband has sworn to commit, she would have been capable of dashing the brain out of a nursing baby. The imagined capacity of a mother to kill her nursing baby is not supposed to horrify her husband, but to encourage him to carry out his oedipal wish. This statement is a continuation of the earlier one she made: to carry out this murder all libidinal relationships have to be severed, even the most profound one, between mother and nursing child; no traces of the milk of human kindness should remain. We should note that milk is used both concretely—"the babe that milks me"—and metaphorically—the "milk of human kindness". There is no sign that the subject of childlessness was of concern before the murder. It will become a central problem after the murder, but only to Macbeth, as evidenced when he states, "Upon my head they placed a fruitless crown, / And put a barren sceptre in my gripe" (III.i.61–62).

What Lady Macbeth is saying is not true, or at least there is nothing in the play to suggest that Macbeth ever "swore", as he is accused of doing. From the very beginning he was in conflict and he needed encouragement from his wife to commit the crime.

Macbeth is struck with admiration for her determination and says:

MACBETH: Bring forth men-children only;
            For thy undaunted mettle should compose
            Nothing but males. (I.vii.72–74)

There is no reference to infertility or the inability to bear a child in Lady Macbeth's soliloquy. The vivid description of the murder of the nursling has achieved its purpose: Macbeth has overcome his hesitation to commit the murder. The unconscious logic is probably as follows: If a mother can kill her nursing baby, Macbeth should be able to commit regicide. This is not logical "secondary process" thinking but typical unconscious thinking, namely, if a mother can kill her babe, nothing else should be as abhorrent.

As the murder of Duncan takes place Shakespeare presents the couple in opposite moods. Lady Macbeth is confident.

LADY MACBETH: That which hath made them drunk hath made me bold
What hath quench'd them hath given me fire. Hark! Peace!
It was the owl that shriek'd, the fatal bell-man,
Which gives the stern'st good-night. (II.ii.1–4)
At the same time, Macbeth has a frightening hallucination.

MACBETH: Is this a dagger which I see before me,
The handle toward my hand? Come, let me clutch thee.
I have thee not, and yet I see thee still.
Art thou not, fatal vision, sensible
To feeling as to sight? Or art thou but
A dagger of the mind, a false creation,
Proceeding from the heat-oppressed brain?
I see thee yet, in form as palpable
As this which now I draw. (II.i.33–41)

Once again it is remarkable how Shakespeare presents hallucinations. There are real daggers and daggers "of the mind", and the daggers of the mind are false creations "Proceeding from the heat-oppressed brain".

After the murder Macbeth feels he has murdered not the king but sleep itself.

MACBETH: Methought I heard a voice cry "Sleep no more!
Macbeth does murder sleep", the innocent sleep,
Sleep that knits up the ravell'd sleave of care,
The death of each day's life, sore labour's bath,
Balm of hurt minds, great nature's second course,
Chief nourisher in life's feast—(II.ii.35–40).

This is a magnificent tribute to the role of sleep in our lives, told by a man who can no longer sleep.

Macbeth experiences guilt feelings and remorse while Lady Macbeth remains calm.

MACBETH: One cried, "God bless us!" and "Amen" the other,
As they had seen me with these hangman's hands.
List'ning their fear I could not say "Amen",
When they did say "God bless us!"

LADY MACBETH: Consider it not so deeply.

MACBETH: But wherefore could not I pronounce "Amen"?
I had most need of blessing, and "Amen"
Stuck in my throat.

LADY MACBETH: These deeds must not be thought
After these ways. So, it will make us mad. (II.ii.27–35)

The way Lady Macbeth attempts to help her husband face the enormous guilt that Duncan's murder evokes in him is reminiscent of Jocasta's attempt to cope with the guilt that was overwhelming Oedipus. Her advice, not to consider it so deeply, advocates denial. Familiarity with psychoanalytic concepts only increases our admiration for Shakespeare. Lady Macbeth's prediction that her husband lacks the will necessary to accomplish the murder has come true. Macbeth is overwhelmed with guilt and like any good wife Lady Macbeth is doing her best to make it easier for him.

It was the interaction within the couple that interested Freud when he discussed the play in his 1916 essay "Some Character Types Met With in Psychoanalytic Work".

The germs of fear that break out in Macbeth on the night of the murder do not develop further in *him* but in *her*. It is he who has the hallucination of the dagger before the crime; but it is she who afterwards falls ill of a mental disorder. It is he who after the murder hears the cry in the house: "Sleep no more! Macbeth does murder sleep …" and so "Macbeth shall sleep no more"; but we never hear that *he* slept no more, while the Queen, as we see, rises from her bed and, talking in her sleep, betrays her guilt. It is he who stands helpless with bloody hands, lamenting that "all great Neptune's ocean" will not wash them clean, while she comforts him: "A little water clears us of this deed"; but later it is she who washes her hands for a quarter of an hour and cannot get rid of the bloodstains: "All the perfumes of Arabia will not sweeten this little hand". Thus what he feared in his pangs of conscience is fulfilled in her; she becomes all remorse and he all defiance. Together they exhaust the possibilities of reaction to the crime, like two disunited parts of a single psychical individuality, and it may be that they are both copied from a single prototype. (Freud, 1916: p. 324)

Freud attributed to Shakespeare the insight that within the couple the partners can exchange identities.

In a magnificent example of the exchange of roles that can take place in a couple, Macbeth fears insomnia and Lady Macbeth develops somnambulism. What is striking is that Shakespeare treats both as purely psychological events based on feelings of guilt. What breaks down in her somnambulism is Lady Macbeth's capacity to keep the murder of King Duncan a secret between herself and her husband. Anyone who watches her desperate efforts to remove the blood spots on her hands can surmise the reason for her agitation.

Just before the murder Macbeth is resolved not to carry it out but is overruled by his wife. There is a long soliloquy of guilt I will quote only in part.

MACBETH: He's here in double trust;
                    First, as I am his kinsman and his subject,
                    Strong both against the deed; then, as his host,
                    Who should against his murderer shut the door,
                    Not bear the knife myself. Besides, this Duncan
                    Hath borne his faculties so meek, hath been
                    So clear in his great office, that his virtues
                    Will plead like angels, trumpet-tongued, against
                    The deep damnation of his taking-off. (I.vii.12–20)

To kill your guest, who is also a relative, and a king, whose subject you are, and whose character you deeply respect, is indeed an abominable crime, but Shakespeare chose in this play to portray such a murderer, not as a villain but rather as a person with a normal capacity to feel guilt. Macbeth can kill the king because he identified himself with his now masculine wife and her lack of conflict. Shakespeare gave a profound psychological meaning to the term joint murder.

It is a special achievement of this play that regicide, a symbolic form of parricide, is carried out not by the traditional villain devoid of guilt feelings but by a man with strong guilt feelings. What overrides the power of the superego is the castration of her own femininity conveyed to Macbeth by his wife.

After the murder, when he has become king, Macbeth is haunted by the fact that he and his wife have no children.

MACBETH: Upon my head they placed a fruitless crown,
And put a barren sceptre in my gripe,
Thence to be wrench'd with an unlineal hand,
No son of mine succeeding. (III.i.60–63)

There is no implication that Lady Macbeth is troubled by her barrenness. I am not sure whether Shakespeare had this connection in mind but to us the connection occurs. The woman who asked to be "unsexed" and who was so willing to kill her nursing baby has, by these wishes, forfeited her right to be a mother and has condemned the couple to remain childless.

I come now to what may be the most significant insight I have to offer to the unconscious meaning of this play. It may also be the one most difficult to accept. In Shakespeare's unconscious the Macbeths are not meant to be a man and a woman but a mother and child. If this interpretation is accepted Macbeth presents a most daring variation on the Oedipus complex: that the murder of the father be accomplished by the mother and child together, with the mother as the more steadfast one. We also gain new insight into the unsexing scene. In Lady Macbeth's mind if she assists in Duncan's murder she herself will become masculine and the baby she promises she would kill must refer unconsciously to Macbeth himself. The oedipal feat is committed by mother and son. Once we realise that the boy could imagine that the mother would help him kill the father, one wonders why no other creative writer imagined this most powerful variant on the oedipal theme. The unconscious message conveyed to Macbeth is: "If I don't kill her, she is capable of killing me".

I come now to the core of what I mean by a psychoanalytic interpretation of the play. There is a variant on the oedipal theme, not discussed by Freud, but possibly active in Shakespeare's unconscious, that may help us to further understand the gripping power of *Macbeth*: the deeply repressed wish of the son that the mother help him in murdering the father. This may well be the most horror evoking variant on the oedipal theme. If any readers feel that such a thought cannot be possible, let me admit that I am not saying this thought was conscious to Shakespeare. All I claim is that this thought motivated Macbeth even if it never became conscious to Shakespeare himself. There are mythological parallels to this wish. Kronos eats his children, but Rhea, his wife, helps their son Zeus to escape him and replace him as the king of the gods. Milder variances on this theme are encountered in the analysis of both sons and mothers whenever mother and son are jointly attacking or criticising the father. Shakespeare came close to dealing with this theme in at least two plays.

In *Hamlet*, after the murder of Polonius, the queen exclaims, "Oh, what a rash and bloody deed is this?" (*Hamlet*, III.iv.27) and Hamlet answers: "A bloody deed! almost as bad, good mother, / As kill a king, and marry with his brother" (III.iv.28–29). Hamlet accuses his mother of this joint oedipal crime projected onto the king's brother. What seemed like a strange hypothesis in *Macbeth* was actually verbalised by Hamlet against his mother. Throughout the play the role of the queen is left uncertain; the ghost that demands revenge explicitly tells Hamlet to "leave her to heaven" (I.v.86) rather than punish her. However, the suspicion hovers that Gertrude may have had a sexual liaison with her brother-in-law even while her husband was alive. Hamlet suspects that she was an accomplice in his father's murder.

In *Macbeth*, composed in 1606, six years after *Hamlet*, Shakespeare may have returned to the same theme in a different disguise. King Duncan is killed by a joint act of the couple but they are husband and wife, not mother and son. A couple's joint decision to murder a father figure is horror evoking, but in this play it is made tolerable by Shakespeare's skill as a dramatist. Macbeth is only unconsciously Lady Macbeth's son, so her role as the mother instigating the son to kill the father is obscured.

As a further piece of evidence for my interpretation I cite "Venus and Adonis". The poem was published in 1593, thirteen years before *Macbeth*. Today it is not nearly as well known as the play but it was popular when it first appeared, going through at least sixteen editions (Burrow, 2002). In the poem Venus, an older and more sexually experienced woman, is trying to seduce what could almost be called a child in psychological terms.

VENUS: "I have been wooed as I entreat thee now
               Even by the stern and direful god of war,

Whose sinewy neck in battle ne'er did bow,
Who conquers where he comes in every jar;
Yet hath he been my captive and my slave,
And begged for that which thou unasked shalt have. (*Venus and Adonis*, 97–102)

Venus stands for the mother trying to seduce Adonis, a son figure, by telling him that he can have her sexually without asking, while the father figure—the god of war, Mars—had to beg for the favour. She is trying to arouse him by evoking competitive oedipal wishes. But Adonis is only interested in the aggressive component of the oedipus complex, killing the boar. In spite of his resistance to Venus, Adonis is killed by a father, represented by a boar. The unconscious message of *Venus and Adonis* is that even resisting the mother's seduction does not prevent the punishment of the child.

Eventually Macbeth will die in personal combat with Macduff although he tries to avoid the encounter. "But get thee back; my soul is too much charged / With blood of thine already" (*Macbeth*, V.viii.5–6). Macbeth learns that Macduff was not "of woman born" (V.viii.13) because "Macduff was from his mother's womb / Untimely ripp'd". (V.viii.15–16). Macduff's superiority turns out to be due to the fact that he was symbolically motherless. This is one more example of Shakespeare's persistent effort to eliminate the mother. Other examples are found in *King Lear* and *The Tempest*.

Macbeth's response to Lady Macbeth's death is that life has no meaning. This response is memorable because the speech expresses some of Shakespeare's most memorable lines but it contains not one word of personal loss or mourning.

MACBETH: Tomorrow, and tomorrow, and tomorrow,
Creeps in this petty pace from day to day
To the last syllable of recorded time,
And all our yesterdays have lighted fools
The way to dusty death. Out, out, brief candle!
Life's but a walking shadow, a poor player
That struts and frets his hour upon the stage
And then is heard no more: it is a tale
Told by an idiot, full of sound and fury,
Signifying nothing. (V.v.19–28)

This is a strange speech of mourning for a dead wife and hardly in keeping with Macbeth's personality, since Macbeth shows no interest in actors and theatre, but what a magnificent expression for Shakespeare the actor and playwright. In these lines Shakespeare himself takes over; this soliloquy may not rightly belong to Macbeth but it expresses Shakespeare's philosophy.

One further scene is of special interest to us as therapists. In the doctor scene that opens Act V Shakespeare comes very close to discovering psychotherapy but refrains from doing so. How close he came and why Shakespeare did not discover psychotherapy could make an interesting chapter in the history of the discipline. We first hear an agitated discussion between the doctor and a gentlewoman who has waited upon the queen.

DOCTOR: I have two nights watched with you, but can perceive no
              truth in your report. When was it she last walked?
GENTLEWOMAN: Since his majesty went into the field, I have seen her rise
              from her bed, throw her night-gown upon her, unlock her
              closet, take forth paper, fold it, write upon't, read it, after-
              wards seal it, and again return to bed; yet all this while in a
              most fast sleep.
DOCTOR: A great perturbation in nature, to receive at once the benefit
              of sleep, and do the effects of watching! In this slumbery agi-
              tation, besides her walking and other actual performances,
              what, at any time, have you heard her say?
GENTLEWOMAN: That, sir, which I will not report after her.
DOCTOR: You may to me: and 'tis most meet you should.
GENTLEWOMAN: Neither to you nor any one; having no witness to confirm
              my speech. (V.i.1–21)

The doctor acts as a therapist. He is interested in the details and his diagnosis is "A great perturbation in nature" because the somnambulism combines two opposites, "the benefits of sleep" and the effects of walking. Like a resisting psychoanalytic patient, the gentlewoman wants the doctor to cure Lady Macbeth without telling him what she knows.

GENTLEWOMAN: Lo you, here she comes! This is her very guise; and, upon
              my life, fast asleep. Observe her; stand close.

DOCTOR:	How came she by that light?
GENTLEWOMAN:	Why, it stood by her: she has light by her continually; 'tis her command.
DOCTOR:	You see, her eyes are open.
GENTLEWOMAN:	Ay, but their sense is shut.
DOCTOR:	What is it she does now? Look, how she rubs her hands.
GENTLEWOMAN:	It is an accustomed action with her, to seem thus washing her hands: I have known her continue in this a quarter of an hour.
LADY MACBETH:	Yet here's a spot.
DOCTOR:	Hark! she speaks: I will set down what comes from her, to satisfy my remembrance the more strongly. (V.i.22–38)

Like many psychotherapists the doctor wants to take notes because he does not trust himself to remember everything.

A bit further in the scene are the famous lines:

LADY MACBETH:	Here's the smell of the blood still: all the perfumes of Arabia will not sweeten this little hand. Oh, oh, oh!
DOCTOR:	What a sigh is there! The heart is sorely charged.
GENTLEWOMAN:	I would not have such a heart in my bosom for the dignity of the whole body.
DOCTOR:	Well, well, well,—
GENTLEWOMAN:	Pray God it be, sir.
DOCTOR:	This disease is beyond my practice: yet I have known those which have walked in their sleep who have died holily in their beds. (V.i.56–67)

It is astonishing how much Shakespeare's doctor knows about mental illness:

DOCTOR:	Foul whisperings are abroad. Unnatural deeds Do breed unnatural troubles; infected minds To their deaf pillows will discharge their secrets. More needs she the divine than the physician. (V.i.79–82)

Later in Act V, in scene three, Macbeth expresses in striking words the task of the therapist, giving a magnificent statement that the therapist should undo the impact of the trauma:

MACBETH: Canst thou not minister to a mind diseased,
             Pluck from the memory a rooted sorrow,
             Raze out the written troubles of the brain
             And with some sweet oblivious antidote
             Cleanse the stuff'd bosom of that perilous stuff
             Which weighs upon the heart? (V.iii.40–45)

The doctor replies: "Therein the patient / Must minister to himself" (V.iii.45–46).

Three hundred years later a Viennese doctor ministered to himself in a self-analysis and discovered a way to minister to "a mind diseased".

CHAPTER EIGHT

Antony and Cleopatra: dangerous dotage

A nyone approaching this play with a psychoanalytic frame in mind will see it first as a magnificent description of an intra-psychic conflict. If I imagine teachers of psychoanalysis or even secondary education teachers trying to convey to their students what an inner conflict is, they could hardly do better than to suggest reading this play. Antony is a Roman general in competition with several other men for the position of leader of the known world. In his outlook and in his ego ideal, he is a Roman at a moment in history when the days of Republican Rome are over and the heritage of Julius Caesar was up for grabs. This very same man falls into submissive love with Cleopatra and the play is a description of his conflict and its dire consequences.

As the play opens Antony has developed a dotage on Cleopatra, queen of Egypt. Neither Antony nor Cleopatra are as young as Romeo and Juliet; they are middle aged. Speaking of Cleopatra's past relationship with Caesar, Agrippa says:

AGRIPPA: Royal wench!
            She made great Caesar lay his sword to bed,
            He ploughed her, and she cropp'd (*Antony and Cleopatra*,
            II.ii.236–238)

131

It is easy to miss this casual remark that plays no further role in the unfolding story, but if we pay attention to the unconscious we cannot ignore that Antony's stormy love relationship is, on a symbolic level, a sexual relationship with his mother. Julius Caesar was symbolically Antony's father and Antony's fame rested on the fact that he punished Caesar's murderers in his role of loyal son. Now he is deeply in love with the woman Caesar "ploughed".

In chapter six on *Julius Caesar* I stressed the analogy of this murder to Freud's *Totem and Taboo*. There was no Antony in the primal horde that killed the primal father. Antony's story is Shakespeare's variation on the oedipal theme: the loyal son who avenges the murder of the father and is rewarded by a sexual relationship with the father's widow.

On an unconscious level *Antony and Cleopatra* is the story of a son who won over his mother and a celebration of this union. Antony, standing for the son, is so overwhelmed by this experience that nothing else matters. With fine intuition, Shakespeare conveys to his audience the fact that if the mother becomes the love object the obedience to the mother will be carried into the new relationship, which Shakespeare calls doting, and this doting will bring about Antony's downfall. In terms of the unconscious, *Antony and Cleopatra* is the story of oedipal success and the price that was paid for it.

Antony is engaged in a love affair with the same woman who bore a child to his father figure. Shakespeare introduces no more than a hint of an oedipal relationship to the audience, but the plowing metaphor makes it certain that this hint registers in the unconscious.

Shakespeare and his audience know that Antony was the one who stirred up the crowd after Caesar's assassination and ultimately defeated Brutus and Cassius. In so far as Antony avenged the murder of Caesar he accomplished what Hamlet could not. Since he was Caesar's avenger and not his murderer, he was entitled to Cleopatra without oedipal guilt; but what part of the unconscious allows, the other part forbids and punishes. I am not assuming that this was consciously known or even surmised by Shakespeare. It represents a psychoanalytic reconstruction.

Not billed as a love relationship but of equal significance in this play is the homosexual love-hate relationship between Antony and Octavius Caesar. At the end of the play the two relationships merge into a triangle.

In every play there is likely to be more than one theme and that the poet is trying to weave together or synthesise a number of themes with which he is struggling.

The theme of a conflict between Antony's military career and his dotage upon Cleopatra is introduced already in the opening lines of the play.

PHILO: Nay, but this dotage of our general's
        O'erflows the measure: those his goodly eyes,
        That o'er the files and musters of the war
        Have glow'd like plated Mars, now bend, now turn,
        The office and devotion of their view
        Upon a tawny front: his captain's heart,
        Which in the scuffles of great fights hath burst
        The buckles on his breast, reneges all temper,
        And is become the bellows and the fan
        To cool a gipsy's lust. Look, where they come.

Flourish. Enter Antony, Cleopatra, her Ladies, the Train, with Eunuchs fanning her

        Take but good note, and you shall see in him.
        The triple pillar of the world transform'd
        Into a strumpet's fool: behold and see. (I.i.1–13)

Technically Philo is a follower of Antony but dramatically he is an observer and judge, and being a Roman soldier he disapproves of his general's dotage. Antony is condemned by him because he "O'erflows the measure" and violates the Greek ideal of everything in moderation and nothing in excess.

Reality breaks in with a messenger from Rome. Antony does not want to hear him but Cleopatra insists.

ANTONY: Let Rome in Tiber melt, and the wide arch
        Of the ranged empire fall! Here is my space.
        Kingdoms are clay: our dungy earth alike
        Feeds beast as man: the nobleness of life
        Is to do thus; when such a mutual pair
        Embracing

> And such a twain can do't, in which I bind,
> On pain of punishment, the world to weet
> We stand up peerless. (I.i.35–42)

Antony is now the spokesman for the unbridled pleasure principle.

ANTONY: Now, for the love of Love and her soft hours,
           Let's not confound the time with conference harsh:
           There's not a minute of our lives should stretch
           Without some pleasure now. What sport tonight? (I.i.46–49)

As a lover Antony reminds us of Theseus, the tense lover who is always in need of entertainment for fear of boredom, in *A Midsummer Night's Dream*.

Within this very same scene we hear the other aspect of Antony asserting itself. After Cleopatra has left and he speaks with the messenger and his attendants, he says:

ANTONY: These strong Egyptian fetters I must break,
           Or lose myself in dotage. (I.ii.112–113)

We get to know a different aspect of Antony in Acts II and III. He has just returned to Rome, and Agrippa, (to cement the relationship between Octavius Caesar and Antony), proposes that Antony marry Octavia, Caesar's sister, as Antony's first wife, Fulvia, had died. Shakespeare has repeatedly shown how difficult it is for a father to give away his daughter, but in this play we sense the deep attachment between brother and sister. Caesar has the traditional power of father over Octavia.

ANTONY: May I never
           To this good purpose, that so fairly shows,
           Dream of impediment! Let me have thy hand;
           Further this act of grace, and from this hour
           The heart of brothers govern in over loves
           And sway our great designs!
CAESAR: There is my hand.
           A sister I bequeath you, who no brother
           Did ever love so dearly; let her live
           To join our kingdoms and our hearts, and never
           Fly off our loves again! (II.ii.153–162)

Cleopatra is all but forgotten, nor is Octavia consulted. The transaction takes place between two men. The sister given in marriage to Antony is the symbol of the two men's love for one another. We recall that Shakespeare used the same word employed by Antony, "impediment", in Sonnet 116: "Let me not to the marriage of true minds / Admit impediments" (lines 1–2).

As Shakespeare portrays Antony he is split and can be sincere with both Cleopatra and Octavius Caesar. Antony reflects, "And though I make this marriage for my peace, / I' the east my pleasure lies" (II.iii.39–40), while one of Pompey's servants remarks, "it raises the greater war between him and his discretion" (II.vii.8–9). Psychoanalysis turns the "war between him and his discretion" into a conflict between id and ego.

In this scene Shakespeare gives us a description of intrapsychic conflict, an aspect of psychic life that psychoanalytic investigation would make its special field of study.

Antony is at his noblest when his relationship to Octavia's brother has deteriorated to the point of war.

OCTAVIA: The good gods will mock me presently,
          When I shall pray, 'O! bless my lord and husband;'
          Undo that prayer, by crying out as loud,
          'O! bless my brother!' Husband win, win brother,
          Prays, and destroys the prayer; no midway
          'Twixt these extremes at all.
ANTONY: Gentle Octavia,
          Let your best love draw to that point which seeks
          Best to preserve it. If I lose mine honour
          I lose myself; better I were not yours
          Than yours so branchless. (III.iv.15–24)

What Antony conveys to Octavia are indeed very noble thoughts. Free from anger and self-serving thoughts, he asks her to preserve her love and not lose it in the quarrel between husband and brother. Then comes the wonderful metaphor comparing a man who has lost his honour to a tree that has lost its branches.

Octavia decides to go to Rome with the hope of restoring peace between her brother and husband, only to learn that Antony has returned to Cleopatra. Now that Antony is reunited with Cleopatra, Shakespeare introduces us to a neurotic Antony. He can fight Octavius Caesar either by land or by sea. Although he is much stronger by land he decides to fight by sea. When asked why he has chosen to fight by sea it is really out of submission to his enemy: "For that he dares us to 't" (III.vii.30). In vain, his friend and follower Enobarbus warns him, "Most worthy sir, you therein throw away / The absolute soldiership you have by land" (III.vii.42–43). Antony's inner conflict becomes self-destructive. The results of the sea battle are reported in a conversation between Enobarbus and Scarus.

SCARUS: With very ignorance; we have kiss'd away
           Kingdoms and provinces. (III.x.7–8)

The battle was just starting when Cleopatra, "like a cow in June / Hoists sails and flies" (III.x.14–15).

SCARUS: She once being loof'd,
           The noble ruin of her magic, Antony,
           Claps on his sea-wing, and like a doting mallard,
           Leaving the fight in height, flies after her.
           I never saw an action of such shame;
           Experience, manhood, honour, ne'er before
           Did violate so itself. (III.x.17–23)

The mallard, a wild duck, was thought to be a coward. As the sea battle started Cleopatra, overcome by fear, fled with her ships and then the catastrophe happened: Antony, unable to tolerate the separation, followed her.

In Act III, scene eleven Antony is devastated.

ANTONY: Hark! the land bids me tread no more upon 't;
           It is asham'd to bear me. Friends, come hither:
           I am so lated in the world that I
           Have lost my way for ever. I have a ship
           Laden with gold; take that, divide it; fly,
           And make your peace with Caesar. (III.xi.1–6)

Iras, one of Cleopatra's servants, urges her to comfort Antony.

IRAS: Go to him, madam, speak to him;
         He is unqualitied with very shame. (III.xi.42–43)

The wonderful word "unqualitied", meaning to lose one's quality, appears nowhere else in Shakespeare's works and may therefore have been created for this occasion.

> ANTONY: O! whither hast thou led me, Egypt? See,
> How I convey my shame out of thine eyes
> By looking back what I have left behind
> 'Stroy'd in dishonour.
> CLEOPATRA: O my lord, my lord!
> Forgive my fearful sails: I little thought
> You would have follow'd.
> ANTONY: Egypt, thou knew'st too well
> My heart was to thy rudder tied by the strings,
> And thou shouldst tow me after; o'er my spirit
> Thy full supremacy thou knew'st, and that
> Thy beck might from the bidding of the gods
> Command me. (III.xi.50–60)

We tarry to admire how much Shakespeare understood. Dotage finds expression in a regression to a very early state of feelings, particularly the early dependency of the child on the mother and the child's inability to tolerate separation from her. Antony was in such a regressive state of feelings during the sea battle that his metaphor is apt: "My heart was to thy rudder tied by the strings".

Shakespeare found a way to illustrate two different neurotic behaviours of the two lovers, which sealed their doom. The fault is equally divided between them. Cleopatra contributed to it by becoming frightened of entering the battle and retreating, Antony by submissively following her example.

Cleopatra's character and skill

Harold Bloom has this to say about Cleopatra.

> Of Shakespearean representations of women, Cleopatra's is the most subtle and formidable, by universal consent …. Cleopatra at last wears Antony out: it would take Hamlet or Falstaff not to be upstaged by her. Cleopatra never ceases to play Cleopatra, and her perception of her role necessarily demotes Antony to the equivocal

status of her leading man. It is her play, and never quite his. (Bloom, 1998: p. 546).

Bloom goes further, to voice that she also wore out Shakespeare, as after this play he gave up further quests into human motivation. The two title characters are mutually destructive to each other. It must have been conscious to Shakespeare that he was portraying a fatal woman of whom the man should beware. As Bloom observed, the art consisted in making her into such a memorable character. We have already learned that she is a scheming woman in Act I, scene three, where she instructs her attendant Charmian to find Antony with the following instructions:

CLEOPATRA: See where he is, who's with him, what he does;
             I did not send you: if you find him sad,
             Say that I am dancing; if in mirth, report
             That I am sudden sick: quick, and return. (I.iii.2–5)

An interesting exchange takes place between Cleopatra and Charmian as to how best to win a man.

CHARMIAN: Madam, methinks, if you did love him dearly,
             You do not hold the method to enforce
             The like from him.
CLEOPATRA: What should I do, I do not?
CHARMIAN: In each thing give him way, cross him nothing.
CLEOPATRA: Thou teachest like a fool; the way to lose him.
CHARMIAN: Tempt him not so too far; I wish, forbear:
             In time we hate that which we often fear. (I.iii.6–12)

Shakespeare conveys two different philosophies for women to maintain their hold over a man. Who is right, Cleopatra or Charmian, will forever be debated.

Cleopatra's dependency on Antony is expressed in another exchange between her and her attendant.

CLEOPATRA: Ha, ha! Give me to drink mandragora.
CHARMIAN: Why, madam?
CLEOPATRA: That I might sleep out this great gap of time
             My Antony is away. (I.v.3–6)

This is followed by a famous passage.

CLEOPATRA: O Charmian,
Where think'st thou he is now? Stands he, or sits he?
Or does he walk? or is he on his horse?
O happy horse, to bear the weight of Antony! (I.v.19–22)

Cleopatra continues to dwell on her love for Antony and his absence.

CLEOPATRA: Give me some music; music, moody food
Of us that trade in love.

         ...

Give me mine angle; we'll to the river: there,
My music playing far off, I will betray
Tawny-finn'd fishes; my bended hook shall pierce
Their slimy jaws; and, as I draw them up,
I'll think them every one an Antony,
And say "Ah, ha! you're caught". (II.v.1–2, 10–15)

In this metaphor Shakespeare conveys both Cleopatra's love and her aggression towards Antony.

Cleopatra then tells Charmian an episode whose significance no psychoanalytic observer can afford to miss.

CLEOPATRA: That time,—O times!—
I laugh'd him out of patience; and that night
I laugh'd him into patience; and next morn,
Ere the ninth hour, I drunk him to his bed;
Then put my tires and mantles on him, whilst
I wore his sword Philippan. (II.v.18–23)

Cleopatra brags that she persuaded a drunken Antony to cross dress in her jewellry while she wore his sword. To a psychoanalyst, Cleopatra is betraying her unconscious wishes to exchange roles with Antony, to feminise him and assume a masculine role herself. Behind her very prominent femininity we discover her masculine wishes and castration wishes towards Antony. It is a very short scene and very easy to miss, but it might give us insight into her betrayal of Antony at the battle of Actium. Shakespeare discloses that Cleopatra playfully persuaded

Antony to exchange gender roles as part of their lovemaking. What Shakespeare does not tell us, but of which the audience is at least momentarily aware, is that by her behaviour such a woman must evoke castration anxiety of becoming a woman in the man, at least unconsciously.

Cleopatra receives the news that Antony has married Octavia and almost kills the messenger, but then Shakespeare adds another master-stroke to the portrait of Cleopatra. She is curious about Octavia, a trait that emphasises the feminine aspect of her character.

CLEOPATRA: Go to the fellow, good Alexas; bid him
              Report the feature of Octavia, her years,
              Her inclination, let him not leave out
              The colour of her hair: bring me word quickly. (II.v.113–16)

There is yet another aspect of Shakespeare's skill that is of psycho-analytic interest. Cleopatra is praised in magnificent language not by Antony but by Enobarbaus, who is closely associated with Antony but will eventually leave him to go to the enemy's camp. Enobarbus describes the first meeting between Antony and Cleopatra.

ENOBARBUS: I will tell you.
              The barge she sat in, like a burnish'd throne,
              Burn'd on the water: the poop was beaten gold;
              Purple the sails, and so perfumed that
              The winds were love-sick with them; the oars were silver,
              Which to the tune of flutes kept stroke, and made
              The water which they beat to follow faster,
              As amorous of their strokes. For her own person,
              It beggar'd all description: she did lie
              In her pavilion—cloth-of-gold of tissue—
              O'er-picturing that Venus where we see
              The fancy outwork nature: on each side her
              Stood pretty dimpled boys, like smiling Cupids,
              With divers-colour'd fans, whose wind did seem
              To glow the delicate cheeks which they did cool,
              And what they undid did. (II.ii.200–215)

              ...

              Antony,

> Enthroned i' the market-place, did sit alone,
> Whistling to the air; which, but for vacancy,
> Had gone to gaze on Cleopatra too,
> And made a gap in nature. (II.ii.224–228)
>
> ...
>
> Age cannot wither her, nor custom stale
> Her infinite variety: other women cloy
> The appetites they feed: but she makes hungry
> Where most she satisfies; for vilest things
> Become themselves in her: that the holy priests
> Bless her when she is riggish. (II.ii.245–250)

The praise of Cleopatra—"she makes hungry / Where most she satisfies"—is one of the great praises of a woman's sexuality that Shakespeare bestows. Its opposite, sexual satiety, is one of Shakespeare's great fears. This line is reminiscent of Venus' promise to Adonis:

I'll smother thee with kisses:

> 'And yet not cloy thy lips with loath'd satiety, (*Venus and Adonis*, lines 18–19)

Enobarbus praises and Antony is the lover; something of a homosexual tie between the two men is implied in this division.

The relationship between Antony and Enobarbus can be understood as a desexualised homosexual relationship. When Enobarbus finally defects from Antony's camp to join Caesar and leaves his treasure behind, Antony sends it after him. Eventually Enobarbus feels so guilty over his betrayal that he too commits suicide.

Shakespeare so structured Cleopatra's personality that she is all desire and knows few moral restraints. She sends Mardian to let Antony assume that she is dead.

CLEOPATRA: Mardian, go tell him I have slain myself;
                Say, that the last I spoke was 'Antony,'
                And word it, prithee, piteously: hence, Mardian,
                And bring me how he takes my death. (IV.xiii.7–10)

The effect on Antony is devastating.

ANTONY: I will o'ertake thee, Cleopatra, and
           Weep for my pardon. So it must be, for now
           All length is torture: since the torch is out
           Lie down and stray no farther.
           …
           Since Cleopatra died,
           I have lived in such dishonour, that the gods
           Detest my baseness. I, that with my sword
           Quarter'd the world, and o'er green Neptune's back
           With ships made cities, condemn myself to lack
           The courage of a woman; less noble mind
           Than she which by her death our Caesar tells
           'I am conqueror of myself'. (IV.xiv.44–47, 55–62)

Antony's suicide wish is a mixture of the desire to emulate what
Cleopatra has supposedly done and also to escape the power of Caesar.
Antony asks Eros to kill him but Eros kills himself instead. Committing
suicide by falling upon his sword, Antony addresses the dead Eros
with the proclamation "Thy master dies thy scholar" (IV.xiv.102).
Before he dies Antony learns that Cleopatra did not in fact kill herself
and is taken to her. Two hundred years before Wagner created the term
Liebestod, combining love and death in *Tristan and Isolde*, Shakespeare
let Antony die such a death in the presence of his beloved. Death is
personified when Cleopatra proclaims "And make death proud to take
us" (IV.xv.93).

   We are now in Act V, scene two. Caesar has sent two messengers
to Cleopatra and will make a personal appearance himself. The first
messenger, Proculeius Gallus, prevents a suicide attempt by Cleopatra.
He is replaced by Dolabella and now something strange happens.
Cleopatra does not know him and yet confides a dream to him.

CLEOPATRA: I dream'd there was an Emperor Antony:
              O, such another sleep, that I might see
              But such another man!
DOLABELLA: If it might please ye,—
CLEOPATRA: His face was as the heavens; and therein stuck
              A sun and moon, which kept their course,
              and lighted
              The little O, the earth.

DOLABELLA: Most sovereign creature,—

CLEOPATRA: His legs bestrid the ocean: his rear'd arm
              Crested the world: his voice was propertied
              As all the tuned spheres, and that to friends;
              But when he meant to quail and shake the orb,
              He was as rattling thunder. For his bounty,
              There was no winter in't; an autumn 'twas
              That grew the more by reaping: his delights
              Were dolphin-like; they show'd his back above
              The element they lived in: in his livery
              Walk'd crowns and crownets; realms and islands were
              As plates dropp'd from his pocket.

DOLABELLA: Cleopatra!

CLEOPATRA: Think you there was, or might be, such a man
              As this I dream'd of?

DOLABELLA: Gentle madam, no.

CLEOPATRA: You lie, up to the hearing of the gods.
              But, if there be, or ever were, one such,
              It's past the size of dreaming: nature wants stuff
              To vie strange forms with fancy; yet, to imagine
              And Antony, were nature's piece 'gainst fancy,
              Condemning shadows quite. (V.ii.75–99)

We are presented with a psychologically complex exchange between the queen and the enemy's messenger. Cleopatra tells a personal dream in which Antony is idealised; when Dolabella does not confirm the idealisation she berates him. This idealisation is a preparation for her suicide and is needed psychologically to bring them together as she merges with him in suicide. There is no indication in the play that this idealisation of Antony was part of their relationship while he was alive.

Cleopatra's death at the very end of the play is one of the high points of Shakespeare's art: a love suicide in which she joins Antony.

CLEOPATRA: Give me my robe, put on my crown; I have
              Immortal longings in me: now no more
              The juice of Egypt's grape shall moist this lip:
              Yare, yare, good Iras; quick. Methinks I hear
              Antony call; I see him rouse himself
              To praise my noble act; I hear him mock

> The luck of Caesar, which the gods give men
> To excuse their after wrath: husband, I come:
> Now to that name my courage prove my title!
> I am fire and air; my other elements
> I give to baser life. (V.ii.274–284)

Suicide is a theme that must have meant a great deal to Shakespeare. All we need to think of is Ophelia's suicide and Hamlet's continual preoccupation with suicide. *Antony and Cleopatra* was written six years after *Hamlet* and the number of suicides in the play is striking: Enobarbus, Eros, Antony, Cleopatra, Charmian, and Iras.

Antony and Octavius Caesar

The relationship between Antony and Octavius Caesar parallels in intensity the relationship between Antony and Cleopatra. They first attempt to seal their relationship by becoming brothers-in-law but then the rivalry between them takes over. Before the last battle, Octavius Caesar lets it be known that Antony is not to be killed but captured alive. After his defeat, Antony invites Octavius Caesar to a personal combat, which Octavius Caesar refuses. At the end of the play, Octavius Caesar comes to Egypt for no other reason than to woo Cleopatra away from Antony. For both Antony and Cleopatra, the victory over Octavius Caesar plays a significant role in their suicides. The complex balancing of the homosexual and heterosexual relationships is one of the achievements of *Antony and Cleopatra*.

CHAPTER NINE

Coriolanus: an astounding description of a destructive mother–child relationship

S hakespeare wrote a number of plays where the mother is conspicuously absent—*The Merchant of Venice, King Lear* and *The Tempest* are examples—but only one play where the mother-son conflict is central, *Coriolanus*. This fact alone would make this play of interest within the frame of reference of this book, but there is yet another reason why the play brings Shakespeare and psychoanalysis closer.

In *Coriolanus* Shakespeare showed an astonishing understanding of a mother-son relationship. Today, largely under the influence of psychoanalysis, we take it for granted that the early years and the relationship to the parents are decisive in forming our characters, but in Shakespeare's time none of this was known. Even today psychoanalytic patients discover to their astonishment how decisive the father or mother was in the formation of their characters.

Act I, scene three takes place in Coriolanus' house, between his mother Volumnia and his wife Virgilia.

VOLUMNIA: I pray you, daughter, sing, or express yourself in a more
comfortable sort. If my son were my husband, I should freelier
rejoice in that absence wherein he won honour than in the

embracements of his bed where he would show most love. When yet
he was but tender-bodied and the only son of my womb, when youth with comeliness plucked all gaze his way, when for a day of kings' entreaties a mother should not sell him an hour from her beholding, I, considering how honour would become such a person—that it was no better than picture-like to hang by th'wall, if renown made it not stir—was pleased to let him seek danger where he was like to find fame. To a cruel war I sent him, from whence he returned, his brows bound with oak. I tell thee, daughter,
I sprang not more in joy at first hearing he was a man-child than now in first seeing he had proved himself a man. (*Coriolanus*, I.iii.1–14)

The phrase, "If my son were my husband" would probably not occur to an ordinary mother, and if it did, it would not be allowed to be told to the daughter-in-law because it betrays a sexualised attitude towards the son. It can pass censorship in this case because the sexuality is negated in the second sentence.

Volumnia goes on, ecstatically visualising how her son terrorises the Volsces even though his brow is bloody. Virgilia objects by saying, "His bloody brow? O Jupiter, no blood!" (I.iii.33).

VOLUMNIA: Away, you fool! it more becomes a man
             Than gilt his trophy. The breasts of Hecuba,
             When she did suckle Hector, look'd not lovelier
             Than Hector's forehead when it spit forth blood
             At Grecian sword, contemning. (I.iii.34–38)

Shakespeare took the plot for Coriolanus from Plutarch's "Life of Caius Marcius Coriolanus". Plutarch had already noted the absent father in Coriolanus' life and that his upbringing was solely due to his mother. Even after his marriage and becoming a father to two children he continued to live with his mother. When such a borrowing takes place we can say that Shakespeare allowed himself to deal with material that was personally difficult by attributing the plot to someone else. The creative act begins passively by borrowing the plot, and deviations from the original version of the story are of special interest because they tell us what was particularly important to the author rewriting the plot. (My comparison is based on the Scott-Kilvert translation of Plutarch).

Plutarch noted that Gaius Marcius (who later becomes known as Coriolanus) lost his father when he was young and was brought up by his mother, who never remarried. Plutarch uses the opportunity to tell his readers that the early loss of the father may impose disadvantages on a boy but it "does not prevent him from living a virtuous or a distinguished life" (Scott-Kilvert, 1965: p. 15). Plutarch, like Shakespeare, portrays the character of Marcius as naturally generous and of noble disposition, but lacking discipline. Plutarch compares him to fertile soil that did not receive the proper tilling. The future Coriolanus achieved much for Rome and he was admired for "his indifference to hardship, to pleasure and to the temptations of money" (ibid.) "but these qualities were combined with a violent temper and an uncompromising self-assertion, which made it difficult for him to cooperate with others" (ibid.). He trained his body so thoroughly for every type of combat that he acquired the speed of an athlete and the muscular strength of a wrestler. "But while other men displayed their courage to win glory for themselves, Marcius's motive was always to please his mother" (Scott-Kilvert, 1965: p. 18). Shakespeare follows Plutarch closely but there is one notable difference: The encounter between Volumnia and Virgilia is absent in Plutarch. We assume that if an author deviates from the sources being followed, the change has a personal meaning. Plutarch's Coriolanus has heroic Roman qualities whereas Shakespeare's Coriolanus is self-destructive because he has an ambivalent relationship with his mother.

In Plutarch the character of Marcius is his very own and it was he who wanted to please his mother, whereas in Shakespeare Marcius / Coriolanus was created by his mother's glorification of his wounds. In Plutarch's version Marcius wants to please his mother while in Shakespeare's retelling his violent life is a response to his mother's unconscious wish to destroy him.

To become consul, Coriolanus is asked to reveal his wounds to the plebeian crowd; this he will not do. He is not the type of man suitable for electioneering, but why does he refuse? The wounds unconsciously may represent his submission to his mother's will; to put it in psychoanalytic terms, he is asked to exhibit his castration and this he refuses to do.

The scene gains significance from the psychoanalytic understanding that he is asked to exhibit himself to the mob and at the very same moment to exhibit his wounds, which are, in psychoanalytic vocabulary, his castration. Having failed to be elected consul, Coriolanus now goes over to the enemy Aufidius. He is without weapons at his enemy's house and since he is thus symbolically castrated he is welcomed.

Often in Shakespeare's plays when someone wishes to convert a former enemy into a lover he offers to let the adversary kill him. Coriolanus gives Aufidius such an opportunity and when Aufidius refuses a bond is established between them.

CORIOLANUS: Make my misery serve thy turn: so use it,
That my revengeful services may prove
As benefits to thee, for I will fight
Against my canker'd country with the spleen
Of all the under fiends. But if so be
Thou darest not this and that to prove more fortunes
Thou'rt tired, then, in a word, I also am
Longer to live most weary, and present
My throat to thee and to thy ancient malice;
Which not to cut would show thee but a fool,
Since I have ever follow'd thee with hate,
Drawn tuns of blood out of thy country's breast,
And cannot live but to thy shame, unless
It be to do thee service. (*Coriolanus*, IV.v.85–98)

As a play *Coriolanus* consists of the interweaving of two different themes: the catastrophic relationship between mother and child and the latent homosexual relationship between Marcius and Aufidius.

The crisis in the mother-son relationship reaches a high point in Act V. The Volces, led by Coriolanus and Aufidius, are at the gates of Rome. They plan to conquer the city and burn it down. First Menenius, a friend whom Coriolanus regards as a father, enters, pleading for him not to destroy Rome, but Coriolanus, with a "crack'd heart", sends him away even though he recalls being loved by him "above the measure of a father" (V.iii.10).

Next his mother, his wife, his son and Virgilia's friend Valeria enter, all in mourning habits. Coriolanus is deeply shaken by their appearance but remains resolute.

CORIOLANUS: But, out, affection!
All bond and privilege of nature, break!
Let it be virtuous to be obstinate.

...

but stand,
As if a man were author of himself
And knew no other kin.

...

Like a dull actor now,
I have forgot my part, and I am out,
Even to a full disgrace. (V.iii.24–25, 35–37, 40–42)

The metaphor of the dull actor does not fit into this very complex situation and represents a moment of Shakespeare the actor's identification with Coriolanus in conflict between his hetero- and homosexual feelings. Once more we note an affinity between Shakespeare and psychoanalysis.

Shakespeare the dramatist is at his very best when he portrays the inner conflict within Coriolanus. The family ties to mother, wife, and child pull him in one direction while his loyalty to his former enemies, his thirst for revenge and the homosexual tie to Aufidius pull him in another.

His mother is also in conflict.

VOLUMNIA: Alas, how can we for our country pray.
Whereto we are bound, together with thy victory,
Whereto we are bound? (V.iii.107–109)

The difficulty in praying when one is in a conflict-filled situation was already noted by Plutarch. Volumnia, speaking to the assembled voices as well as to her son, says:

VOLUMNIA: And even to pray to the gods, which others may find a comfort in their misfortunes, has become impossible for us, since we cannot ask them in the same breath to make our country victorious and to keep you safe. (Scott-Kilvert, 1965: p. 48)

In *Antony and Cleopatra* Shakespeare gave the same dilemma to Octavia, Antony's wife and Octavius Caesar's sister when the two men become enemies.

Volumnia tells her son that she will not wait to find out the result of the war between Rome and her son. She will kill herself rather than face the consequences.

VOLUMNIA: I purpose not to wait on fortune till
These wars determine: if I cannot persuade thee
Rather to show a noble grace to both parts
Than seek the end of one, thou shalt no sooner
March to assault thy country than to tread—
Trust to't, thou shalt not—on thy mother's womb,
That brought thee to this world. (*Coriolanus*, V.iii.119–125)

The attack on Rome was always symbolic matricide; Volumnia makes the symbolic concrete.

Virgilia reminds him that she "brought you forth this boy, to keep your name / Living to time" (V.iii.126–127). Eventually his mother appeals to her son's narcissism: he can gain fame by making peace between the Romans and the Volsces.

VOLUMNIA: The end of war's uncertain, but this certain,
That, if thou conquer Rome, the benefit
Which thou shalt thereby reap is such a name,
Whose repetition will be dogg'd with curses;
Whose chronicle thus writ: 'The man was noble,
But with his last attempt he wiped it out;
Destroy'd his country, and his name remains
To the ensuing age abhorr'd'. (V.iii.141–148)

Volumnia gets increasingly bitter in her denunciation of her son.

VOLUMNIA: Thou hast never in thy life
Show'd thy dear mother any courtesy,
When she, poor hen, fond of no second brood,
Has cluck'd thee to the wars and safely home,
Loaden with honour. Say my request's unjust,
And spurn me back: but if it be not so,
Thou art not honest; and the gods will plague thee,
That thou restrain'st from me the duty which
To a mother's part belongs. (V.iii.160–168)

It is left to Coriolanus to express the tragedy of the mother-son relationship.

CORIOLANUS: O mother, mother!
What have you done? Behold, the heavens do ope,
The gods look down, and this unnatural scene
They laugh at. O my mother, mother! O!
You have won a happy victory to Rome;
But, for your son,—believe it, O, believe it,
Most dangerously you have with him prevail'd,
If not most mortal to him. But, let it come. (V.iii.183–190)

We should note a significant change in the character of Volumnia. On the basis of what we learned about her previously we would have expected her to be on her son's side and be indifferent to her own death as long as she is identified with her son's humiliation at his expulsion and with his subsequent victory over Rome, but we meet a different Volumnia. She is no longer totally allied with her son's injuries to his honour. She shows a concern for her own safety, a love for Rome and a much greater independence from her son. It is the encounter with a different mother that shakes the narcissistic foundation of her son's resolve and will soon bring about his death.

The second subplot of the play, the relationship between Coriolanus and Aufidius

In many plays we have the chance to see that Shakespeare the dramatist is not satisfied to follow one plot but prefers two interacting themes to convey the complexity of life. In this play the relationship between Coriolanus and the general of the Volsces supplies the second plot.

In the first act the news comes that the Volsces are in arms and we learn about a peculiar attitude of almost erotic admiration that Marcius has for Tullus Aufidius, their leader.

CORIOLANUS: I sin in envying his nobility,
And were I any thing but what I am,
I would wish me only he.

...

> he is a lion
> That I am proud to hunt. (I.i.214–216, 219–220)

Aufidius reciprocates this sentiment when he says: "'Tis sworn between us we shall ever strike / Till one can do no more" (I.ii.35–36).

In psychoanalytic work we encounter men who wish to be someone other than who they are. When they find the person who is what they would like to be, this feeling can become transformed into a homosexualised or desexualised attraction. Marcius envies Aufidius' nobility and comes near to stating that he would like to be him. The next metaphor is particularly interesting, as if the majesty of the lion conveys nobility on the hunter. The relationship deepens when Coriolanus seeks refuge in Aufidius' house.

Coriolanus leaves it up to Aufidius to avenge himself by killing him or to use him for revenge against Rome, which would punish his banisher for exiling him. The first alternative is masochistic while the second one gratifies his own wishes for revenge.

Coriolanus gives his enemy a choice, but dramatically speaking there was no choice: what kind of plot would it be if Aufidius had decided to kill his helpless guest? Of particular note is the line "Drawn tuns of blood out of thy country's breast" (IV.v.106). Earlier I commented on Volumnia's words when she compared Hector's bleeding head with Hecuba's breasts; now Shakespeare returns to the same fixation point, the mother's breasts, but in this case the mother is the country and Coriolanus accuses himself of drawing blood from them. The metaphor is highly original and once more the hostility between the baby and the nursing mother is affirmed.

The hostility between Aufidius and Coriolanus turns into a friendship or more likely a homosexual love. Aufidius responds to Coriolanus' overture with deep emotion:

AUFIDIUS:　O Marcius, Marcius!
　　　　　　Each word thou hast spoke hath weeded from my heart
　　　　　　A root of ancient envy. If Jupiter
　　　　　　Should from yond cloud speak divine things,
　　　　　　And say 'Tis true,' I'ld not believe them more
　　　　　　Than thee, all noble Marcius. (IV.iv.98–103)

The bond between the two men holds until the scene where Coriolanus yields to his mother's request. Aufidius is present during Coriolanus' encounter with his family. The relationship between the two men breaks down when the heterosexuality of Coriolanus asserts itself when he meets with his wife. Coriolanus asks Aufidius:

CORIOLANUS: Were you in my stead, would you have heard
                A mother less? or granted less, Aufidius?
AUFIDIUS: I was moved withal. (V.iii.193–195)

It is in Act V, scene five in Antium that a change takes place in Aufidius. He recognises that he became Coriolanus' follower and not his partner. The last exchange between the two men is dramatic.

AUFIDIUS: Ay, traitor, Marcius!
CORIOLANUS: Marcius!
AUFIDIUS: Ay, Marcius, Caius Marcius: dost thou think
                I'll grace thee with that robbery, thy stol'n name
                Coriolanus in Corioli?
                You lords and heads o' the state, perfidiously
                He has betray'd your business, and given up,
                For certain drops of salt, your city Rome,
                I say 'your city', to his wife and mother;
                Breaking his oath and resolution like
                A twist of rotten silk, never admitting
                Counsel o' the war, but at his nurse's tears
                He whined and roar'd away your victory,
                That pages blush'd at him and men of heart
                Look'd wondering each at other.
CORIOLANUS: Hear'st thou, Mars?
AUFIDIUS: Name not the god, thou boy of tears!
CORIOLANUS: Ha!
AUFIDIUS: No more.
CORIOLANUS: Measureless liar, thou hast made my heart
                Too great for what contains it. Boy! O slave!
                Pardon me, lords, 'tis the first time that ever
                I was forced to scold. Your judgments, my grave lords,
                Must give this cur the lie: and his own notion—
                Who wears my stripes impress'd upon him; that
                Must bear my beating to his grave—shall join
                To thrust the lie unto him. (V.v.88–112)

The fact that the two turn against each other so vehemently suggests that their previous relationship, although desexualised, was based on homosexual love.

I am certain that many generations of readers who compared Plutarch with Shakespeare have noticed the differences in their use of language. Shakespeare's language is richer in metaphors and more adorned, while Plutarch's account is simple and direct. However, the general conclusion must have been that Shakespeare essentially followed Plutarch's model. It is psychoanalysis that opens our eyes to see the gulf that separates the two interpretations: Plutarch is an educating author who conveys the importance of self-discipline and the Greek virtue of moderation, while Shakespeare tells us of a mother so unfeminine that she raises a son to love battle and eventually, in obedience to her unconscious wishes he must destroy himself. The self-destructive behaviour of the son found temporary relief in a homosexual friendship between two former enemies but the restoration of heterosexual ties doomed the hero of this play.

CHAPTER TEN

King Lear: the daughter as a replacement for the mother

If a student were struggling to understand what psychoanalysis means by regression, King Lear's wish to abdicate his kingdom and crawl towards death unburdened would be an excellent example. The metaphor arouses psychoanalytic interest. Lear crawled as an infant before he learned to walk and now he wishes to crawl again, this time towards death. To be unburdened he has to be taken care of by his daughters; the wish is based on a "role reversal" and therefore must fail. Today, when medicine has done so much to prolong life and so many adults are burdened by the need to take care of older parents, the problems in the play have a new urgency. In clinical psychoanalytic practice such a wish is often encountered when the mother has transferred her oedipal wishes for her father to her son at the expense of the husband or a father prefers his daughter to his wife.

According to Kermode, King Lear was entered in the Stationer's Register in November 1607, while the play was performed in December 1606. We have no record of how it was received. Kermode writes that the audience "lacked the desire, or perhaps the terminology, to record its reaction". (Kermode, 1969: p. 12)

Hazlitt, writing in 1817, opens the King Lear chapter thus: "We wish that we could pass this play over and say nothing about it .... To attempt to give a description of the play itself or its effect upon the mind, is mere impertinence". Harold Bloom writes: "*King Lear*, together with *Hamlet*, ultimately baffles commentary" (Bloom, 1998: p. 476) and later he says, "*King Lear* is arguably the most powerful and inescapable of literary works" (Bloom, 1998: p. 496). It is possible that Bloom reached his deepest understanding of the play when he saw Lear as "surpassing even Hamlet as death's ambassador to us" (Bloom, 1998: p. 512). He describes the impact of the play as "altogether uncanny .... We are at once estranged and uncomfortable". Some critics, notably Tolstoy, hated the play, and many were shocked by it. Shakespeare made no effort to protect the reader or audience from experiencing a sense of traumatic shock. In this sense *King Lear* is a modern play, where the wish to protect the audience from a traumatic response has been abandoned.

In the memory of most people, *King Lear* opens with the abdication scene of King Lear, when he bequeaths the greatest part of his kingdom to the daughters who profess that they love him the most. However, the play actually opens on a very different note, with a short and almost bawdy scene between three men: the Earl of Kent, the Earl of Gloucester and Gloucester's son Edmund. Kent asks Gloucester whether Edmund is his son and in return receives a confession, that the young man's mother "had...a son for her cradle ere she had a husband for her bed". (*King Lear*, I.i.12–13). He then goes on to make a further confession:

GLOUCESTER: ... though this knave
came something saucily into the world before he was sent for, yet was his mother fair, there was good sport at his making. (I.i.16–18)

One can easily imagine the audience at the Globe roaring with laughter. As it turns out in the course of the play, the very son who was born as a result of this "good sport" will blind his father; in psychoanalytic terms blindness stands for castration. Edmund will also be responsible for Cordelia's death and develop into one of Shakespeare's great villains, but in this first scene he is a passive bystander. The "manifest" reason for Edmund's engineering of his father's blinding is jealousy of Edgar, his half-brother and the legitimate son; the unconscious reason is likely because the father awakened or created primal scene jealousy in the son and thus stirred his oedipal jealousy by describing so vividly his sexual pleasure with his son's mother.

Lear has three daughters, Gloucester two sons, thus giving the play balance. Lear has one good daughter and two unreliable ones, while Gloucester has one loving son and one who blinds him.

Lear invites his three daughters to a love contest for him. The scene is a parody of the classical theme where Paris is asked to choose which one of the three goddesses is the most beautiful. Goneril and Regan flatter their father and receive their share of his kingdom; Cordelia, like Desdemona in *Othello* and Hermia in *A Midsummer Night's Dream*, has resolved her Oedipus complex enough to stand up to the father who cannot let his daughter belong to another man. In psychoanalytic terms Cordelia represents a phase in the life of every young woman who has to overcome her oedipal attachment to her father to make room for the capacity to love a man of her own choosing.

CORDELIA: Unhappy that I am, I cannot heave
             My heart into my mouth: I love your majesty
             According to my bond, no more nor less.
   LEAR: How, how, Cordelia? Mend your speech a little,
             Lest you may mar your fortunes.
CORDELIA: Good my lord,
             You have begot me, bred me, loved me. I
             Return those duties back as are right fit,
             Obey you, love you, and most honour you.
             Why have my sisters husbands, if they say
             They love you all? Happily, when I shall wed,
             That lord whose hand must take my plight shall carry
             Half my love with him, half my care and duty.
             Sure, I shall never marry like my sisters,
             To love my father all. (I.i.86–99)

Although they flatter their father, both Goneril and Regan are capable of a realistic appraisal of their father.

GONERIL: You see how full of changes his age is; the observation we have
            made of it hath not been little: he always loved our sister most,
            and with what poor judgment he hath now cast her off appears too
            grossly.
REGAN: 'Tis the infirmity of his age, yet he hath ever but slenderly known
            himself.

GONERIL: The best and soundest of his time hath been but rash; then must we look from his age to receive not alone the imperfections of long-engraffed condition, but therewithal the unruly waywardness that infirm and choleric years bring with them. (I.i.280–290)

The scene is brief but we should not overlook the reference to self-knowledge that is so very important to Shakespeare. We should also note the expression "imperfections of long-engraffed condition". The word engraffed is Shakespeare's way of implying that the traumatic event was imprinted on the person by the outside world, while "long-engraffed" suggests that Shakespeare knew that the injury could have been inflicted long ago.

The 100 knights

From a psychoanalytic point of view the knights play a significant role. They are responsible for the break between Lear and his daughters Regan and Goneril. They are very important to Lear and the daughters' attempt to eliminate them created the conflict with the daughters.

When Lear plans to "unburdened crawl towards death" he is speaking only about himself. At the end of Act I we hear from Goneril that Lear has kept 100 knights. 100 idle knights guarding the king's dotage is a very different kind of regression than to "unburdened crawl toward death".

Goneril is afraid of the knights, and although her husband, Albany, urges her not to overreact, she disregards his advice.

GONERIL: This man hath had good counsel. A hundred knights?
            'Tis politic and safe to let him keep
            At point a hundred knights? Yes, that on every dream,
            Each buzz, each fancy, each complaint, dislike,
            He may enguard his dotage with their powers
            And hold our lives in mercy. Oswald, I say!
ALBANY: Well, you may fear too far.
GONERIL: Safer than trust too far. (I.iv.276–282)

Lear complains to Regan, "She hath abated me of half my train" (II.iv.151), but Regan asks for a further reduction from fifty knights to twenty-five. Lear is now willing to go back to Goneril.

LEAR: Thy fifty yet doth double five and twenty,
        And thou art twice her love.
GONERIL: Hear me, my lord:
        What need you five and twenty? ten? or five?
        To follow in a house where twice so many
        Have a command to tend you? (II.iv.252–256)

Goneril argues that her own servants can take care of her father's needs
and that he therefore needs no knights to serve him directly. The discussion ends with Regan's statement, "For his particular, I'll receive him
gladly, / But not one follower". (II.iv.285–286)

What do the 100 knights represent and what does the bargaining
down from 100 to fifty to twenty-five, and finally, to their total elimina-
tion stand for? The knights are there to play with; I suggest that they
symbolise the masturbation of childhood, the penis with which the boy
can "play", as distinguished from the adult penis that can impregnate
and therefore do useful work. The old king is no longer potent; he has
regressed to prepubescent masturbation. Goneril and Regan have symbolically become Lear's mothers; when they reduce the number of his
knights they are symbolically prohibiting masturbation and castrating
him. The daughters not only find the knights unnecessary but also are
revolted by them, symbolising the mother's rejection of Lear's infantile sexuality. The sought-after good mother turns into the bad mother
when she prohibits the infantile sexuality of the son.

Deprived of his knights, Lear becomes desperate and an inner struggle takes place between anger and the wish to weep. Anger seems masculine to him and he prefers it to tears.

LEAR: You heavens, give me that patience, patience I need.
        You see me here, you gods, a poor old man,
        As full of grief as age, wretched in both;
        If it be you that stir these daughters' hearts
        Against their father, fool me not so much
        To bear it tamely. Touch me with noble anger,
        And let not women's weapons, water-drops,
        Stain my man's cheeks. No, you unnatural hags,
        I will have such revenges on you both,
        That all the world shall—I will do such things—
        What they are, yet I know not, but they shall be

The terrors of the earth! You think I'll weep;
No, I'll not weep. (II.iv.264–276)

Facing a choice between anger and depression because his wishes to regress have not yielded what he hoped for, Lear prefers fury to tears. If this episode is an example of the role of the unconscious in Shakespeare's play, we face a further question: Was it unconscious to Shakespeare or only to the audience? Furthermore, it is likely that the audience derived pleasure from the quarrel, even if my interpretation never occurred to theatre goers. It is even possible that men will side with Lear and women with the prohibiting sisters.

The fool

We meet the fool in Act I, scene four. As he enters, he offers Kent his coxcomb, implying that Kent is a fool.

FOOL: There, take my coxcomb; why, this fellow has banished two on's daughters and did the third a blessing against his will; if thou follow him, thou must needs wear my coxcomb. (I.iv.88–91)

Next the fool offers the kind of advice that Polonius has made famous.

FOOL: Have more than thou showest,
         Speak less than thou knowest,
         Lend less than thou owest,
         Ride more than thou goest,
         Learn more than thou trowest,
         Set less than thou throwest,
         Leave thy drink and thy whore,
         And keep in-a-door,
         And thou shalt have more,
         Than two tens to a score. (I.iv.103–112)

The fool has many functions in this play. He offers relief from the tensions evoked by the play; he offers time out for reflection; he is entertaining, but his main function is to help Lear come back to sanity, to wake the king up from the nightmare of his regression. It is the fool who tells Lear: "… thou mad'st thy daughters / thy mothers". (I.iv.133–134); this is the kind of insight we today call psychoanalytic insight. When Lear asks, "Who is it that can tell me who I am?" (I.iv.189) the fool answers, "Lear's shadow" (I.iv.190). Earlier, Lear asks, "Dost thou call me fool, boy?" (I.iv.96), to which the fool replies, "All thy other titles thou hast given away" (I.iv.97). The fool is a Shakespearean proto-therapist conveying insight in metaphorical language.

FOOL: I can tell why a snail has a house.
LEAR: Why?
FOOL: Why, to put 's head in, not to give it away to his daughters, and leave his horns without a case. (I.v.23–26)

At times Shakespeare lets us know that the therapy of the fool is effective.

FOOL: If thou wert my fool, nuncle, I'd have thee beaten for being old before thy time.
LEAR: How's that?
FOOL: Thou shouldst not have been old till thou hadst been wise.
LEAR: O, let me not be mad, not mad, sweet heaven!
        Keep me in temper, I would not be mad. (I.v.33–38)

It is evident that the fool succeeded in his efforts as Lear is struggling to regain his sanity. Shakespeare's fool is not a participant in the play itself. He is a detached observer, akin to the chorus in Greek tragedy in observing and commenting, anticipating the role of a therapist.

After Lear has quarrelled with his two eldest daughters he is alone with the fool in a storm when he is spotted by Kent.

KENT: But who is with him?
GENTLEMAN: None but the fool, who labours to out-jest
             His heart-struck injuries. (III.i.8–10)

We should stop to admire Shakespeare the wordsmith; to "outjest" is to attempt to cure by humour.

When patients use humour about their mental problems psychoanalysts consider it a good sign, because to treat oneself with humour means that one has learned to look at oneself more objectively, and it is usually a sign that the superego has lost some of its harshness.

King Lear, who in the first scene was so childish and narcissistic in his behaviour, grows to acquire a kind of wisdom. We may assume that in the following lines Lear is speaking for Shakespeare:

LEAR: Thou must be patient. We came crying hither.
        Thou know'st the first time that we smell the air
        We wawl and cry.
        …
        When we are born, we cry that we are come
        To this great stage of fools. (IV.v.170–172, 174–175)

That life is a stage is one of Shakespeare's favourite metaphors, but here life has become a "stage of fools".

Edgar's therapy

Lear and Gloucester are parallel figures. Lear is driven to madness, Gloucester to blindness and attempted suicide.

In Act IV, scene 1 the blinded Gloucester asks his disguised son Edgar to lead him to Dover.

GLOUCESTER: There is a cliff whose high and bending head
              Looks fearfully in the confinèd deep.
              Bring me but to the very brim of it,
              And I'll repair the misery thou dost bear
              With something rich about me. From that place
              I shall no leading need. (IV.i.68–73)

In Act IV, scene five Edgar claims to have reached that spot, although in reality they remain on level ground. Edgar describes to his blind father where they are supposed to be.

EDGAR: Give me your hand. You are now within a foot
         Of th'extreme verge. For all beneath the moon
         Would I not leap upright. (IV.v.25–27)
         …
GLOUCESTER: (Kneels) O you mighty gods!
              This world I do renounce, and in your sights

Shake patiently my great affliction off.
If I could bear it longer and not fall
To quarrel with your great opposeless wills,
My snuff and loathèd part of nature should
Burn itself out. If Edgar live, O, bless him.
Now, fellow, fare thee well. (IV.v.34–41)

Gloucester has become suicidal and Edgar devises a "mock suicide" for him: he thinks he is jumping down into an abyss but in fact stays on level ground. The device works and Gloucester is cured of his suicide wish. In an aside to the audience, Edgar says, "Why I do trifle thus with his despair / Is done to cure it" (IV.vi.33–34). After he fails to kill himself Gloucester regains the wish to live. No school of therapy has adopted Edgar's technique.

The scene is short and powerful. One cannot read it without being struck that it refers to the stage, as if Shakespeare were telling us that one way of curing suicidal wishes is to allow the experience of suicide to take place without the actual commitment of the act. Could it be that this scene is a veiled confession that Shakespeare went through a suicidal depression and was cured by a mock suicide represented by writing *King Lear*? This hypothesis may be an organising hypothesis that gives the play a further meaning.

Lear's cursing vocabulary

Shakespeare gave Lear a magnificent imagery and vocabulary for cursing. The capacity of a father to curse his daughters is not one we are likely to admire but to our unconscious it gives Lear a kind of vitality. We may not approve but we are nevertheless impressed that his anger and frustration are expressed in such magnificent language. Cordelia is denounced with the lines:

LEAR: Let it be so, thy truth then be thy dower.
For by the sacred radiance of the sun,
The mysteries of Hecate and the night,
By all the operation of the orbs
From whom we do exist and cease to be,
Here I disclaim all my paternal care,

Propinquity and property of blood,
And as a stranger to my heart and me
Hold thee from this for ever. (I.i.102–110)

Next we come to Lear's curse of Goneril:

LEAR: Hear, nature, hear, dear goddess, hear:
Suspend thy purpose, if thou didst intend
To make this creature fruitful!
Into her womb convey sterility,
Dry up in her the organs of increase;
And from her derogate body never spring
A babe to honour her! If she must teem,
Create her child of spleen, that it may live
To be a thwart disnatur'd torment to her.
Let it stamp wrinkles in her brow of youth,
With cadent tears fret channels in her cheeks;
Turn all her mother's pains and benefits
To laughter and contempt, that she may feel
How sharper than a serpent's tooth it is
To have a thankless child. (I.iv.230–244)

Lear failed to transform Goneril into his wished-for mother; he therefore curses her capacity to become a mother. "Derogate" means debased and "child of spleen" means an entirely malicious child; "thwart" means perverse in this instance and "disnatur'd" is unnatural. The last two lines are among the best remembered from this play.

We are reminded of the famous unsexing scene that Shakespeare gave to Lady Macbeth. Lady Macbeth evokes feminine sterility in order to carry out symbolic parricide and here the father imposes sterility on the ungrateful daughter. The curse is a highly sexualised statement involving the father in the daughter's sexual organs.

In Act Four, scene six Lear's anger at Goneril is generalised to hatred of all women. Once more, the anger is directed at the female sexual organ.

LEAR: Down from the waist they are Centaurs,
Though women all above:
But to the girdle do the gods inherit,

Beneath is all the fiends':
There's hell, there's darkness, there's the sulfurous pit,
Burning, scalding, stench, consumption. (IV.vi.126–131)

This speech powerfully expresses the familiar disdain of homosexual men for the female genitalia.

Dying together

A long European tradition combines love and death; Wagner's *Tristan and Isolde* is perhaps the best-known example. Shakespeare may well be the artist who popularised the idea of combining love and death as in *Romeo and Juliet*. The love declaration of King Lear to the dead Cordelia is one of the high points of Western literature. When Lear and Cordelia are led to prison by Edmund's order in Act V, Lear woos his youngest daughter:

LEAR: Come, let's away to prison.
We two alone will sing like birds i' th' cage.
When thou dost ask me blessing, I'll kneel down
And ask of thee forgiveness. So we'll live,
And pray, and sing, and tell old tales, and laugh
At gilded butterflies, and hear poor rogues
Talk of court news, and we'll talk with them too—
Who loses and who wins, who's in, who's out—
And take upon 's the mystery of things
As if we were God's spies. And we'll wear out
In a walled prison packs and sects of great ones
That ebb and flow by the moon. (V.iii.8–19)

Psychologically, Lear is not going to prison; he is a child who found his mother. One is struck by the beauty of the term "God's spies". What Lear is proposing is that they not be active in the affairs of the world but become onlookers of the world's follies. They will "take upon ... the mystery of things". Here too, Shakespeare may have smuggled into the play his own philosophy of life. The playwright is not an actor in the world but an observer. He is entitled to call himself God's spy. But what about God himself? The last time he interfered in human history was when he allowed the crucifixion and resurrection of his son. It is not far-fetched to think that God is no longer active but is spying on humanity.

Edmund

Edmund is one of the great villains in Shakespeare's oeuvre, a detested human being. In Act I he explains why he became a villain:

EDMUND: Why "bastard"? Wherefore "base"?
           When my dimensions are as well compact,
           My mind as generous, and my shape as true
           As honest madam's issue? Why brand they us
           With "base", with "baseness", "bastardy", "base", "base"—
           Who in the lusty stealth of nature take
           More composition and fierce quality
           Than doth within a dull, stale, tirèd bed
           Go to th' creating a whole tribe of fops
           Got 'tween a sleep and wake? (I.ii.6–15)

Both sisters have rejected their father's wish to become his tolerant mother who allows him to entertain his hundred knights. Shakespeare combines the two themes of the play by making them both fall in love with Edmund.

EDMUND: To both these sisters have I sworn my love,
           Each jealous of the other as the stung
           Are of the adder. Which of them shall I take?
           Both? One? Or neither? Neither can be enjoyed
           If both remain alive. (V.i.44–48)

Coleridge, writing in 1810–11, understood the psychology of Edmund.

> He hears his mother and the circumstances of his birth spoken of with a most degrading a licentious levity—described as a wanton by her own paramour, and the remembrance of the animal sting, the low gratifications connected with her wantonness and prostituted beauty assigned as the reason why "the whoreson must be acknowledged". (Coleridge, 1811–1812: p. 35)

Coleridge understood that Edmund, listening to his father's description of how he came into the world, understood that he was an unwanted child. The psychoanalyst Sandor Ferenczi wrote a famous paper, "The unwelcome child and his death instinct", in 1929, in which he showed that a child who is not wanted has no desire to live and has a strong wish to die. In *King Lear* Shakespeare pursued another alternative: the unwanted child turns the hostility not against himself but against the father who begot him, unwanted.

The last act

Act V opens with an encounter between Edmund and Regan. She asks him for assurance, using a remarkable language to enquire whether he had sexual relations with her sister Goneril: "But have you never found my brother's way / to the forfended place?" (*King Lear*, V.i.10–11). She then becomes more explicit: "I am doubtful that you have been conjunct / And bosom'd with her". (V.i.12–13). To be "conjunct" is Shakespeare's terminology for sexual intercourse and "bosom'd" is what today is called petting. Both words appear in Shakespeare's work only here. We learn that both Regan and Goneril were in love with Edmund, and he confesses, "I was contracted to them both" (V.iii.202). Earlier, the Earl of Gloucester tried to save their father and had been captured.

REGAN: Hang him instantly.
GONERIL: Pluck out his eyes. (III.vii.3–4)

Regan and Goneril interrogate him as to why he helped the king escape to Dover.

GLOUCESTER: Because I would not see thy cruèl nails
Pluck out his poor old eyes, nor thy fierce sister
In his anointed flesh stick boarish fangs. (III.vii.55–57)

When Cornwall plucks out one of Gloucester's eyes Regan encourages him to remove the other, saying, "One side will mock another—th' other too" (III.vii.70). After this scene we can no longer doubt the evil nature of the two sisters.

It is a strange world that Shakespeare unfolds in *King Lear*. The king and Gloucester have no wives and, what is even odder, no memory of these wives; the play takes place in a motherless world. Edmund's mother is recalled but only as a sexual partner and not as a mother.

Lear's need for mothering is intense but directed towards his daughters. Of the five main characters of the second generation—Goneril, Regan, Cordelia, Edgar, and Edmund—none have children. Throughout the play we inhabit a motherless world.

Freud on King Lear

In an essay written in 1913, "The theme of the three caskets", Freud included a paragraph on *King Lear*.

> King Lear's dramatic story is intended to inculcate two wise lessons: that one should not give up one's possessions and rights during one's lifetime, and that one must guard against accepting flattery at its face value. (Freud, 1913: p. 300)

Freud continues:

> But Lear is not only an old man: he is a dying man. In this way the extraordinary premises of the division of his inheritance loses all its strangeness. But the doomed man is not willing to renounce the love of women; he insists on hearing how much he is loved. Let us now recall the moving final scene, one of the culminating points of tragedy in modern drama. Lear carries Cordelia's dead body on to the stage. Cordelia is Death. If we reverse the situation it becomes intelligible and familiar to us. She is the Death-goddess who, like the Valkyrie in German mythology, carries away the dead hero from the battlefield. Eternal wisdom, clothed in the primaeval myth, bids the old man renounce love, choose death and make friends with the necessity of dying. (Freud, 1913: p. 301)

The way in which Freud ended "The theme of the three caskets" is memorable and poetic.

> But it is in vain that an old man yearns for the love of woman as he had it first from his mother; the third of the Fates alone, the silent Goddess of Death, will take him into her arms. (Freud, 1913: p. 301)

If the play is treated like a dream we can say that in the manifest dream Lear carries the dead Cordelia but in the latent content Cordelia "is" death and she carries the old man. Freud made no claim to have interpreted the play itself. The basic idea of the three women in a man's life, expressed in "The theme of the three caskets", was not Shakespeare's idea but Freud's.

On 25 March 1934, in a letter to James S. H. Branson Freud discussed *King Lear*:

> ... the last small section of the book discloses the secret meaning of the tragedy, the repressed incestuous claims on the daughter's love.
>
> ...
>
> The elder sisters have already overcome the fateful love for the father and become hostile to him; to speak analytically, they are resentful at the disappointment in their early love. Cordelia still clings to him; her love for him is her holy secret. When asked to reveal it publicly she has to refuse defiantly and remain dumb. I have seen just that behavior in many cases. (Jones, 1957: p. 457)
>
> ...
>
> Is it not curious, by the way, that in the play that deals with the father's relations to his three daughters there is no mention whatever of the mother, and after all there must have been one. This is one of the traits that gives the tragedy a rather hard note of inhumanity. (ibid. p. 458)

At the end of the play, when Lear offers Cordelia the chance of becoming one of "God's spies" with him, a special kind of voyeuristic incestuous relationship, a longed-for father-daughter relationship, is expressed. Had the play ended on this note the poet would have permitted a disguised incestuous relationship to gain dominance. It would have granted gratification to sublimated incestuous wishes. Tragedy takes the needs of the superego into account. The oedipal yearning of both father and daughter are not allowed even symbolic gratification: both of them die.

King Lear as self-therapy

To discuss any play from a psychoanalytic point of view assumes that every playwright's work is also an attempt to solve an inner conflict. Shakespeare's overriding wish behind the writing of *King Lear* is likely to have been Shakespeare's own wish to retire, regress to early childhood and be taken care of by his daughters. When he wrote *King Lear* he not only gave us a profound play but also gave himself the signal that his wishes to make his daughters his mother were dangerous and should be resisted. The play makes conscious the otherwise repressed wish not as Shakespeare's wish but as King Lear's wish. Did Shakespeare have any inkling that he was writing about himself? We do not know.

King Lear wishes to refind the indulgent mother of childhood in his daughters and what he refinds is the harsh mother who prohibits masturbation. When Shakespeare created the title character he gave us a unique combination of an old man acting as a petulant child but then, when adversity strikes, the petulant child metamorphoses into a philosopher of life. There is another important theme: Had Regan and Goneril been ideal daughters, would Lear's regressive wish have met with success? The play could have ended either on the note that Regan and Goneril could have given Lear the good mother for whom he was looking but they were not good enough daughters, or Shakespeare could have implied that this kind of regression could not have ended well no matter what. He chose to leave the question unresolved.

CHAPTER ELEVEN

Richard II: abdication as a father's reaction to the Oedipus complex

Abdication was a theme of great interest to Shakespeare. *Richard II* is only the first play in which abdication plays a central role; *King Lear* and *The Tempest* will follow. Only a king can abdicate; the rest of us can only resign.

We noted in an earlier chapter that Shakespeare was in conflict about his calling as a poet. To him, being a poet seems to be the equivalent of being a magician. In this play the assumption is made that he imagined himself as a king forced to abdicate.

Richard II was written in 1595, some three years after *Richard III*. William Hazlitt, writing in 1817, left us a great psychological description of *Richard II*.

> *Richard II* is a play little known compared with *Richard III* which last is a play that every unfledged candidate for theatrical fame chuses to strut and fret his hour upon the stage in; yet we confess that we prefer the nature and feeling of the one to the noise and bustle of the other; at least, as we are so often forced to see it acted. In *Richard II* the weakness of the king leaves us leisure to take a greater interest in the misfortunes of the man. After the first act, in which the arbitrariness of his behaviour only proves his want of resolution, we see

him staggering under the unlooked-for blows of fortune, bewailing his loss of kingly power, not preventing it, sinking under the aspiring genius of Bolingbroke, his authority trampled on, his hopes failing him, and his pride crushed and broken down under insults and injuries, which his own misconduct had provoked, but which he has not courage or manliness to resent. (Hazlitt, 1817: pp. 178–179)

Hazlitt's description of Richard's character is excellent; being pre-Freudian he has no need or space to deal with the unconscious.

In the third act Richard, facing Bolingbroke's rebellion, is still confident in his election as king and the special sanctity that his position gives him.

RICHARD II: Not all the water in the rough rude sea
Can wash the balm off from an anointed king;
The breath of worldly men cannot depose
The deputy elected by the Lord.
For every man that Bolingbroke hath press'd
To lift shrewd steel against our golden crown,
God for his Richard hath in heavenly pay
A glorious angel: then, if angels fight,
Weak men must fall, for heaven still guards the right. (*Richard II*, III.ii.54–62)

And yet in the very same scene Richard, not unlike Shylock in *The Merchant of Venice*, asks for our sympathy and wants to be seen as an ordinary person.

RICHARD: For you have but mistook me all this while:
I live with bread like you, feel want,
Taste grief, need friends: subjected thus,
How can you say to me, I am a king? (III.ii.174–177)

In the next scene we find Richard forcing himself to accept his abdication.

RICHARD II: What must the King do now? Must he submit?
The king shall do it: must he be depos'd?
The king shall be contented: must he lose

The name of king? o' God's name, let it go:
I'll give my jewels for a set of beads,
My gorgeous palace for a hermitage,
My gay apparel for an almsman's gown,
My figured goblets for a dish of wood,
My sceptre for a palmer's walking staff,
My subjects for a pair of carved saints
And my large kingdom for a little grave. (III.iii.143–153)

In Act IV, the abdication discussion between Richard and Bolingbroke
is of psychological interest. Richard still regards himself as king of his
grief, a poetic description of masochism.

BOLINGBROKE: I thought you had been willing to resign.
RICHARD: My crown I am; but still my griefs are mine:
You may my glories and my state depose,
But not my griefs; still am I king of those.
BOLINGBROKE: Part of your cares you give me with your crown.
RICHARD: Your cares set up do not pluck my cares down.
My care is loss of care, by old care done;
Your care is gain of care, by new care won:
The cares I give I have, though given away;
They tend the crown, yet still with me they stay.
BOLINGBROKE: Are you contented to resign the crown?
RICHARD: Ay, no; no, ay; for I must nothing be;
Therefore no no, for I resign to thee.
Now mark me, how I will undo myself;
I give this heavy weight from off my head
And this unwieldy sceptre from my hand,
The pride of kingly sway from out my heart;
With mine own tears I wash away my balm,
With mine own hands I give away my crown,
With mine own tongue deny my sacred state,
With mine own breath release all duty's rites:
All pomp and majesty I do forswear;
My manors, rents, revenues I forego;
My acts, decrees, and statutes I deny:
God pardon all oaths that are broke to me!
God keep all vows unbroke that swear to thee!

> Make me, that nothing have, with nothing grieved,
> And thou with all pleased, that hast all achieved!
> Long mayst thou live in Richard's seat to sit,
> And soon lie Richard in an earthly pit!
> God save King Harry, unking'd Richard says,
> And send him many years of sunshine days! (IV.i.190–221)

The expression of the masochistic needs and the struggle against them can be considered the unconscious motivation of writing this play.

When Richard says, "My crown I am; but still my griefs are mine" he indicates that both the crown and his "griefs" have become part of his sense of identity. We may add that Richard calls his "griefs", which we may be tempted to call his neuroses, have become very dear to him and constitute a treasured part of the self. They determine his sense of identity. Psychoanalytic experience has time and again demonstrated that it is much harder to give up a neurosis when it has become the carrier of one's identity, and renouncing it evokes strong resistance. Upon abdication he will give up his crown but still retain his grief.

Bolingbroke demands a yes or no answer. Richard, being neurotic, knows the complexity of his psychology and why he cannot answer yes or no. Then comes the magnificent line "With mine own tears I wash away my balm". Unlike King Lear (although that play was not yet written when Shakespeare composed these lines), King Richard II has no wish to crawl towards death. What he does may look like abdication, but he knows that he has allowed himself to be overthrown. Bolingbroke, the victor and man of action, knows nothing of the unconscious, while Richard II, the flawed king, has a deep understanding of the unconscious.

The scene continues with the same magnificent language. The Earl of Northumberland offers Richard a paper to sign as a mere formality. Richard's answer is regal. In his downfall he identifies himself with Christ, as if Christ too had abdicated.

RICHARD: Nay, all of you that stand and look upon,
            Whilst that my wretchedness doth bait myself,
            Though some of you with Pilate wash your hands
            Showing an outward pity; yet you Pilates
            Have here deliver'd me to my sour cross,
            And water cannot wash away your sin. (IV.i.237–242)

The original masochistic surrender turns into identification with the betrayed Christ and an attack on his former followers.

NORTHUMBERLAND: My lord,—
RICHARD: No lord of thine, thou haught insulting man,
Nor no man's lord; I have no name, no title,
No, not that name was given me at the font,
But 'tis usurp'd: alack the heavy day,
That I have worn so many winters out,
And know not now what name to call myself!
O that I were a mockery king of snow,
Standing before the sun of Bolingbroke,
To melt myself away in water-drops!
Good king, great king, and yet not greatly good,
An if my word be sterling yet in England,
Let it command a mirror hither straight,
That it may show me what a face I have,
Since it is bankrupt of his majesty. (IV.i.253–266)

It is questionable whether Richard asked for a mirror concretely or metaphorically, but Bolingbroke is not a man to understand metaphor. He orders a mirror to be brought. When the looking glass arrives it evokes another storm of self-accusation from Richard.

RICHARD: Give me the glass, and therein will I read.
No deeper wrinkles yet? hath sorrow struck
So many blows upon this face of mine,
And made no deeper wounds? O flattering glass,
Like to my followers in prosperity,
Thou dost beguile me! Was this face the face
That every day under his household roof
Did keep ten thousand men? was this the face
That, like the sun, did make beholders wink?
Was this the face that faced so many follies,
And was at last out-faced by Bolingbroke?
A brittle glory shineth in this face:
As brittle as the glory is the face. (IV.i.276–288)

He then dashes the glass against the ground.

I have quoted the mirror scene in full because in portraying it Shakespeare conquered new psychic terrain. It is not easy to match this scene in the vehemence of the attack upon the self. On the analytic couch we hear similar self-denunciations but these are brought about because the analysand was urged to censor nothing. To describe such an attack on the self, Shakespeare could not go anywhere to find it except in the depths of his own unconscious.

Shakespeare has given us what may well be the first description of masochism in Western literature. The way he presents Richard II to us is remarkable; we understand him and sympathise with him but Shakespeare took care that we do not identify with him.

There is yet another quality in King Richard II that Shakespeare took pains to show us: his detachment. He is unemotional and cold because he is addicted to remaining the self-observer. Richard II cannot tolerate any intensity of feeling and certainly not one between a man and woman. In Act V, scene one the queen knows that he will be brought to the tower and waits for him.

> QUEEN: And must we be divided? must we part?
>
> RICHARD: Ay, hand from hand, my love, and heart from heart.
>
> QUEEN: Banish us both and send the king with me.
>
> NORTHUMBERLAND: That were some love but little policy.
>
> QUEEN: Then whither he goes, thither let me go.
>
> RICHARD: So two, together weeping, make one woe.
> Weep thou for me in France, I for thee here;
> Better far off than near, be ne'er the near.
> Go, count thy way with sighs; I mine with groans.
>
> QUEEN: So longest way shall have the longest moans.
>
> RICHARD: Twice for one step I'll groan, the way being short,
> And piece the way out with a heavy heart.
> Come, come, in wooing sorrow let's be brief,
> Since, wedding it, there is such length in grief;
> One kiss shall stop our mouths, and dumbly part;
> Thus give I mine, and thus take I thy heart.
>
> QUEEN: Give me mine own again; 'twere no good part
> To take on me to keep and kill thy heart.
> So, now I have mine own again, be gone,
> That I might strive to kill it with a groan.
>
> RICHARD: We make woe wanton with this fond delay:
> Once more, adieu; the rest let sorrow say. (V.i.81–102)

We are entitled to wonder whether this is the way a husband and wife speak when they both know they will never see each other again. The words they exchange are noble and we can feel the queen's love, but not Richard's love for his queen. In terms of Shakespeare's unconscious the separation between a husband and a wife may represent Shakespeare's own wish to live separated from his wife. In couples that wish to separate but cannot do so, we encounter dreams that they are forced to separate.

In Act V, scene five, Richard is alone in prison. Shakespeare gave Richard a very long soliloquy, which I quote in part.

RICHARD: I have been studying how I may compare
                  This prison where I live unto the world:
                  And for because the world is populous
                  And here is not a creature but myself,
                  I cannot do it; yet I'll hammer it out.
                  My brain I'll prove the female to my soul,
                  My soul the father; and these two beget
                  A generation of still-breeding thoughts,
                  And these same thoughts people this little world
                  …
                  Thus play I in one person many people,
                  And none contented: sometimes am I king;
                  Then treasons make me wish myself a beggar,
                  And so I am: then crushing penury
                  Persuades me I was better when a king;
                  Then am I king'd again: and by and by
                  Think that I am unking'd by Bolingbroke,
                  And straight am nothing. (V.v.1–9, 31–38)

The very same Richard whose weaknesses we have learned to know appears in this last scene in a new light. Alone in the cell he tries to achieve what psychoanalysis has designated as splitting the ego: to divide himself into two parts so that he can become two persons who entertain each other. We thus find that Shakespeare already knew another mechanism discovered by psychoanalysis, namely splitting. Alone in his cell, Richard is trying to achieve what his creator, Shakespeare, has achieved when he writes a play.

In 1927, under the title "A father pleads for the death of his son", M. P. Taylor focused on two scenes, Act V, scenes two and three, which are "in no way essential for the action of the drama". The Duke of York discovers that his son, Aumerle, is plotting to restore the recently deposed Richard II to the throne. He rushes to meet the usurper, Henry IV, asking that his son be put to death. Aumerle and his mother also arrive and the three kneel before the king, the mother and son pleading for the son's life. The mother believes that the duke does not think that Aumerle is his son but is a bastard.

The mother pleads with her husband not to kill their son.

DUCHESS: Hadst thou groan'd for him
            As I have done, thou wouldst be more pitiful.
            But now I know thy mind; thou dost suspect
            That I have been disloyal to thy bed,
            And that he is a bastard, not thy son:
            Sweet York, sweet husband, be not of that mind:
            He is as like thee as a man may be,
            Not like to me, or any of my kin,
            And yet I love him. (*Richard II*, V.ii.101–109)

This is a milder version of what will take place in *The Winter's Tale*, where a paranoid father suspects that his child is a bastard. In this play the father, mother, and son, rush to Bolingbroke. The father accuses the son, and the mother is successful in obtaining pardon for him. Dramatically the scene builds Bolingbroke's good image but from other plays we know that the accusation of marital infidelity and the feeling that the child is a bastard was a favourite theme to express paranoid feelings. This may also be the case in this play, although here it has only a minor role not connected to the main theme.

In 1968 Martin Wangh published a psychoanalytic interpretation of *Richard II*. He studied the actual historical records about the real Richard II. Richard was the second son of Edward of Woodstock, later know as the Black Prince. He was born in Bordeaux on 6 January 1367; an older brother died when he was four and his father died when he was nine. A year later he became king of England, succeeding his grandfather, Edward III. He abdicated in 1399 and was murdered in 1400. Wangh assumes that Shakespeare believed that Richard II suffered from survivor's guilt, and the rumour that he was a bastard must have added to his feeling of not being entitled to the crown. Richard compared himself to Phaeton, who tried to drive his father Apollo's sun chariot but could not master the divine horses.

RICHARD: I have no name, no title
              No, not that name was given me at the font,
              But 'tis usurped. (IV.i.254–256)

Richard tries to "ward off the pressure of his unconscious guilt but it unconsciously compelled to follow its dictates" (Wangh, 1968: pp. 213–214). When he surrenders his crown there is a momentary relief from the pressure of his unconscious guilt: "Here, cousin, seize the crown, / On this side my hand and on that side thine" (*Richard II*, IV.i.181–182). Not only the crown but Richard's very name has been usurped.

As a psychological study of a very complex personality, *Richard II* is a masterpiece. Only a very great psychologist could have created such a personality. Richard is a very guilty man and a masochist, long before the term was coined. I would describe the play as one in which the psychologist won over the dramatist. We are more interested in Richard II as an individual than in the play.

PART IV

INTRAPSYCHIC CONFLICT

CHAPTER TWELVE

Measure for Measure: the disintegration of a harsh superego

The title of this play is derived from Matthew 7: 1–2:

> 1) Judge not, that ye be not judged. 2) For with what judgment ye judge, ye shall be judged: and with what measure ye mete, it shall be measured to you again.

The title suggests that the play deals with justice and punishment and it is believed that Shakespeare wrote it in 1604, the same year as *Othello* and a year before *King Lear*. It is hard to classify *Measure for Measure* since it is neither a comedy nor a tragedy. It is of psychoanalytic interest because it deals with the need for and the disappointment in the harshness of the superego, as well as the development of the relationship of Isabella and Angelo, who are both in search of a stricter superego. We find ourselves in a situation that recalls the time when progressive education was introduced. Angelo introduces the problem with an original metaphor.

ANGELO: We must not make a scarecrow of the law,
            Setting it up to fear the birds of prey,

183

> And let it keep one shape till custom make it
> Their perch and not their terror. (*Measure for Measure*, II.i.1–4)

Vincentio, the Duke of Vienna, is in agreement.

VINCENTIO: Now, as fond fathers
            Having bound up the threatening twigs of birch,
            Only to stick it in their children's sight
            For terror, not to use—in time the rod
            More mocked than feared—so our decrees,
            Dead to infliction, to themselves are dead,
            And Liberty plucks Justice by the nose,
            The baby beats the nurse, and quite athwart
            Goes all decorum. (I.iii.24–32)

At the opening of the play Duke Vincentio, the ruler of Vienna, decides on a temporary abdication. He will leave Vienna in the hands of his deputy Angelo, known for being much stricter than the duke. The theme of abdication has a long history in Shakespeare's work, recalling *King Lear*, *Richard II*, and Prospero in *The Tempest*. In this play, however, Vincentio does not leave his kingdom but remains there disguised as a friar in order to see what will happen under Angelo's stricter rule.

At this point we encounter Shakespeare's irony: the supposedly corrupt Vienna can find no worse a criminal than a man who impregnated his fiancée before, rather than after, their wedding.

After being arrested Claudio meets his friend Lucio and requests that he ask his sister to intervene on his behalf with the new ruler.

CLAUDIO: I prithee, Lucio, do me this kind service:
          This day my sister should the cloister enter
          And there receive her approbation.
          Acquaint her with the danger of my state,
          Implore her, in my voice, that she make friends
          To the strict deputy: bid herself assay him.
          I have great hope in that; for in her youth
          There is a prone and speechless dialect
          Such as move men; beside, she hath prosperous art
          When she will play with reason and discourse,
          And well she can persuade. (I.ii.157–167)

The speech is sufficiently enigmatic that one does not know whether Claudio anticipates the price Isabella will be asked to pay to win his pardon. Much depends on how we interpret "make friends/to the strict deputy". Is he sending his sister to plead for him or to seduce Angelo into pardoning him?

When we first meet Isabella in Act I, scene four, she is visiting a nunnery she plans to join. The following exchange takes place between Isabella and the nun Francesca.

ISABELLA: And have you nuns no farther privileges?
FRANCISCA: Are not these large enough?
ISABELLA: Yes, truly; I speak not as desiring more,
        But rather wishing a more strict restraint
        Upon the sisterhood, the votarists of Saint Clare. (I.iv.1–5)

Isabella, mirroring the duke, is not asking for more freedom but more restrictions as a pre-condition for her joining the nunnery. Subtly, Shakespeare shows us that the duke, Angelo, and Isabella have in common a need and search for a harsher superego.

The second scene of Act II, where Isabella visits Angelo and pleads with him to save her brother, shows us Shakespeare the dramatist as a great psychologist. Isabella herself is as harsh as Angelo and in basic sympathy with the law that punishes extramarital sex by death. When she pleads with Angelo for the life of her brother she is really in sympathy with the death penalty and betrays her inner conflict. She starts the interview by confessing her dilemma and her plea for her brother's life is ambivalent.

ISABELLA: There is a vice that most I do abhor,
        And most desire should meet the blow of justice;
        For which I would not plead, but that I must,
        For which I must not plead, but that I am
        At war 'twixt will and will not.
ANGELO: Well; the matter?
ISABELLA: I have a brother is condemned to die. (II.ii.30–35)

Angelo has no difficulty refusing her request for Claudio's pardon.

ANGELO: Condemn the fault, and not the actor of it?
        Why, every fault's condemn'd ere it be done.

> Mine were the very cipher of a function
> To fine the faults, whose fine stands in record,
> And let go by the actor. (II.ii.38–42)

Isabella is defeated, ready to leave, and in sympathy with the man who will execute her brother. What we have witnessed is an encounter between a man and a woman who both believe in a strict morality, with the woman surrendering to the man. Isabella persists only because Lucio, Claudio's friend who persuaded Isabella to plead for her brother's life, is fully aware how much in conflict she is and how ineffective her pleading is and urges her to continue her suit.

LUCIO
(ASIDE TO ISABELLA):   Give't not o'er so: to him again, entreat him,
                        Kneel down before him, hang upon his gown.
                        You are too cold. If you should need a pin,
                        You could not with more tame a tongue desire it.
                        (II.ii.44–47)

Lucio is successful and Isabella resumes her pleading. She is now markedly more effective when she praises the virtue of marriage. Skillfully she introduces the distinction between the law and Angelo's power to alter Claudio's sentence. Angelo says he will not pardon Claudio, to which Isabella replies, "But can you if you would?" (II.ii.52). Angelo's claims that there is no distinction between the two "Look what I will not, that I cannot do" (II.ii.53). The relationship between the two has radically changed; Isabella is on the offensive.

ISABELLA: If he had been as you, and you as he,
             You would have slipt like him, but he like you
             Would not have been so stern. (II.ii.65–67)

At one point Angelo is almost ready to yield.

ANGELO: I will bethink me. Come again tomorrow.
ISABELLA: Hark how I'll bribe you—good my lord, turn back.
ANGELO: How? Bribe me?
ISABELLA: Ay, with such gifts that heaven shall share with you. (II.ii.149–152)

We are now in a position to make a psychoanalytic construction. The phrase of "I'll bribe you" is akin to a slip of the tongue; Isabella is hinting at a sexual reward. The hint is not lost on Angelo. Isabella has to extricate herself from this embarrassing admission; she has no way out and has to say that prayer is a form of bribery.

Angelo, feeling the power of her seduction, tells her, "Pray you be gone" (II.ii.67). Once Isabella leaves, Angelo is shaken and confused.

ANGELO: Can it be
          That modesty may more betray our sense
          Than woman's lightness? Having waste ground enough
          Shall we desire to raze the sanctuary
          And pitch our evils there? Oh, fie, fie, fie,
          What dost thou or what art thou, Angelo?
          Dost thou desire her foully for those things
          That make her good? Oh, let her brother live:
          Thieves for their robbery have authority
          When judges steal themselves. What, do I love her
          That I desire to hear her speak again
          And feast upon her eyes? What is't I dream on?
          O cunning enemy that, to catch a saint,
          With saints dost bait thy hook! Most dangerous
          Is that temptation that doth goad us on
          To sin in loving virtue. Never could the strumpet
          With all her double vigour, art and nature,
          Once stir my temper; but this virtuous maid
          Subdues me quite. Ever till now,
          When men were fond, I smiled, and wondered how. (II.ii.172–191)

Since Angelo has such a harsh superego, what interests him first is who is to blame, the tempter or the tempted. He has forgotten that it was Isabella who used the term "I'll bribe you" and accuses himself of "desire to raze the sanctuary". In psychoanalytic language, he realises that his sexuality was aroused by an aggressive wish to destroy Isabella's "sanctuary". We know from *Richard III* that the question of who is guilty, the tempter or the tempted, interested Shakespeare greatly.

Angelo exonerates Isabella and takes all the blame himself, and next wonders if "modesty may more betray our sense / Than woman's lightness?" (II.ii.173–174). In the last two lines he interprets his attraction as derived not from the sexual but from the aggressive drive and condemns himself: "Shall we desire to raze the sanctuary / And pitch our evils there? Oh, fie, fie, fie" (II.ii.175–176). What Angelo understands, and Shakespeare himself must have known to give Angelo this insight, is that sexual attraction need not always be motivated by love. It can also be an expression of aggressive wishes.

If Angelo were a psychoanalytic patient one would grant that he has insight into his desires and feelings but the insight is under the domination of a severe superego. When insight and condemnation appear together the insight will not bring about any change for the better but rather exhaust itself in condemnation.

Another interpretation must also be considered. The technique Isabella used was emphasising the similarities between Claudio and Angelo, with Claudio being less harsh. Angelo's unconscious responds to the comparison, but how is he to sin like Claudio? Since Isabella is advocating leniency and since she also hinted at bribery, Angelo believes she should yield to him. If she suggests that like her brother he too could slip, then with whom should this slip take place? Obviously with Isabella herself.

Measure for Measure contains a further insight that we can call psychoanalytic in its structure. We are in Act III, scene one. Isabella is visiting her brother in jail.

ISABELLA: If I would yield him my virginity,
             Thou might'st be freed!
CLAUDIO: Oh, heavens, it cannot be!
ISABELLA: Yes, he would give't thee, from this rank offence:
             So to offend him still. This night's the time
             That I should do what I abhor to name,
             Or else thou diest to-morrow.
CLAUDIO: Thou shalt not do't.
ISABELLA: Oh, were it but my life
             I'd throw it down for your deliverance
             As frankly as a pin.
CLAUDIO: Thanks, dear Isabel.
ISABELLA: Be ready, Claudio, for your death tomorrow. (III.i.97–106)

A few lines later Claudio weakens.

CLAUDIO: Death is a fearful thing.

ISABELLA: And shamèd life a hateful.

CLAUDIO: Ay, but to die and go we know not where,
To lie in cold obstruction and to rot,
This sensible warm motion to become
A kneaded clod, and the delighted spirit
To bathe in fiery floods or to reside
In thrilling region of thick-ribbed ice,
To be imprisoned in the viewless winds
And blown with restless violence round about
The pendent world, or to be worse than worst
Of those that lawless and incertain thought
Imagine howling; 'tis too horrible.
The weariest and most loathèd worldly life
That age, ache, penury and imprisonment
Can lay on nature, is a paradise
To what we fear of death. (III.i.116–132)

Shakespeare has given to Claudio the same fear of what may come after death that he had earlier given to Hamlet. This fear is a denial of death. Those who burn in hell, strictly speaking, are not dead, for they suffer the pain associated with being burnt alive.

CLAUDIO: Sweet sister, let me live.
What sin you do to save a brother's life,
Nature dispenses with the deed so far
That it becomes a virtue.

ISABELLA: Oh, you beast!
Oh faithless coward, oh dishonest wretch!
Wilt thou be made a man out of my vice?
Is't not a kind of incest, to take life
From thine own sister's shame? (III.i.133–140)

Logically there is no connection between sex to save a brother's life and committing incest with him but Shakespeare gave Isabella the capacity to surmise the logic of the unconscious.

Shakespeare had a striking capacity to make his actors express the kind of thinking that included the unconscious but he never allowed these insights to be effective or influence the action. One is reminded of the Chinese, who invented gunpowder but used it only for firecrackers.

What Angelo plans to do to Isabella is truly villainous. If his plan had succeeded, within twenty-four hours Isabella's brother would have been executed and her virginity, which she esteems so highly, sacrificed in vain.

Angelo and Isabella are very similar to one another. They are both excessively moral, strict, and rigid, with little capacity for sensual pleasure. Angelo's attack on Isabella's chastity may have been an attack on his own rigidity as well, and the attraction was based on the unconscious realisation that she mirrored him. The very same mirroring will also attract the duke to Isabella.

At the very end of the play the duke proposes marriage to Isabella, but his proposal is probably the briefest and least romantic proposal ever recorded, and Isabella's response is not even given. It is evident that Shakespeare wanted to finish the play and marrying the duke was a way to conclude it. The duke and Isabella share a yearning for a stricter world.

Mariana enters and confesses that she had a sexual encounter with Angelo in Isabella's "imagined person" (V.i.209). Shakespeare has followed a fallacy popular in Western literature: that in the dark a man cannot know with whom he is having sexual intercourse. It is Isabella, at Mariana's request, who pleads for Angelo's pardon.

VINCENTIO: He dies for Claudio's death.
ISABELLA: (*kneeling*) Most bounteous sir,
              Look if it please you on this man condemned
              As if my brother lived. I partly think
              A due sincerity governed his deeds,
              Till he did look on me. Since it is so,
              Let him not die. My brother had but justice,
              In that he did the thing for which he died.
              For Angelo,
              His act did not o'ertake his bad intent,
              And must be buried but as an intent
              That perish'd by the way. Thoughts are no subjects,
              Intents but merely thoughts. (V.i.436–447)

Why is Isabella pleading to save Angelo's life? Does she feel guilty because she aroused sexual wishes in him? Or has she fallen in love with him while pleading for her brother? Could this be a return of what Shakespeare read in his sources: that Isabella and Angelo got married? The fact that she says, "Till he did look on me" suggests that she accepted Angelo's argument that the tempter is as guilty as the tempted. The line "His act did not o'ertake his bad intent" refers to that fact that he did not actually have sexual relations with her and therefore does not deserve to die.

The lesson Shakespeare may have wanted us to draw from this play may be that no one, including Isabella and Angelo, is immune to temptation; therefore, no one is entitled to judge others because, like them, they may be tempted. Saving a brother's life does not justify the loss of chastity.

We are astonished to discover that Isabella pleads to the duke for Angelo even when she still believes he killed her brother. We are left to wonder why. Is she so harsh that she feels her brother deserved to be killed? Is she secretly in love with Angelo? The lines "His act did not o'ertake his bad intent, / And must be buried but as an intent" is an important psychological statement but it is wasted in this situation. It so happens that psychoanalysis has found that the power of the superego to punish the person is significantly based on blurring this line of difference between "act" and "intent". In psychoanalytic terms to commit adultery in one's heart is not the same as committing it in actuality.

We know that Shakespeare was himself guilty of the "crime" of Claudio: impregnating his future wife before their marriage. What we did not know until we read *Measure for Measure* is how guilty Shakespeare felt, at least unconsciously. In subsequent plays, notably in *The Tempest*, the father makes sure that the future son-in-law waits until the marriage ceremony has taken place before the relationship is consummated.

The other striking feature of the play is that it is a comedy without gaiety. Eros is not triumphant. True, the duke and Isabella plan to get married but they are so inhibited as individuals that one cannot imagine them in love, or capable of pleasure, or enjoying each other.

The place of death in the play

Although *Measure for Measure* was not written as a tragedy the role death plays in it is nearly as important as it is in *Hamlet*.

The duke's gives Claudio the following advice about his impending death:

CLAUDIO: Be absolute for death: either death or life
            Shall thereby be the sweeter. Reason thus with life:
            If I do lose thee I do lose a thing
            That none but fools would keep; a breath thou art,
            Servile to all the skyey influences
            That dost this habitation where thou keepest
            Hourly afflict. Merely, thou art death's fool;
            For him thou labour'st by thy flight to shun
            And yet runn'st toward him still. (III.i.5–13)

The prisoner Barnardine represents a very different attitude towards death; the provost describes him as:

PROVOST: A man that apprehends death no more dreadfully but as a
            drunken sleep: careless, reckless, and fearless of what's past,
            present, or to come: insensible of mortality and desperately mortal.
            (IV.ii.125–128)
            ...
            We have very oft awaked him, as if to carry him to execution, and
            showed him a seeming warrant for it. It hath not moved him at all.
            (IV.ii.132–141)

When the warrant to be beheaded comes, Barnardine has been drinking all night and says, "I will not consent to die this day, that's certain" (IV.iii.47–48). The line is comic because we do not usually think of an execution as asking permission of the condemned.

Claudio, who expresses fully the fear of death, represents the third attitude towards death. The three attitudes support the idea that we have already derived from *Hamlet*: that Shakespeare was very much preoccupied with death and the fear of what comes after death.

Angelo represents a fourth attitude: he welcomes death.

ANGELO: I am sorry that such sorrow I procure,
           And so deep sticks it in my penitent heart
           That I crave death more willingly than mercy.
           'Tis my deserving, and I do entreat it. (V.i.467–470)

There is dignity in Angelo's response. When he sentences himself to death because of his transgressions he once more rises in our esteem, so that as an audience we no longer demand as strongly that he be punished. Angelo is the opposite of Claudio. Shakespeare must have sensed something of Freud's death instinct for he makes Angelo "crave death". In psychoanalytic language we would say that both Angelo's superego and ego have accepted that he deserves death and therefore there is no fear of death. This dignity suggests that Shakespeare had a deeper sympathy for this man than the audience is likely to have. It suggests that Shakespeare may have been more identified with Angelo than we would have otherwise assumed. We understand what we had difficulty comprehending earlier: that Angelo represents Shakespeare's guilt.

PART V

THE BATTLE AGAINST PARANOIA

CHAPTER THIRTEEN

Othello: motiveless malignity or latent homosexuality?

Shakespeare's *Othello* is probably the greatest literary work on the subject of jealousy. The source for the play was Cinthio's *Hecatommithi*, published in Venice in 1566. In the original, the jealousy is a simple heterosexual one, in which an ensign, Iago, passionately desires Desdemona. When she fails to respond he becomes convinced that she loves another officer, a Moorish captain named Cassio; the love turns into a murderous jealousy and Desdemona is killed. In this version the Moor is not in love with or married to Desdemona.

Shakespeare transformed this relatively simple story into the tale of the capacity of one man, Iago, to transform the sexually non-consummated love relationship between the Moor, Othello, and the young white woman, Desdemona, into her murder by Othello in a fit of jealousy. Iago leaves us with an uncanny impression because he kindles this jealousy and at the same time warns Othello against it.

IAGO: O! beware, my lord, of jealousy;
        It is the green-eyed monster which doth mock
        The meat it feeds on; that cuckold lives in bliss
        Who, certain of his fate, loves not his wronger;

> But O! what damned minutes tells he o'er
> Who dotes, yet doubts; suspects, yet soundly loves. (*Othello*, III.
> iii.165–170)

These are difficult lines, conveying a complex message. Jealousy is said to be a "green-eyed monster" that mocks "the meat it feeds on", meaning that it renders ridiculous the very person who succumbs to it. But in the middle of the third line a very different message is transmitted. According to Iago, one is particularly a victim of the green-eyed monster if one both dotes (loves submissively) and suspects one's lover at the same time. These very complex lines are uttered not by a thinker on the nature of jealousy, but by a man planning to snare another man by evoking his jealousy and causing him to kill the woman he loves.

Othello assures Iago that he is immune "To such exsufflicate and blown surmises" (III.iii.182) and thereby becomes more susceptible to Iago's ensnarement. Jealousy is also discussed between Iago's wife Emilia and Desdemona.

DESDEMONA: Alas the day! I never gave him cause.
EMILIA: But jealous souls will not be answer'd so;
They are not ever jealous for the cause,
But jealous for they are jealous. It is a monster
Begot upon itself, born on itself. (III.iv.158–162)

Both Iago and Emilia call jealousy a monster but Emilia calls it a monster "Begot upon itself", a metaphorical way of saying that jealousy needs no external cause but can start without provocation. Jealousy remains a monster all through this play. Iago's jealousy is a bisexual one, for he not only instigates Desdemona's death at the hands of Othello but also orchestrates Cassio's murder by Roderigo.

Iago makes yet another observation on jealousy:

IAGO: He hath a daily beauty in his life
That makes me ugly. (V.i.19–20)

One can be jealous not only of a relationship but also of what another person is that one cannot be. Iago is jealous of Desdemona while Cassio and Desdemona have a desexualised relationship that Iago cannot abide.

IAGO: Our general cast us thus early for the love of his Desdemona: who let us not therefore blame: he hath not yet made wanton the night with her; and she is sport for Jove.

CASSIO: She's a most exquisite lady.

IAGO: And, I'll warrant her, full of game.

CASSIO: Indeed, she's a most fresh and delicate creature.

IAGO: What an eye she has! methinks it sounds a parley to provocation.

CASSIO: An inviting eye; and yet methinks right modest.

IAGO: And when she speaks, is it not an alarum to love?

CASSIO: She is indeed perfection.

IAGO: Well, happiness to their sheets! (II.iii.14–29)

Every one of Iago's lines expresses his jealousy of Desdemona's sexuality and every response by Cassio is desexualised praise of her. Shakespeare lets us know how very differently the two perceive Desdemona. Cassio is reverent and respectful of her, while Iago sees her as sexual and promiscuous, and hates her for being so. Othello and Desdemona have retired to consummate their marriage. Once more, as in Venice, Iago cannot allow their union. He gets Cassio drunk and a loud scene forces Othello to interrupt his lovemaking; Iago must always disturb the sexual union between Othello and Desdemona. Unconsciously, Iago stands for the child who cannot tolerate the parents' sexual relations and gets the father to murder the mother.

Shakespeare scholars have accepted Emilia's interpretation that jealousy is a monster "Begot upon itself" and therefore make no further interpretation. Marjorie Garber cites with approval Coleridge's term "motiveless malignity", which is close to "a monster / Begot upon itself" (Garber, 2004, p. 605) and here we are touching on a basic difference of viewpoint. Those who are not psychoanalytically oriented can accept the concept of "motiveless malignancy" but psychoanalysts will not rest until they find the motive.

Harold Bloom opens his chapter on *Othello* with a quote from Hazlitt:

> The character of Iago ... belongs to a class of characters common to Shakespeare, and at the same time peculiar to him—namely, that of great intellectual activity, accompanied with a total want of moral principle, and therefore displaying itself at the constant expense of others. (Bloom, 1998: p. 423)

Bloom himself writes:

> Shakespeare's finest achievement in Othello is Iago's extraordinary mutations, prompted by his acute self-overhearing as he moves through his eight soliloquies, and their supporting asides .... Iago is always at the center of the web; ceaselessly weaving his fiction, and snaring us with dark magic. (Bloom, 1998. pp. 455–456)

He also notes that "No villain in all literature rivals Iago as a flawless conception" (Bloom, 1998: p. 453). This is Iago's nature and no further exploration of motives is necessary.

Nuttall finds that Iago has no motive for his actions; he adds that those critics who sense latent homosexuality in Iago could be right (Nuttall, 2007: p. 286). Iago has consciously decided to treat a suspicion that could be false (that Othello slept with his wife) as true and by doing so he has successfully induced a violent emotion in himself. Iago persuades himself to transform a surmise into a surety.

Psychoanalysis sees jealousy as an important emotion of childhood. It has two major sources: the jealousy the child feels towards the parents, which is the wish to replace either the father or the mother's love for the other parent. This jealousy leads to the formation of the Oedipus complex in its many forms. The other jealousy emerges from sibling rivalry, the wish to be the favourite child of father or mother. What adults regard as a monster begat upon itself is, in psychoanalytic terms, a return from repression of childhood jealousy.

In his 1922 paper "Some neurotic mechanisms in jealousy, paranoia and homosexuality" Freud differentiated three types of jealousy: competitive (a normal jealousy that has its roots in the Oedipus complex of the child or in sibling rivalry), projected jealousy (in which one's own impulses towards unfaithfulness are projected on the innocent partner), and delusional jealousy (which arises out of the denial of homosexual impulses in oneself that are projected on the partner as "I do not love him; she loves him").

Freud reports a delusional jealousy that overwhelmed a man after a successful heterosexual relationship had taken place. Freud explained this behaviour by assuming that after the heterosexual libido was satisfied the homosexual needs asserted themselves and those needs found expression in the accusation that the wife had been unfaithful (Freud, 1922: p. 223). We are now dealing with a basic psychoanalytic concept. Psychoanalysis believes human happiness can be of short duration only, for when one group of needs has been met, after a while, it arouses the dormant counter-needs and the happiness is undone by the return of the intrapsychic conflict.

One of Freud's original ideas was that delusional jealousy is the expression of a repressed homosexual wish. The man then accuses the woman of having a sexual relationship with another man who is desired unconsciously by the man himself.

As an example of projected jealousy Freud quoted from Desdemona's song:

> I called my love false love; but what said he then?
>
> …
>
> If I court moe women, you'll couch with moe men.
> (*Othello*, IV.iii.55, 57)

It is possible that *Othello* helped Freud formulate the concept of projective and delusional jealousy, as *Hamlet* helped him understand the Oedipus complex.

In 1932, in the paper "Jealousy as a mechanism of defense", Joan Riviere offered a psychoanalytic interpretation of Othello. She emphasised that the first act shows;

> Desdemona's old father, his grief and fury aroused by Othello's abduction of his daughter, his bitter reproaches and accusations, his threats and prophecies of disaster. Othello had won this love object by seizure from her owner—her father. (*Riviere*, 1932: p. 424)

This has evoked psychic guilt in Othello. What adds to the guilt is Othello's race, his blackness, which contrasts with Desdemona's white skin. According to Riviere, Iago is only Othello's alter ego. Othello cannot "endure the evil in himself. He must make Desdemona black instead" (Riviere, 1932: p. 424).

A very different psychoanalytic interpretation was made by Martin Wangh in his paper "*Othello*: the tragedy of Iago". In Wangh's interpretation Iago is unconsciously in love with Othello and jealous of Desdemona. Out of his jealousy he goads Othello into suspicion of Desdemona's faithfulness and brings about her murder. "It is he who is jealous of Desdemona and hates her. Iago loves Othello.... It is Iago who is the absorbing personality, the evil genius of the play"

(Wangh, 1950: pp. 203–204). In Venice as well as in Cyprus Iago creates disturbances wherever Othello and Desdemona have retired to have sexual intercourse; he cannot tolerate the idea that the two have sexual relations. In Iago infantile jealousy has returned and he wishes to replace Desdemona. Wangh points out that if Iago's jealousy had been "projective jealousy" the object of the jealousy would have been Emilia, Iago's wife, and therefore Iago should have either cuckolded Othello by sleeping with Desdemona or have murdered him. Since neither of these events happen the jealousy is of the delusional type, based on unconscious homosexuality. The supposed dream that Iago relates to Othello about Cassio is further proof of Iago's repressed homosexuality; the handkerchief Wangh interprets as a fetish.

Wangh's paper not only interpreted the unconscious meaning of Iago's behaviour but also influenced the way the role was played. Under the influence of Wangh's paper, the actor portraying Iago often displayed homosexual traits; what Shakespeare left implicit the actor makes explicit. Wangh's essay was often cited and reprinted. It succeeded to shift the interest from Othello to Iago. Those who do not accept the psychoanalytic interpretation fall back on "motiveless malignity" while those who accept the unconscious perceive the same behaviour as due to latent homosexuality.

What is so shocking in this play is that the unconsciously implied homosexuality had lost all connection to any sexual desire. Iago does not wish to replace Desdemona as a lover but only to bring about her death. It is the triumph of aggression over love, or, in Freud's terms, the victory of the death instinct over libido.

Psychoanalysis further assumes that Shakespeare, by writing *Othello*, gained enough insight into his own unconscious to prevent himself from Othello's fate.

In the first act Brabantio, Desdemona's father, accuses Othello of winning her through witchcraft:

BRABANTIO: She is abus'd, stol'n from me, and corrupted
              By spells and medicines bought of mountebanks;
              For nature so preposterously to err,
              Being not deficient, blind, or lame of sense,
              Sans witchcraft could not. (*Othello*, I.iii.60–64)

Othello defends himself against the accusation:

OTHELLO: I did consent,
And often did beguile her of her tears,
When I did speak of some distressful stroke
That my youth suffer'd. My story being done,
She gave me for my pains a world of sighs:
She swore, in faith, 'twas strange, 'twas passing strange,
'Twas pitiful, 'twas wondrous pitiful:
She wish'd she had not heard it, yet she wish'd
That heaven had made her such a man: she thank'd me,
And bade me, if I had a friend that loved her,
I should but teach him how to tell my story.
And that would woo her. Upon this hint I spake:
She loved me for the dangers I had pass'd,
And I loved her that she did pity them. (I.iii.155–168)

Shakespeare gives us stages in the process of Desdemona falling in love. At first she struggles against her love when she says she wishes she had not heard it, then a masculine wish takes over. She wishes "That heaven had made her such a man". As she overcomes her masculine wishes her jealousy is transformed into love. She now loves Othello but disguises this love by telling him that his story is the way to win her love. Othello himself does not fall in love with Desdemona as a woman but with the Desdemona who loves Othello: his response is what is called in psychoanalysis narcissistic love and such love is always a weaker form of love than object love.

It is now Desdemona's turn to be interrogated.

BRABANTIO: Do you perceive in all this noble company
Where most you owe obedience? (I.iii.179–180)
DESDEMONA: My noble father,
I do perceive here a divided duty:
To you I am bound for life and education;
My life and education both do learn me
How to respect you; you are the lord of duty;
I am hitherto your daughter: but here's my husband,
And so much duty as my mother show'd
To you, preferring you before her father,
So much I challenge that I may profess
Due to the Moor, my lord. (I.iii.180–189)

We recall that this is also the answer Cordelia gives to her father in *King Lear*:

CORDELIA: I love your majesty
             According to my bond; nor more nor less.

             ...

             Good my lord,
             You have begot me, bred me, loved me: I
             Return those duties back as are right fit,
             Obey you, love you, and most honour you.
             Why have my sisters husbands, if they say
             They love you all? Haply, when I shall wed,
             That lord whose hand must take my plight shall carry
             Half my love with him, half my care and duty:
             Sure, I shall never marry like my sisters,
             To love my father all. (*King Lear*, I.i.94–95, 97–106)

What we hear from Desdemona and Cordelia is what psychoanalysis calls resolution of the Oedipus complex. The father is still loved and respected but the duty is divided and the lion's share goes to the husband.

When Othello stands before the Doge of Venice asking for Desdemona's hand he is eager to prove that it is not sexual lust that draws him to her.

OTHELLO: Let her have your voice.
            Vouch with me, heaven, I therefore beg it not,
            To please the palate of my appetite,
            Nor to comply with heat—the young affects
            In my distinct and proper satisfaction.
            But to be free and bounteous to her mind:
            And heaven defend your good souls, that you think
            I will your serious and great business scant
            For she is with me: no, when light-wing'd toys
            Of feather'd Cupid seal with wanton dullness
            My speculative and officed instruments,
            That my disports corrupt and taint my business (*Othello*,
            I.iii.256–267)

To speak about his potency to the doge of Venice seems inappropriate. Is Othello impotent, or is he aware of the exaggerated potency usually ascribed to men of African ancestry and defending himself against that image? The intense sexual jealousy that Iago experiences is an imaginary one: the potency of the Moor exist only in Iago's mind. If Othello was indeed impotent and the marriage unconsummated, Othello's vulnerability to believe Iago's insinuations becomes more understandable.

Desdemona's capacity to love Othello remains intact to the very end. Ironically it is to Iago that she says these magnificent words of loyalty:

DESDEMONA: I know not how I lost him. Here I kneel:
If e'er my will did trespass 'gainst his love,
Either in discourse of thought or actual deed,
Or that mine eyes, mine ears, or any sense,
Delighted them in any other form;
Or that I do not yet, and ever did.
And ever will—though he do shake me off
To beggarly divorcement—love him dearly,
Comfort forswear me! Unkindness may do much;
And his unkindness may defeat my life,
But never taint my love. (IV.ii.151–161)

Shakespeare could describe a woman's deep capacity to love, even when her life is endangered by her lover.

Is Desdemona a real person? We would like to believe she is, but the total absence of aggression towards Othello and the love that knows no limits for him up to the very end, suggests that she may be an idealised representation of love itself, deserving the idealisation that Cassio has bestowed upon her.

How Iago ensnared Othello

Othello and Desdemona, in spite of all the limitations of their relationship, both love and respect each other. Shakespeare had to devise a method that would transform a lover into a murderer. When we trace this technique we may learn something about the nature of jealousy. I will now reconstruct the steps.

First, Cassio himself behaves in a way that enables Iago to plant suspicion in Othello. Cassio, although innocent, is afraid to be caught in the company of Desdemona by Iago.

IAGO: Ha! I like not that.

OTHELLO: What dost thou say?

IAGO: Nothing, my lord: or if—I know not what.

OTHELLO: Was not that Cassio parted from my wife?

IAGO: Cassio, my lord! No, sure I cannot think it
           That he would steal away so guilty-like,
           Seeing you coming. (III.iii.35–40)

Iago's technique is to plant the suspicion and act as if he cannot believe it to be true. In the next step Desdemona adds to the suspicion by advocating strongly that Cassio be reinstated in Othello's good opinion. Iago then resumes his technique of hinting and denying the hints that makes Othello increasingly suspicious.

OTHELLO: What dost thou think?

IAGO: Think, my lord?

OTHELLO: Think, my lord! By heaven, he echoes me,
           As if there were some monster in his thought
           Too hideous to be shown. Thou dost mean something.
           (III.iii.105–109)

As Othello's suspicion takes hold Iago resorts to another technique: he warns Othello against becoming suspicious. Othello assures him that he is immune to jealousy. Othello's own feelings of inadequacy now gain the upper hand.

OTHELLO: Haply, for I am black,
           And have not those soft parts of conversation
           That chamberers have, or for I am declined
           Into the vale of years. (III.iii.265–268)

Othello expresses his feelings of inadequacy: He is black, he lacks the skills of "chamberers" and he feels old, expressed as "the vale of years".

    We come now to a particularly interesting moment when Othello is resisting Iago's impact.

OTHELLO: Avaunt, be gone! thou hast set me on the rack.
           I swear 'tis better to be much abused
           Than but to know't a little.

IAGO: How now, my lord!
OTHELLO: What sense had I of her stolen hours of lust?
          I saw't not, thought it not, it harm'd not me.
          I slept the next night well, fed well, was free and merry;
          I found not Cassio's kisses on her lips.
          He that is robbed, not wanting what is stolen,
          Let him not know't, and he's not robb'd at all.
IAGO: I am sorry to hear this. (III.iii.336–345)

Othello's argument is familiar, under the heading ignorance is bliss, but what is unexpected and implies latent homosexuality is Othello's statement that he would have been happy if everyone in the army "had tasted" Desdemona's "sweet body" if he had not known it. This is followed by anger towards Iago.

OTHELLO: Villain, be sure thou prove my love a whore;
          Be sure of it. Give me the ocular proof,
          Or by the worth of mine eternal soul,
          Thou hadst been better have been born a dog
          Than answer my waked wrath! (III.iii.360–364)

The ambivalence that has overtaken Othello encourages Iago to go further, to the fabrication of the final "evidence". He becomes even bolder and reports an event that implies that Cassio and Desdemona are in fact lovers.

IAGO: I lay with Cassio lately;
          And, being troubled with a raging tooth,
          I could not sleep.
              ...
          In sleep I heard him say "Sweet Desdemona,
          Let us be wary, let us hide our loves";
          And then, sir, would he gripe and wring my hand,
          Cry "O sweet creature!" and then kiss me hard,
          As if he pluck'd up kisses by the roots
          That grew upon my lips: then laid his leg
          Over my thigh, and sigh'd, and kiss'd; and then
          Cried "Cursed fate that gave thee to the Moor!" (III.iii.413–416,
          419–426)

Then Iago once more pretends to defend Cassio:

IAGO: Nay, this was but his dream. (III.iii.427)

The jealousy Freud describes is libidinal in nature; it is the wish to receive the love of the parent. The jealousy that Shakespeare describes is purely destructive and aims to kill the parent. Iago does not wish to replace Desdemona as Othello's love but to destroy her.

Shakespeare's capacity to understand Iago's sadism comes out in Act IV. Iago not only wants Othello to murder Desdemona, but also to dictate the way she should be killed.

OTHELLO: Get me some poison, Iago; this night. I'll not expostulate with her, lest her body and beauty unprovide my mind again. This night, Iago.
IAGO: Do it not with poison, strangle her in her bed, even the bed she hath contaminated. (IV.i.204–208)

In psychoanalytic terms Othello wants to poison Desdemona, using a form of murder that is oral in nature. However, Iago wants her to be strangled on the bed in which she had sexual intercourse with Othello. Strangling can be understood as the aggressive equivalent of sexual intercourse. Iago derives pleasure from his sadistic wishes. We will learn later that Othello does not experience this sadistic pleasure.

The significance of the handkerchief

The word handkerchief occurs in Shakespeare's work thirty-six times, with twenty-seven appearances in *Othello*. It is the only play where such an object plays a central role.

We encounter the handkerchief first in Act III, scene three. Emilia has obtained Desdemona's handkerchief for her husband.

EMILIA: What handkerchief!
            Why, that the Moor first gave to Desdemona;
            That which so often you did bid me steal.
IAGO: Hast stol'n it from her?
EMILIA: No, 'faith; she let it drop by negligence.
            And, to the advantage, I, being here, took't up.
            Look, here it is.

IAGO: A good wench; give it me.
EMILIA: What will you do with 't, that you have been so earnest
To have me filch it?

IAGO
[SNATCHING IT.]:   Why, what's that to you?
EMILIA: If it be not for some purpose of import,
Give't me again: poor lady, she'll run mad
When she shall lack it.
IAGO: Be not acknown on 't; I have use for it. (III.iii.307–319)

Emilia, who is otherwise so loyal to Desdemona, betrays her here; the reason for this behaviour is never explained. She immediately regrets what she has done. In the very same scene Iago mentions the handkerchief to Othello.

IAGO: Have you not sometimes seen a handkerchief
Spotted with strawberries in your wife's hand?
OTHELLO: I gave her such a one; 'twas my first gift. (III.iii.434–436)

Iago now tells Othello that he saw Cassio wipe his beard with it, to which Othello replies:

OTHELLO: All my fond love thus do I blow to heaven.
'Tis gone.
Arise, black vengeance, from thy hollow cell!
Yield up, O love, thy crown and hearted throne
To tyrannous hate! Swell, bosom, with thy fraught,
For 'tis of aspics' tongues! (III.iii.445–450)

"Arise, black vengeance" suggests an insight: that vengeance has long laid in its "hollow cell" and "tyrannous hate" is a shade too welcome. What is missing is the expected sense of loss and depression.

The next time we encounter the handkerchief is in Act III, scene four. Othello asks for it and Desdemona cannot produce it.

OTHELLO: That's a fault. That handkerchief
Did an Egyptian to my mother give;
She was a charmer, and could almost read
The thoughts of people. She told her, while she kept it,
'Twould make her amiable and subdue my father
Entirely to her love, but if she lost it
Or made gift of it, my father's eye

> Should hold her loathed and his spirits should hunt
> After new fancies. She, dying, gave it me;
> And bid me, when my fate would have me wive,
> To give it her. I did so: and take heed on't;
> Make it a darling like your precious eye;
> To lose't or give't away were such perdition
> As nothing else could match. (III.iv.55–68)

When Desdemona hears the story, she responds: "Then would to God that I had never seen't!" (III.iv.77). At the very end of the play the fact that Desdemona cannot produce the handkerchief becomes the ultimate proof of her disloyalty and supposed whoredom.

We are not told when and with what explanation Othello gave her the handkerchief. Is she only now, when she has lost it, learning what power it has over her life, or is Othello just reminding her of what she already knows? Desdemona's response implies that this is the first time she learns of its importance. This is also the first time that we, the audience, learn why the handkerchief was important to Othello.

In theory the handkerchief is a talisman to guarantee heterosexual fidelity, but in Othello's case as long as Desdemona has it in her possession he is subservient, obedient, and loyal to her. In psychoanalytic terms the handkerchief gives the woman power over the man; it is supposed to prevent heterosexual infidelity but as it turns out the handkerchief protects the woman against the man's wish to destroy her.

In 1946 the psychoanalyst Robert Bak wrote a paper, "Masochism in paranoia", in which he showed how sublimated homosexuality could undergo regression to masochism. Bak concluded that paranoia is delusional masochism. Shakespeare had an astonishing understanding of this masochism. As long as Desdemona has the handkerchief Othello is submissive, or masochistic, in his relationship with her, but if she looses it the repressed paranoia breaks out. Iago makes her lose it and thereby facilitates Othello's outbreak of paranoia.

The final scene

Just before the terrible ending Shakespeare the dramatist gives us an exchange between Desdemona and Emilia on the subject of jealousy.

EMILIA: But I do think it is their husbands' faults
           If wives do fall: say that they slack their duties,

And pour our treasures into foreign laps,
Or else break out in peevish jealousies,
Throwing restraint upon us; or say they strike us,
Or scant our former having in despite;
Why, we have galls, and though we have some grace,
Yet have we some revenge. Let husbands know
Their wives have sense like them: they see and smell
And have their palates both for sweet and sour,
As husbands have. (IV.iii.82–92)

In the last scene between Othello and Desdemona, Shakespeare the dramatist is at his very best. Othello enters the bedroom where Desdemona is asleep. We hear in his soliloquy a state of profound ambivalence:

OTHELLO: It is the cause, it is the cause, my soul,—
Let me not name it to you, you chaste stars!—
It is the cause. Yet I'll not shed her blood;
Nor scar that whiter skin of hers than snow,
And smooth as monumental alabaster.
Yet she must die, else she'll betray more men.
Put out the light, and then put out the light:
If I quench thee, thou flaming minister,
I can again thy former light restore,
Should I repent me: but once put out thy light,
Thou cunning'st pattern of excelling nature,
I know not where is that Promethean heat
That can thy light relume. When I have pluck'd the rose,
I cannot give it vital growth again.
It must needs wither: I'll smell it on the tree.
Kissing her
Ah balmy breath, that dost almost persuade
Justice to break her sword! One more, one more.
Be thus when thou art dead, and I will kill thee,
And love thee after. (V.ii.1–19)

The thought "I will kill thee, / And love thee after" tells us how profoundly Shakespeare understood the nature of ambivalence. Once she is dead, that is, once the aggressive wishes have obtained the upper hand, love will return full force.

He will not name what he is about to do; it is too much for the "chaste stars" to hear. Desdemona's murder is compared to putting out the light, the opposite of what Prometheus did when he gave humans power over fire. Othello kills Desdemona because only after he kills her will he be able to love her again.

Before he kills Desdemona, Othello wants to make sure she has prayed and asked forgiveness for her sins; it is an expression of concern and even love at the very moment he is about to murder her.

There is one particular accusation by Othello that should give us pause.

> O perjured woman! thou dost stone my heart,
> And makest me call what I intend to do
> A murder, which I thought a sacrifice: (V.ii.63–65)

The differentiation between murder and sacrifice at that crucial moment should make us reflect. To murder is an expression of lustful hate; to sacrifice is to perform a duty and to maintain moral order. When Othello entered and kissed Desdemona he loved her but considered it his moral duty to kill her, but now that she expresses feelings for the murdered Cassio his jealousy has been aroused and the sacrifice turns into murder. Othello then refers to the handkerchief.

Desdemona awakens and Othello asks her whether she prayed at night.

OTHELLO: If you bethink yourself of any crime
            Unreconciled as yet to heaven and grace,
            Solicit for it straight.
DESDEMONA: Alas, my lord, what do you mean by that?
OTHELLO: Well, do it, and be brief; I will walk by:
            I would not kill thy unprepared spirit;
            No; heaven forfend! I would not kill thy soul.
DESDEMONA: Talk you of killing?
OTHELLO: Ay, I do.
DESDEMONA: Then heaven
            Have mercy on me!
OTHELLO: Amen, with all my heart! (V.ii.26–34)

After Othello kills Desdemona remorse sets in. He goes to the bed.

OTHELLO: Now, how dost thou look now? O ill-starr'd wench!
         Pale as thy smock! when we shall meet at compt,
         This look of thine will hurl my soul from heaven,
         And fiends will snatch at it. Cold, cold, my girl!
         Even like thy chastity. O cursed slave!
         Whip me, ye devils,
         From the possession of this heavenly sight!
         Blow me about in winds! roast me in sulphur!
         Wash me in steep-down gulfs of liquid fire!
         O Desdemona! Desdemona! dead!
         Oh! Oh! Oh! (V.ii.270–280)

Othello visualises that they will meet again "at compt", that is, on Judgment Day, and he will be hurled into hell to burn. Killing Desdemona did not bring the expected satisfaction and the aggression turned onto Othello himself.

Our analysis of *Julius Caesar* has prepared us to understand the difference between sacrifice and murder. A murder is called sacrifice when it is undertaken as a moral obligation free from feelings of aggression towards the victim. Unlike Brutus, Othello does not succeed in making Desdemona's murder a sacrifice.

How are we to understand that Othello planned to "sacrifice" Desdemona but now he has to murder her? He had hoped that, facing certain death and aware that he had found out her perfidy, Desdemona would agree that she deserved her death, making it a deserved punishment and therefore a sacrifice. Increasingly infuriated, Othello does not even grant Desdemona what he twice asked: for her to say a prayer. The scene is horrifying because, when Othello comes in he gives Desdemona a kiss and he wants her to die after a prayer to assure her salvation; he does not want to kill her soul, only her sinful body. However, all that is left of his love for her is swept away by the growing fury of his jealousy.

Othello's last soliloquy before he commits suicide, like Hamlet's last words, is addressed to posterity.

OTHELLO: Soft you; a word or two before you go.
         I have done the state some service, and they know't.
         No more of that. I pray you, in your letters,
         When you shall these unlucky deeds relate,

> Speak of me as I am; nothing extenuate,
> Nor set down aught in malice: then must you speak
> Of one that loved not wisely but too well;
> Of one not easily jealous, but being wrought
> Perplex'd in the extreme. (V.ii.334–342)

The soliloquy is psychologically addressed to jealousy. Othello believes he loved "not wisely but too well" and that he was not easily aroused to jealousy but once he yielded to it he was "Perplex'd in the extreme". The phrase was Shakespeare's coinage for what we call ambivalence.

CHAPTER FOURTEEN

The Winter's Tale: latent homosexuality and paranoia

*O*thello was written in 1604 and *The Winter's Tale* in 1610–11. Both plays have paranoia as their central theme. Shakespeare's need to return to this subject suggests that writing Othello did not succeed in liberating its author from this dangerous capacity. The two plays may add to our understanding of this aspect of Shakespeare's unconscious.

Leontes, King of Sicily, and Polixenes, King of Bohemia, grew up together as children. Polixenes has been Leontes' guest for nine months and as the play opens he wishes to return home. In the first act Camillo, a lord in attendance on Leontes, introduces the theme of the play.

CAMILLO: They were trained together in their childhoods; and
there rooted betwixt them then such an affection,
which cannot choose but branch now. Since their
more mature dignities and royal necessities made
separation of their society, their encounters,
though not personal, have been royally attorneyed
with interchange of gifts, letters, loving
embassies; that they have seemed to be together,
though absent, shook hands, as over a vast, and

215

> embraced, as it were, from the ends of opposed
> winds. The heavens continue their loves! (*The Winter's Tale*,
> I.i.25–35)

This happiness does not come true because of Leontes' paranoid fear
that Polixenes had a sexual relationship with Hermione, Leontes' wife.
Recalling Freud's classification of different types of jealousy, discussed
in the chapter on *Othello*, we conclude that Leontes' jealousy is of the
delusional type.

Intense desexualised love relationships between children of the
same gender are not uncommon. Shakespeare himself described such
a relationship between Helena and Hermione in *A Midsummer Night's
Dream*.

Polixenes is ready to return home when Leontes, like many hosts,
is trying to detain his guest longer. He fails and asks his wife to try.
Hermione gives her guest only one choice: whether to stay as a guest or
as a prisoner. Polixenes prefers to be treated as a guest. The encounter
between them is rich in connotations.

HERMIONE: ... You'll stay?
POLIXENES: I may not, verily.
HERMIONE: Verily!
             You put me off with limber vows; but I,
             Though you would seek to unsphere the stars with oaths,
             Should yet say 'Sir, no going.' Verily,
             You shall not go: a lady's 'Verily' 's
             As potent as a lord's. Will you go yet?
             Force me to keep you as a prisoner,
             Not like a guest; so you shall pay your fees
             When you depart, and save your thanks. How say you?
             My prisoner? or my guest? by your dread 'Verily,'
             One of them you shall be.
POLIXENES: Your guest, then, madam:
             To be your prisoner should import offending;
             Which is for me less easy to commit
             Than you to punish. (I.ii.45–59)

We should note that Hermione does not invite Polixenes to stay as the
wife of the host but converts it into a combat between the two of them.

She speaks and is effective in her own name and symbolically Polixenes has already become her prisoner.

The dialogue is elegant. Is Hermione joking? Is she really threatening a guest who is also a king with imprisonment? Is he playing at yielding or really scared of becoming a prisoner? Is she promising him a sadomasochistic relationship, with him obedient to her will? Did Shakespeare convey that there is more in the relationship between the two than meets the eye? The two may not be lovers, as Leontes suspects, but they definitely have their own relationship. From clinical experience we know that paranoia is all too often based on a kernel of truth that undergoes a quantitative change in the mind of the paranoid individual.

We can stop to admire Shakespeare's technique. Leontes' paranoia has been dormant since his guest arrived nine months ago; why does it break out now? Is it because Polixenes was persuaded to stay not when Leontes asked him but rather when Hermione spoke to him? Did Leontes become jealous of his wife's success? Or is it because Polixenes is threatening the equilibrium established by the three of them by making plans to leave?

LEONTES: Is he won yet?
HERMIONE: He'll stay my lord.
LEONTES: At my request he would not.
            Hermione, my dearest, thou never spokest
            To better purpose. (I.ii.86–89)

Hermione asks her husband "Never?" and gets the response she was hoping for, that the first time she spoke so well was when she agreed to his proposal or marriage.

HERMIONE: 'Tis grace indeed.
            Why, lo you now, I have spoke to the purpose twice:
            The one for ever earn'd a royal husband;
            The other for some while a friend. (I.ii.105–108)

We learn about Leontes' paranoia from an aside.

LEONTES: [*Aside*] Too hot, too hot!
            To mingle friendship far is mingling bloods.

> I have *tremor cordis* on me: my heart dances;
> But not for joy; not joy. This entertainment
> May a free face put on, derive a liberty
> From heartiness, from bounty, fertile bosom,
> And well become the agent; 't may, I grant;
> But to be paddling palms and pinching fingers,
> As now they are, and making practised smiles,
> As in a looking-glass, and then to sigh, as 'twere
> The mort o' the deer; O, that is entertainment
> My bosom likes not, nor my brows! (I.ii.108–119)

Hermione is pregnant, and at the very moment she succeeds in making Polixenes stay on as a guest Leontes becomes convinced that the two are lovers. Furthermore, he believes the child she is carrying is not his child but the bastard of Polixenes and Hermione. We owe to Freud the insight that paranoia can express repressed homosexuality. Leontes is himself sexually attracted to his visiting childhood friend and represses this wish by projecting it onto his wife. We are led to understand that Hermione must have become pregnant at the very time Polixenes' visit began, and now he is ready to leave as she is due to deliver. The suspicion is aroused in Leontes that the child is not his but Polixenes' offspring.

On psychoanalytic grounds we can assume that the pregnancy was an attempt to protect his heterosexuality against the homosexual temptations aroused by this long visit and the very defense failed and turned into the opposite: a paranoid suspicion. From the sonnets we know that Shakespeare was troubled by the same suspicion: that his male lover and the dark lady established their own sexual liaison. The invitation to stay even longer must have intensified the homosexual desire. To dilute this desire Leontes asks his wife to participate but when the guest yields to his wife rather than to his own invitation the hitherto latent paranoia is confirmed in Leontes' mind.

For Leontes a *ménage à trois* has been established; he has both the heterosexual relationship with his wife and his homosexual wishes for Polixenes satisfied. However, clinical psychoanalysis has taught us that the two tendencies do not happily live with each other for a long period of time. When Hermione asks the visitor to stay longer she is acting in a way familiar to us from the behaviour of some women who discover their husbands to be homosexual. The wife agrees in principle that her husband can have a male lover but it is the male lover, typically, who will not tolerate the dual relationship.

Shakespeare offers another hint of what may have caused Leontes' suspicion. Recalling his courtship of Hermione, Leontes says she only spoke as well as in persuading Polixenes to stay once before.

LEONTES: Why, that was when
            Three crabbed months had sour'd themselves to death,
            Ere I could make thee open thy white hand
            And clap thyself my love: then didst thou utter
            'I am yours for ever'. (I.ii.101–105)

The three months were "crabbed" and "sour'd themselves to death" because Hermione took time to say yes to his marriage proposal, and we note that it took time to open her "white hand". By contrast, she extends this hand to Polixenes.

As soon as Polixenes agrees to stay Hermione interrogates him on the childhood activities of the two kings. She wants to know their "tricks" and assumes they were "pretty lordings" when they were children. Polixenes seems to be on the defensive, as he reassures her.

POLIXENES: We were, fair queen,
            Two lads that thought there was no more behind
            But such a day to-morrow as to-day,
            And to be boy eternal.
HERMIONE: Was not my lord the verier wag o' the two?
POLIXENES: We were as twinn'd lambs that did frisk i' the sun,
            And bleat the one at the other: what we changed
            Was innocence for innocence; we knew not
            The doctrine of ill-doing, nor dream'd
            That any did. Had we pursued that life,
            And our weak spirits ne'er been higher rear'd
            With stronger blood, we should have answer'd heaven
            Boldly 'not guilty;' (I.ii.62–74)

Polixenes is defending a state of desexualised innocence but there is nevertheless intense love between the two boys. In the search to refind this innocence, Polixenes has spent nine months as a guest in Sicily, leaving his own family and kingdom behind. The plea is not guilty but the accusation is not specified. Polixenes can only mean that there was no sexual relationship between the two boys. Since nobody has raised such an accusation we surmise that Polixenes too is defending himself against an inner accusation of childhood homosexuality.

Hermione may be innocent of the charge of adultery but she sexualises Polixenes' declaration of innocence.

HERMIONE: By this we gather
             You have tripp'd since.
POLIXENES: O my most sacred lady!
             Temptations have since then been born to's; for
             In those unfledged days was my wife a girl;
             Your precious self had then not cross'd the eyes
             Of my young play-fellow.
HERMIONE: Grace to boot!
             Of this make no conclusion, lest you say
             Your queen and I are devils: yet go on;
             The offences we have made you do we'll answer,
             If you first sinn'd with us and that with us
             You did continue fault and that you slipp'd not
             With any but with us. (I.ii.76–86)

Polixenes said nothing that implied that the two wives are devils, but Hermione seizes the opportunity to inquire into the possibilities of premarital or extramarital relationships. Has Polixenes aroused sexual wishes in her? Skillfully, Shakespeare suggests such a possibility.

Hermione understands that the protestation of innocence implies that the boys had no sexual relationship with each other but she is guilty of a non sequitur. Innocence of homosexuality does not mean that the two had no premarital sexual experiences. An implicit sexual play between the two is taking place.

Still within the same scene, only a few lines later, Leontes tells the audience (in an aside), that his jealousy has been aroused. The fact that Shakespeare begrudged Leontes the time to develop his jealousy has often been criticised, but we must remember that in *Othello* Shakespeare had given us a play that centred on this very theme: the slow development of jealousy. It is therefore understandable that he had no wish to repeat this part of the psychological journey.

The paranoia of Leontes becomes evident when he suspects his friend and wife of "paddling palms and pinching fingers", that is, using handshakes to confirm their alliance, and then "making practiced smiles" as a way of communicating secretly with one another. Leontes rambles, as fits a man whose mind is in disarray. He compares himself to a hunted deer, "mort o' the deer". The Variorum edition explains that this is a hunting phrase giving notice that the deer is run down.

LEONTES: There have been,
            Or I am much deceived, cuckolds ere now;
            And many a man there is, even at this present,
            Now while I speak this, holds his wife by the arm,
            That little thinks she has been sluiced in's absence
            And his pond fish'd by his next neighbour, by
            Sir Smile, his neighbour: nay, there's comfort in't
            Whiles other men have gates and those gates open'd,
            As mine, against their will. (I.ii.190–198)

This is the only place in Shakespeare's work where "sluiced" is used in alluding to sexual intercourse. The original metaphor "his pond fish'd by his next neighbor" also appears only here.

Because of Freud's work our awareness for a child's feelings have become more sensitive. It is likely that Shakespeare's audience would not have thought that this father was insensitive to what effect his words have on his son. Even if we allow for this cultural difference it remains true that Shakespeare has done nothing to make this jealousy acceptable to us. Leontes is not a man evoking sympathy in the audience.

As Leontes' madness intensifies, a dread of derealisation overcomes him together with a greater dependency on Hermione.

LEONTES: Why, then the world and all that's in't is nothing;
            The covering sky is nothing; Bohemia nothing;
            My wife is nothing; nor nothing have these nothings,
            If this be nothing. (I.ii.293–296)

The paranoid suspicion is so terrible because Hermione has become so important to him that without her a sense of nothingness takes over. In psychoanalytic language, what Shakespeare is telling us is that when love is lost to paranoia life loses its meaning.

Camillo is Polixenes' cup bearer and he agrees to poison him.

CAMILLO: I must believe you, sir:
            I do; and will fetch off Bohemia for't;
            Provided that, when he's removed, your highness
            Will take again your queen as yours at first,
            Even for your son's sake; and thereby for sealing
            The injury of tongues in courts and kingdoms
            Known and allied to yours.
LEONTES: Thou dost advise me
            Even so as I mine own course have set down:
            I'll give no blemish to her honour, none. (I.ii.333–341)

What Shakespeare is presenting is another strange pact between two men. Camillo will poison Polixenes provided Leontes restores his relationship with Hermione. Camillo plays a role opposite that of Iago. In *Hamlet* the ghost admonishes Prince Hamlet not to take action against his mother but to "leave her to heaven" (I.v.86). Both the ghost and Camillo are afraid of a homosexual situation such as the one that took place in the relationship between Othello and Iago, the part of Shakespeare that feared and suspected women.

Polixenes meets Camillo. He has noticed the change in Leontes' attitude and in Camillo's demeanour and asks Camillo the reason, saying, "Your changed complexions are to me a mirror" (I.ii.381). Camillo then confesses, "I am appointed him to murder you" (I.ii.412); the murder is avoided and the two escape Leontes' realm.

Even though Leontes has no doubt about his wife's infidelity he consults the oracle of Apollo at Delphi.

LEONTES: Though I am satisfied and need no more
            Than what I know, yet shall the oracle
            Give rest to the minds of others. (II.i.189–191)

Until the oracle's verdict arrives Hermione is in prison, and there she gives birth to a daughter. She is visited by Paulina, wife of one of the king's counselors, who wants to present the baby to the king with the hope that the sight of the baby will soften his heart. It is likely that naïve people would share Paulina's belief that the baby would soften the king's heart.

PAULINA: Behold, my lords,
            Although the print be little, the whole matter
            And copy of the father, eye, nose, lip,
            The trick of's frown, his forehead, nay, the valley,
            The pretty dimples of his chin and cheek, his smiles,
            The very mould and frame of hand, nail, finger. (II.ii.97–102)

The effort fails and the king calls the child a bastard. "This brat is none of mine; / It is the issue of Polixenes" (II.ii.92–93). The madness of the king increases. He accuses his councilors, "You are liars all" (II.ii.146). Regaining a measure of sanity, the king pardons Paulina but orders the newly born infant to be banished:

LEONTES: Mark and perform it, see'st thou! for the fail
            Of any point in't shall not only be
            Death to thyself but to thy lewd-tongued wife,
            Whom for this time we pardon. We enjoin thee,
            As thou art liege-man to us, that thou carry
            This female bastard hence and that thou bear it
            To some remote and desert place quite out
            Of our dominions, and that there thou leave it,
            Without more mercy, to its own protection
            And favour of the climate. As by strange fortune
            It came to us, I do in justice charge thee,
            On thy soul's peril and thy body's torture,
            That thou commend it strangely to some place
            Where chance may nurse or end it. Take it up. (II.ii.170–183)

At this point it seems that Shakespeare has adopted a page from Sophocles' *Oedipus Rex*.

The reader will have noticed that I have suggested a number of reasons why Leontes disowned Perdita. In psychoanalysis we often discover numerous reasons working together to bring about a psychic change. This process is called overdetermination and means that a behaviour has more than one cause.

As we enter Act III, scene two the trial of Hermione takes place. She is accused of adultery with Polixenes and of plotting to murder Leontes.

HERMIONE: For Polixenes,
With whom I am accused, I do confess
I loved him as in honour he required,
With such a kind of love as might become
A lady like me, with a love even such,
So and no other, as yourself commanded:
Which not to have done I think had been in me
Both disobedience and ingratitude

...

Sir, spare your threats:
The bug which you would fright me with I seek.
To me can life be no commodity:
The crown and comfort of my life, your favour,
I do give lost; for I do feel it gone,
But know not how it went. My second joy
And first-fruits of my body, from his presence
I am barr'd, like one infectious. My third comfort
Starr'd most unluckily, is from my breast,
The innocent milk in its most innocent mouth,
Haled out to murder: myself on every post
Proclaimed a strumpet: with immodest hatred. (III.ii.62–69, 92–103)

Hermione's declaration is deeply moving. She has lost the love of her husband, her reputation, and the possibility of nursing her baby. She does not understand why because she knows nothing of the force of the unconscious. The relationship of Hermione and Polixenes reminds me of the relationship between Desdemona and Cassio in *Othello*. In both plays the paranoid man cannot accept that a man and a woman can have a relationship that is close but not sexual.

We come now to what may well be, from a psychoanalytic point of view, the high point of this play, or, to put it differently, the point where the special psychoanalytic detective work must be fully employed. The messengers have returned with the verdict of Apollo's oracle. Shakespeare was apparently not aware of the ambiguous language in which this oracle was accustomed to speak; the message is explicit. The queen is chaste and Polixenes not guilty. Camillo too is innocent and Leontes a jealous tyrant. The king's response is as expected from a paranoid person: "There is no truth at all I' the oracle" (III.ii.141). At this point a messenger arrives announcing that Mamillius, Leontes' and Hermione's son, has just died. Hermione faints and is considered dead by her ladies, and a marked change in the behaviour of the king takes place. Paranoia is like a bad dream that takes place in a waking state; when it is over it is similar to awakening from a troubling dream. A recovery from the paranoia has occurred and the king experiences remorse for persecuting the innocent queen.

When I first read this passage I was puzzled and wondered how Shakespeare, who showed such a deep feeling for what it is like to suffer from paranoia, could suddenly make the king awake from it as if it had only been a bad dream. However, reading the passage numerous times, it dawned on me what Shakespeare is telling us in a coded form: the death of the son is the cure for the father's paranoia. Translated into Shakespeare's biography, he may well be telling us that Hamnet's death cured his paranoid feelings. Because I myself had difficulty in accepting this interpretation I assume that it will cause difficulty to other psychoanalysts and will be rejected by those not familiar with the working of the unconscious. What my hypothesis implies (and it cannot be anything else but a hypothesis), is that Leontes unconsciously feared the hostility of his son, who would kill him like Oedipus killed his father Laius. With the death of his son this danger is past and the entire paranoid structure collapsed.

Act Three does not end at this point. Baby Perdita, considered a bastard child by the mad king, is taken to a barren seashore of Bohemia either to die or to be picked up by the proverbial shepherd. The fact that Shakespeare gave a seashore to landlocked Bohemia has often been commented on, but what is interesting from a psychoanalytic point is a comment of the shepherd, made out of context as he enters the play.

SHEPHERD: I would there were no age between ten and three-and-twenty,
             or that youth would sleep out the rest; for there is
             nothing in the between but getting wenches with child, wronging
             the ancientry, stealing, fighting .... (III.iii.58–61)

Perdita was not sired by an immature young man, but such an early and unwelcome pregnancy was the likely cause of Shakespeare's own marriage.

In Act IV we find ourselves in a different world. The act opens with the entrance of Time as a chorus. Time proclaims that it has decided to use its wings and slide across sixteen years. As if skipping ahead so many years were not enough, another and deeper change has taken place in this act. This is how the new Variorum Edition of 1898 (reissued in 1966) explains the change.

> During the first three Acts the interest of the play is mainly tragic; the scene is densely crowded with incidents; the action hurried, abrupt, almost spasmodic; the style quick and sharp, flashing off point after point in brief, sinewy strokes; ... the insane fury of the King, the noble agony of the Queen, the enthusiasm of the Court in her behalf, and the King's violence toward both them and her, ... Far otherwise the latter half of the play. Here the anticipations proper to a long, leisurely winter evening are fully met; the general effect is soothing and composing; .... (Furness, 1966: p. 153).

Harold Bloom has singled out Act IV, scene four as one of Shakespeare's most amazing scenes. It is a long scene of 840 lines of which the following is typical.

PERDITA: Here's flowers for you;
Hot lavender, mints, savoury, marjoram;
The marigold, that goes to bed wi' the sun
And with him rises weeping: these are flowers
Of middle summer, and I think they are given
To men of middle age. You're very welcome. (*The Winter's Tale*, IV.iv.103–108)

Florizel jokingly protests being strewn with flowers like a corpse, to which Perdita replies:

PERDITA: No, like a bank for love to lie and play on;
Not like a corpse; or if, not to be buried,
But quick and in mine arms. (IV.iv.130–132)

Perdita is so captivating, so open and direct in her sexuality, that she compensates us for her father's morbidity. We understand now why a hiatus of sixteen years was necessary between Act III and Act IV: Perdita had to grow up. Shakespeare often saw the creative writer as a kind of magician and in Act IV he plays this role. The latent homosexual relationship between Leontes and Polixenes took a paranoid turn, with disastrous results. Act IV is an attempt to undo the damage in the next generation as the relationship is heterosexualised by the love between their children, Perdita and Florizel.

One question needs to be answered: How could Hermione wish to be reconciled to Leontes after all that he did and after sixteen years of separation? Greenblatt (p. 144) offers a biographical explanation, surmising that the play was written at a time when Shakespeare was planning to give up acting and writing and return to Stratford to redeem the position of honour that his father had all but lost. Shakespeare may have considered reconciliation with his wife. His will, written in 1616 and leaving practically nothing to her, shows that the reconciliation failed. By that time Shakespeare's love had found an outlet in his love for his daughter. *The Winter's Tale*, *King Lear* and *The Tempest* all deal with the father-daughter relationship. The death of Leontes' and Hermione's' son, Mamillius, which cured Leontes' paranoia, could represent the impact of Hamnet's death on Shakespeare's homosexuality and paranoid tendencies.

The fact that Shakespeare wrote two plays on paranoia that are based, in our interpretation, on a denied homosexual tendency, suggests that as a self-therapy *Othello* did not achieve its purpose. The *Othello* model is to let the fictional character kill his innocent wife and then himself, thereby freeing his creator from such a fate. Had *The Winter's Tale* ended after the third act the model would have been similar. It is the fourth act that provides a different model with a happy ending. The *Othello* model gives the audience a similar opportunity as paranoid tendencies in the audience are put to rest by the play's conclusion. The end of *The Winter's Tale* is psychologically less of a catharsis for both author and audience and in our estimate *Othello* ranks higher as a work of literature than the later play.

PART VI

THE HOMOSEXUAL COMPROMISE

CHAPTER FIFTEEN

The Merchant of Venice: a portrayal of masochistic homosexuality

For *The Merchant of Venice* to be included in this book I had to overcome a feeling analogous to what psychoanalysis calls countertransference. Countertransference is defined as a situation in which the analyst's feelings and attitude towards a patient are derived from earlier situations in the analyst's life that have been displaced onto the patient. All the other plays I approached with inherent curiousity and a wish to understand them in psychoanalytic terms; this play's powerful anti-Semitism renders this more difficult. It threatens my idealisation of Shakespeare. I had to overcome a strong resistance expressed in the wish to skip this play. The feeling is not unconscious and strictly speaking not a countertransference, but it did require some extra energy not to be repelled by the play's blatant anti-Semitism. In psychoanalysis the countertransference has to be faced and, if possible, overcome if the analysis is to be successful; an analogous process will have to be undertaken not only by me but also by the readers of this chapter. Shylock is not just a Jewish moneylender; he is the Jew incarnate. We are in Act IV, scene one.

GRATIANO: O learned judge! Mark, Jew: a learned judge.
SHYLOCK: I take this offer then: pay the bond thrice,
And let the Christian go.
BASSANIO: Here is the money.
PORTIA: Soft.
The Jew shall have all justice; soft, no haste;
He shall have nothing but the penalty.
GRATIANO: O Jew, an upright judge, a learned judge!
PORTIA: Therefore prepare thee to cut off the flesh.
Shed thou no blood; nor cut thou less nor more
But just a pound of flesh. If thou tak'st more,
Or less than a just pound, be it but so much
As makes it light or heavy in the substance
Or the division of the twentieth part
Of one poor scruple—nay, if the scale do turn
But in the estimation of a hair,
Thou diest, and all thy goods are confiscate.
GRATIANO: A second Daniel; a Daniel, Jew!
Now, infidel, I have thee on the hip.
PORTIA: Why doth the Jew pause? Take thy forfeiture.
SHYLOCK: Give me my principal, and let me go. (*The Merchant of Venice*,
IV.i.319–332)

As if to add further insult, Gratiano is calling the judge Daniel, an Old Testament figure whom Shylock is expected to respect. Through the whole procedure, Shylock is never called by his name; he is always referred to as "Jew", thus I infer he stands for all Jews.

It is difficult for us to accept that Shakespeare, who was so superior in insight and in understanding the unconscious, shared the popular prejudice against Jews and that we cannot place him among those who helped in the struggle to create a more tolerant world. Christopher Marlowe's Barnabus in *The Jew of Malta* is a mass murderer while Shylock is consumed by his wishes for revenge towards one person, Antonio.

It is a historical fact that the Nazis used this play to persuade the German public to exterminate the Jews, but if we are to succeed in arriving at a psychoanalytic interpretation we must put this knowledge on some psychological backburner. I had to force myself not to think about this aspect of the play to arrive at the psychoanalytic interpretation. It was the source of special gratification when I could formulate the analytic interpretation.

What is to be said about this play from a psychoanalytic point of view? The pound of flesh that Shylock demands makes him, at least in the unconscious of the audience, the castrator, so the play is about the re-awakened castration anxiety. In Freud's thinking this castration anxiety brings about the end of the period of infantile sexuality and ushers in the latency period, which ordinarily lasts between the ages of six and thirteen years. The play re-arouses it. Portia, a woman dressed as a man, saves Antonio, who is in danger of the loss of a pound of flesh. She is therefore a masculine woman or, in psychoanalytic language, a phallic woman, saving Antonio from the castrating Shylock. Had *The Merchant of Venice* been a fairy tale, Antonio, freed from the castration anxiety, should have married Portia out of gratitude, but in the play she marries his friend Bassanio. All this goes on unconsciously, a man freed from his castration anxiety by a woman typically remains not only grateful but also submissive to her. It seems that in this play Shakespeare experimented with this idea but decided against it, leaving Antonio without a mate.

It is the relationship between the two men and Portia that differentiates the play from the clinically more common event of a woman helping a man overcome his castration anxiety.

We turn to the relationship between Antonio and Bassanio.

ANTONIO: In sooth I know not why I am so sad.
           It wearies me, you say it wearies you;
           But how I caught it, found it, or came by it,
           What stuff 'tis made of, whereof it is born,
           I am to learn.
           And such a want-wit sadness makes of me,
           That I have much ado to know myself. (I.i.1–7)

A man who does not understand himself, who is depressed but does not know why and a man who has "much ado" to know himself is not a medieval sinner worried about punishment in hell but a modern man. We can go even further and say he is a man ready for psychoanalysis.

In these opening lines Shakespeare tells us that Antonio is depressed but also invites us to join him in the wish to know himself. When his friends try to guess what makes him sad, Antonio answers with one of Shakespeare's best-known metaphors, repeated in many plays, that life is nothing but a stage on which everyone plays their assigned role.

ANTONIO: I hold the world but as the world, Gratiano;
A stage where every man must play a part,
And mine a sad one. (I.i.77–79)

Writing plays made Shakespeare feel that life itself was a stage and every individual was an actor in a play written by someone else.

In 1917 Freud published his important essay "Mourning and melancholia", which explains Antonio's remark. In mourning, the mourner knows what he has lost and the work of mourning comes to an end. In melancholia the loss is unconscious and therefore the work of mourning cannot be done. Antonio has just helped Bassanio to reach the woman he loves at great cost to himself but Antonio does not know consciously that he is mourning the loss of Bassanio, for whom he has a repressed homosexual love.

The 3,000 ducats obtained from Shylock were to be spent by Bassanio to win Portia and it is for these ducats that Antonio offered a pound of his flesh as a surety. Once more, in psychoanalytic language Antonio exposed himself to castration anxiety so that Bassanio could marry Portia without anxiety. Antonio pays for Bassanio's heterosexuality.

The task of the creative playwright is not to shock us by revealing the hidden homosexuality outright and yet to make us aware of it. It is the veiled language that accomplishes this contradictory aim.

ANTONIO: I pray you, good Bassanio, let me know it,
And if it stand as you yourself still do
Within the eye of honour, be assured
My purse, my person, my extremest means
Lie all unlocked to your occasions. (I.i.134–138)

Antonio is putting all he has at Bassanio's disposal so he can go and win the woman he loves. If we wish we can interpret the passage as friendship between Antonio and Bassanio but reading it carefully should make us suspect that more is involved. "My purse, my person, my extremest means, / Lie all unlock'd to your occasions" (I.i.137–138) sounds too passionate, too submissive, and too eager to be only words of friendship between two men, and then comes the offer to let Shylock have his pound of flesh if the loan cannot be repaid. We are dealing with submissive homosexuality. What sets the play in motion is the masochistic homosexual love of Antonio for Bassanio. The love is masochistic because Antonio is paying to make it possible for Bassanio to have a heterosexual relationship that will remove him further from a homosexual relationship with him. We cannot deny Antonio nobility. In spite of his love for Bassanio he is helping him reach the woman he loves. Shakespeare must have known what psychoanalytic work with homosexuals has demonstrated: that many homosexuals are particularly attracted to heterosexual men, or at least those who appear to be so. Antonio never asks why Bassanio needs so much money or whether he is pretending to Portia that he is rich when he is not. We gain the impression that Antonio is more eager to give the money than Bassanio is to receive it.

Psychoanalysis assumes that neither Shakespeare nor his audience are consciously aware of my interpretation but what remains so admirable in the work of great artists is that they know how to communicate unconscious knowledge in such a way that it becomes "almost" conscious, but without it becoming so conscious that it evokes anxiety in the author or audience. To push the material upward without crossing this line is what Freud called "ars poetica".

With the main work of interpretation behind us I now draw attention to some other interesting aspects of this play.

As to the historical facts, Greenblatt's book reminds us that in 1290 the Jews were expelled from England. In Shakespeare's time there were no Jews practicing their religion in England, but stories about Jews were alive in English folklore. They were feared because of the blood libel and their supposed bisexuality. Jewish men were believed to menstruate. In 1589, when Shakespeare was near the beginning of his career, Christopher Marlowe had written a popular play, *The Jew of Malta*, in which the Jew Barnabas kills sick people with pleasure and poisons wells. We also learn from Greenblatt that Shakespeare lifted the whole plot of *The Merchant of Venice* from the Italian Ser Giovanni's *Il Pecorone* (Greenblatt, 2004: p. 290), published in Milan in 1558.

In this Italian version a merchant of Venice called Ansaldo adopts his orphaned grandson Giannetto. The grandson falls in love with a Belmont woman who tricks men into spending the night with her by giving them drugged wine and Giannetto loses his ship to the lady. Eventually Ansaldo has to borrow money from a Jew who demands a pound of flesh as assurance for the loan. In this version the woman playing Portia's role is as an openly castrating woman, while in Shakespeare's version Portia exhibits this quality only in relation to Shylock. What appears in Ser Giovanni's version as a family relationship between grandfather and grandson, it is transformed by Shakespeare into a thinly disguised homosexual love between Antonio and Bassanio. Greenblatt adds the important observation that Shakespeare's father, like Shylock, was a usurer.

The change that Shakespeare introduced was ambivalence toward the Jew. Ambivalence makes possible a more nuanced and interesting character than the portrayal of a hateful man. If we include the information that for Shakespeare the usurer unconsciously represented his father, the ambivalence is understandable.

SHYLOCK: Signior Antonio, many a time and oft
            In the Rialto you have rated me
            About my moneys and my usances.
            Still have I borne it with a patient shrug
            For suff'rance is the badge of all our tribe.
            You call me misbeliever, cut-throat dog,
            And spit upon my Jewish gaberdine,
            And all for use of that which is mine own.
            Well then, it now appears you need my help.
            Go to, then, you come to me, and you say,
            'Shylock, we would have moneys'—you say so,
            You that did void your rheum upon my beard,
            And foot me as you spurn a stranger cur
            Over your threshold: moneys is your suit.
            What should I say to you? Should I not say
            'Hath a dog money? is it possible
            A cur can lend three thousand ducats?' Or
            Shall I bend low, and in a bondman's key,
            With bated breath and whisp'ring humbleness,
            Say this:
            'Fair sir, you spit on me on Wednesday last,
            You spurned me such a day, another time
            You called me dog: and for these courtesies
            I'll lend you thus much moneys'. (*The Merchant of Venice*,
            I.iii.98–121)

Shylock is willing to lend the money if he can legally murder Antonio and Antonio is so submissive to Bassanio that he accepts the deal.

SHYLOCK: This kindness will I show.
                 Go with me to a notary, seal me there
                 Your single bond, and, in a merry sport,
                 If you repay me not on such a day,
                 In such a place, such sum or sums as are
                 Express'd in the condition, let the forfeit
                 Be nominated for an equal pound
                 Of your fair flesh, to be cut off and taken
                 In what part of your body pleaseth me.
ANTONIO: Content, in faith! I'll seal to such a bond,
                 And say there is much kindness in the Jew.
BASSANIO: You shall not seal to such a bond for me;
                 I'll rather dwell in my necessity. (I.iii.135–148)

In Act III, scene one, Shylock is speaking to Salarino and Solanio; his speech, one of the best-known passages from this play, has often been used to argue that Shakespeare was not anti-Semitic.

SHYLOCK: He hath disgraced me, and hindered me half a million, laughed at
                 my losses, mocked at my gains, scorned my nation, thwarted my
                 bargains, cooled my friends, heated mine enemies—and what's
                 his reason? I am a Jew. Hath not a Jew eyes? Hath not a Jew hands,
                 organs, dimensions, senses, affections, passions? Fed with the same
                 food, hurt with the same weapons, subject to the same diseases,
                 healed by the same means, warmed and cooled by the same winter
                 and summer as a Christian is? If you prick us, do we not bleed? If
                 you tickle us, do we not laugh? if you poison us, do we not die?
                 And if you wrong us, shall we not revenge? (III.i.43–52)

The theme of the three caskets

As early as 1910 Otto Rank, then one of Freud's most gifted disciples, noted that Portia makes what we call a Freudian slip. Portia is obliged by her father's will to take as a husband the man who chooses the right casket. In that portion of the play, the clever Portia manages to get the man she loves in spite of her father's restrictions.

PORTIA: I could teach you
              How to choose right, but then I am forsworn.

> So will I never be. So may you miss me;
> But if you do, you'll make me wish a sin,
> That I had been forsworn. Beshrew your eyes!
> They have o'erlook'd me and divided me:
> One half of me is yours, the other half yours—
> Mine own, I would say: but if mine, then yours,
> And so all yours. (III.ii.10–18)

Consciously, Portia meant to say, "half of me is yours" to convey to Bassanio that she was already half-conquered, but her unconscious prevailed and made her say that the other half was also his. Shakespeare deliberately wrote these lines. He may not have called it the intrusion of unconscious thinking into consciousness but in order to write these lines he must have known that a slip of the tongue expresses an unconscious wish.

The other psychoanalytic work commenting on *The Merchant of Venice* is Freud's 1913 essay "The theme of the three caskets". In Freud's interpretation the choice of one of the caskets is a disguise for its opposite, namely lack of choice or necessity. He concludes that the three caskets stand for "the three inevitable relations that a man has with a woman— the woman who bears him, the woman who is his mate and the woman who destroys him" (Freud, 1913: p. 301). (Inevitable here means not by choice.) These women are mother herself, the beloved who is chosen after her pattern, and lastly mother earth. Freud concludes: "But it is in vain that an old man yearns for the love of the woman as he had it first from his mother; the third of the Fates alone, the silent Goddess of Death, will take him into her arms" (Freud, 1913: p. 301). Freud's essay cannot be called an interpretation of Shakespeare's play; rather, he uses Shakespeare's text to makes an observation of his own.

According to Freud, the second woman, the beloved, is never chosen just for her excellence, as lovers claim, but because "every finding is refinding" (Freud, 1905a: p. 202). Unconsciously, the loved woman represents the refound mother. Today we know that the problem is more complex. The refound beloved need not be only the mother; she could be a sister, a grandmother and at times even the father. With the third woman, Mother Earth, Freud does something strange. In Western culture death was typically a man, the "grim reaper", but Freud feminised and libidinised death. Death is a goddess and she takes the dead man in her arms. Psychoanalytic clinical experience has shown that those who fear death do not experience it as a benevolent mother figure but rather, as Hamlet did, as a nightmare danger.

There is yet another scene that deserves our attention. Shylock is defending his request for the pound of flesh before the doge of Venice.

> SHYLOCK: I have possessed your grace of what I purpose,
> And by our holy Sabaoth have I sworn
> To have the due and forfeit of my bond.
> If you deny it, let the danger light
> Upon your charter and your city's freedom!
> You'll ask me why I rather choose to have
> A weight of carrion flesh than to receive
> Three thousand ducats. I'll not answer that—
> But say it is my humour: is it answered?
> What if my house be troubled with a rat,
> And I be pleased to give ten thousand ducats
> To have it baned? What, are you answered yet? (*The Merchant of Venice*, IV.i.35–46)

Shylock swears by Sabaoth, the Hebrew term for the god of hosts, and then speaks to the doge in a threatening way that one cannot imagine any Jew using: "If you deny it, let the danger light. / Upon your charter and your city's freedom". It is unlikely that the future of the powerful state of Venice will be endangered if Shylock does not receive his bond. Shakespeare thus gives Shylock a boldness one cannot imagine the playwright could have ever displayed to his own queen. Despised as Shylock is, in this subtle way he also represents a republican ego ideal to Shakespeare.

Would any doge of the Serenissima let Shylock fulfill his bond? Would he not immediately condemn him for attempted murder? Would the Venetian population allow him to kill Antonio without Shylock being killed by a mob? Would the Jewish community of Venice allow Shylock to bring about a pogrom on the whole community? Dramatically the impotence of the doge is necessary because otherwise Portia could not have the opportunity to exhibit her sagacity.

> SHYLOCK: Some men there are love not a gaping pig;
> Some that are mad if they behold a cat;
> And others, when the bagpipe sings i'the nose,

> Cannot contain their urine: for affection,
> Masters oft passion, sways it to the mood
> Of what it likes or loathes. Now for your answer:
> As there is no firm reason to be rendered
> Why he cannot abide a gaping pig,
> Why he a harmless necessary cat,
> Why he, a woollen bagpipe, but of force
> Must yield to such inevitable shame
> As to offend, himself being offended:
> So can I give no reason, nor I will not,
> More than a lodged hate and a certain loathing
> I bear Antonio, that I follow thus
> A losing suit against him. Are you answered? (IV.i.47–62)

What we hear, to our astonishment, is that Shakespeare gave Shylock an awareness not only that neuroses exist but also the conviction that they have a right to exist. Shylock's first example, the man who does not love a "gaping pig", is, in our current language, a reference to pigs as phobic objects. This is a strange statement coming from such a self-conscious Jew. Another phobia mentioned concerns cats and the third example, a strange one, refers to men who lose urinary control when they hear bagpipe music. This is a bizarre reference and could refer to a better-known loss of urinary control at night, a common malady called enuresis. Logically the argument has no validity: the wish for a pound of flesh is in no way analogous to either of the two cited phobias or the loss of urinary control.

A further irony is that Jessica, raised by the Jew Shylock, turns out to be an expert on Greek mythology when she is with her lover.

LORENZO: The moon shines bright. In such a night as this,
            When the sweet wind did gently kiss the trees,
            And they did make no noise, in such a night
            Troilus methinks mounted the Troyan walls
            And sighed his soul toward the Grecian tents,
            Where Cressid lay that night.
JESSICA: In such a night
            Did Thisbe fearfully o'ertrip the dew
            And saw the lion's shadow ere himself
            And ran dismay'd away.

LORENZO: In such a night
            Stood Dido with a willow in her hand
            Upon the wild sea-banks, and waft her love
            To come again to Carthage.

JESSICA: In such a night
            Medea gathered the enchanted herbs
            That did renew old Aeson.

LORENZO: In such a night
            Did Jessica steal from the wealthy Jew
            And with an unthrift love did run from Venice
            As far as Belmont.

JESSICA: In such a night
            Did young Lorenzo swear he loved her well,
            Stealing her soul with many vows of faith,
            And ne'er a true one.

LORENZO: In such a night
            Did pretty Jessica (like a little shrew)
            Slander her love, and he forgave it her. (V.i.1–22)

All of Lorenzo's references are positive about the outcome of love, while all of Jessica's references are pessimistic. Were they play-acting, as lovers do, or do these lines indicate that Shakespeare did not have confidence that Lorenzo and Jessica's love would endure as it was based on an attack on the father?

From the analysis of a number of plays including *King Lear* and *The Tempest*, we have learned how the father-daughter relationship that excludes the mother was important to Shakespeare. The Shylock-Jessica relationship fits into this model, but there is a significant difference. Jessica is the only daughter to rob and betray her father. Desdemona and Cordelia make claims to be independent of their fathers in selecting their mates but they never repudiate their fathers as Jessica does.

JESSICA: Farewell, and if my fortune be not crossed,
            I have a father, you a daughter, lost. (II.v.54–55)

Earlier she expressed some guilt about her decision to flee from her father's house.

JESSICA: Alack, what heinous sin is it in me
            To be ashamed to be my father's child!
            But though I am a daughter to his blood

> I am not to his manners. O Lorenzo,
> If thou keep promise, I shall end this strife,
> Become a Christian and thy loving wife. (II.iii.15–20)

Jessica is the only character in Shakespeare's works to be ashamed of her father and to betray him. In all other plays the daughter is portrayed as loving. Only here did Shakespeare permit the possibility of open hostility between daughter and father.

A psychoanalytic summary

Antonio is the masochistic homosexual, Bassanio the ambitious heterosexual and Shylock the castrator, but where shall we put the author of this play? I suggest midway between the three. Portia, the woman who solves the problem, is a masculine woman and finds ways to declare her love for Bassanio before he has made his choice of caskets. Then, disguised as a man, she is highly effective as the doctor of law and she saves Antonio from a symbolic castration. Such masculine women are often a compromise solution between homosexual and heterosexual strivings. If Shakespeare was close to Antonio the masculinity of Portia may make her acceptable as a bisexual individual. If Shakespeare, like Antonio, had an unconscious wish for self-castration as a way of gaining Bassanio's favour, this wish was projected onto Shylock, eliminating the danger of castration emanating from the woman; on the contrary, she protects Antonio from Shylock. We can look upon the play as Shakespeare moving from masochistic and self-castrating homosexuality to a measure of heterosexuality, even though it remains a qualified heterosexuality. This constitutes a psychoanalytic interpretation of this play.

There is yet another problem to consider. If I am right and Antonio, who is so dull, is the psychological centre of the play, why is Shylock the symbolic castrator endowed with so much life and energy, leading us to think that he is the centre of the play? In general we can say that Shakespeare's endowed his villains—including Richard III, Iago and Edmund as well as Shylock—with vitality. He knew how to harness aggression in the service of creativity. A castration wish is allowed to dominate the play. In the end, *The Merchant of Venice* represents an attempt to deal with the sadistic and masochistic part of Shakespeare's unconscious. In the play Portia triumphs over Antonio, Shakespeare's depression, as well as over homosexuality.

CHAPTER SIXTEEN

Twelfth Night: a sublimation of bisexuality in homosexuality

It is well known to us from Sonnet 62 that Shakespeare regarded self-love as a psychic danger. In this play he tried another technique to combat it: ridicule. It may be interesting to compare the two approaches.

Sonnet 62

Sin of self-love possesseth all mine eye
And all my soul, and all my every part;
And for this sin there is no remedy,
It is so grounded inward in my heart.
Methinks no face so gracious is as mine,
No shape so true, no truth of such account;
And for myself mine own worth do define,
As I all other in all worths surmount.
But when my glass shows me myself indeed,
Beated and chopped with tanned antiquity,
Mine own self-love quite contrary I read;
Self so self-loving were iniquity.

> 'Tis thee, myself, that for myself I praise,
> Paintng my age with beauty of thy days.

In this sonnet the poet's biography is condensed. The first eight lines express a self gratifying narcissism but then the poet discovers signs of aging: "chopped with tanned antiquity". Now the poet recognises a split within himself; creativity is expressed as "thee, myself", that is, being praised for myself.

The play consists of the development of five different love relationships: Duke Orsino's love for Countess Olivia, Olivia's love for Cesario (the disguised Viola), Viola's love for Orsino, Malvolio's love for Olivia, and Antonio's love for Sebastian (Viola's twin brother). The opening lines of the play convey the nature of Orsino's love for Olivia.

ORSINO: If music be the food of love, play on;
        Give me excess of it, that, surfeiting,
        The appetite may sicken, and so die.
        That strain again! it had a dying fall:
        O, it came o'er my ear like the sweet sound,
        That breathes upon a bank of violets,
        Stealing and giving odour! Enough; no more:
        'Tis not so sweet now as it was before. (*Twelfth Night*, I.i.1–8)

The speech is not addressed to anyone and is left unanswered. The close association between music and love will be repeated in Cleopatra's famous line "Give me some music—music, moody food / Of us that trade in love" (II.v.1–2).

The idea that love contains within itself the seeds of its own destruction was important to Shakespeare. In *Hamlet*, Claudius says, "There lives within the very flame of love / A kind of wick or snuff that will abate it" (*Hamlet*, IV.vii.115–116).

In Act II, scene 4 the duke once more confides his views on the two genders to the disguised Viola.

ORSINO: There is no woman's sides
        Can bide the beating of so strong a passion
        As love doth give my heart; no woman's heart
        So big, to hold so much; they lack retention
        Alas, their love may be call'd appetite,

> No motion of the liver, but the palate,
> That suffer surfeit, cloyment and revolt;
> But mine is all as hungry as the sea,
> And can digest as much: make no compare
> Between that love a woman can bear me
> And that I owe Olivia. (*Twelfth Night*, II.iv.94–104)

Women's love is seen as nothing more than "appetite", or sexual attraction, while man's love comes from the liver (thought to be the seat of emotion in Shakespeare's time); this feminine appetite soon suffers "surfeit, cloyment and revolt" whereas his own love is supposedly "as hungry as the sea".

Orsino is not a heterosexual man, as we learn from his high evaluation of virginity.

ORSINO: For women are as roses, whose fair flower
           Being once displayed, doth fall that very hour. (II.iv.37–38)

Viola does not dispute this claim and only answers:

VIOLA: And so they are. Alas, that they are so,
          To die even when they to perfection grow! (II.iv.39–40)

In psychoanalytic terms what Shakespeare gives us when he portrays Orsino is a narcissistic man who has talked himself into believing he is in love. The formation of such a character is Shakespeare's achievement but we owe the understanding that this is a description of narcissistic love to Freud's 1914 essay "Narcissism: An introduction".

Viola's love for the duke is as "fantastical" as the duke's for Olivia. She has just escaped drowning when she learns that she is in Illyria, a country ruled by a bachelor duke, and decides that she is in love with him. Shakespeare does not tell us why she thinks she can be more successful in winning him disguised as a man, but the homosexual implication is that the woman can win a man when she first appeals to his homosexual impulses. To the unconscious a woman disguised as a man represents a compromise between homo- and heterosexual wishes.

The duke appoints the disguised Viola as his ambassador to Olivia and, speaking for him, she is most eloquent in her declaration of love to Olivia, who says she cannot love Orsino because she is mourning the death of her brother.

OLIVIA: Your lord does know my mind. I cannot love him.
Yet I suppose him virtuous, know him noble,
Of great estate, of fresh and stainless youth.
In voices well divulged, free, learned, and valiant;
And in dimension and the shape of nature
A gracious person. But yet I cannot love him;
He might have took his answer long ago.
VIOLA: If I did love you in my master's flame,
With such a suffering, such a deadly life,
In your denial I would find no sense;
I would not understand it.
OLIVIA: Why, what would you?
VIOLA: Make me a willow cabin at your gate
And call upon my soul within the house.
Write loyal cantons of contemned love
And sing them loud even in the dead of night.
Halloo your name to the reverberate hills
And make the babbling gossip of the air
Cry out "Olivia!" Oh, you should not rest
Between the elements of air and earth,
But you should pity me. (I.v.231–250)

Such magnificent language will win Olivia's love, but for the messenger, not Orsino.

Olivia falls in love not with the duke but with his messenger. The comic situation of a woman falling in love with another woman disguised as a man must have given Shakespeare pleasure; the implied lesson is that it is not a person we fall in love with but what we imagine that person to be.

When the duke sends Viola to Olivia he seems almost to know that Viola will obtain Olivia's love for herself.

VIOLA: Sure, my noble lord,
If she be so abandon'd to her sorrow
As it is spoke, she never will admit me.
ORSINO: Be clamorous and leap all civil bounds

> Rather than make unprofited return.
>
> VIOLA: Say I do speak with her, my lord, what then?
>
> ORSINO: O, then unfold the passion of my love,
>   Surprise her with discourse of my dear faith:
>   It shall become thee well to act my woes;
>   She will attend it better in thy youth
>   Than in a nuncio's of more grave aspect.
>
> VIOLA: I think not so, my lord.
>
> ORSINO: Dear lad, believe it;
>   For they shall yet belie thy happy years,
>   That say thou art a man. (I.iv.18–31)

Orsino trusts that Olivia is more likely to respond to his love if it is transmitted by a "lad". Viola and the audience know that the victory will go to homosexual love.

When Viola is admitted to meet Olivia her first speech is as narcissistic as Orsino's love.

> VIOLA: Most radiant, exquisite and unmatchable beauty,—I
>   pray you, tell me if this be the lady of the house,
>   for I never saw her: I would be loath to cast away
>   my speech, for besides that it is excellently well
>   penned, I have taken great pains to con it. (I.v.181–185)

Subtly, Viola draws attention to herself as a poet and away from Orsino.

Love yields to narcissism; the poetry of the speech is at issue, not the love Orsino bears Olivia. When, after much negotiation, Olivia draws back her veil so Viola can see her face, Viola exclaims:

> VIOLA: Lady, you are the cruell'st she alive,
>   If you will lead these graces to the grave
>   And leave the world no copy. (I.v.259–261)

We are familiar with Viola's argument from the procreation sonnets, as exemplified in Sonnet 1.

> From fairest creatures we desire increase,
> That thereby beauty's rose might never die, (lines 1–2)

The conversation continues:

OLIVIA: How does he love me?
VIOLA: With adorations, fertile tears,
          With groans that thunder love, with sighs of fire. (*Twelfth Night*,
          I.v.228–230)

Malvolio

Shakespeare has given us many hints that Orsino and Olivia are too narcissistic to establish a love relationship. Olivia falls in love with the eloquence of the messenger. In the audience this narcissism is bound to evoke hostility and Malvolio becomes the target of this hostility.

Malvolio's name, in Latin, means "ill wisher", implying that if he has his way any one contacting him will not fare well. In the play Shakespeare makes him a puritan incapable of joy. Olivia tells him, "O! you are sick of self-love, Malvolio" (I.v.97). Malvolio is steward to Olivia's household and a comic character in his efforts to keep Olivia's uncle Sir Toby and his drinking companion Sir Andrew sober. He has evoked the ire of Maria, Olivia's lady in waiting.

MARIA: The devil a puritan that he is, or anything constantly, but a time-
          pleaser,
          an affectioned ass, that cons state without book and
          utters it by great swarths. The best persuaded of himself: so
          crammed (as he thinks) with excellencies, that it is his grounds of
          faith that all that look on him love him; and on that vice in him
          will my revenge find notable cause to work. (II.iii.124–129)

Imitating Olivia's handwriting, Maria writes a letter that she lets Malvolio find, in which "Olivia" states that she is in love with him and urges him to assume the greatness that will be bestowed upon him by her love. He is instructed to keep smiling and dress in a ridiculous fashion. Malvolio follows the advice in the letter and is humiliated, to the satisfaction of Maria, Sir Toby, and Sir Andrew.

Garber has pointed out that in the letter Malvolio found he was asked to cross-dress sexually as well as cross social lines. In Elizabethan law cross-dressing along social lines was strictly forbidden. The branched velvet gown is a cloth reserved for nobility; Malvolio is "duped into wearing unfashionable and uncomfortable cross-gartered yellow stockings" (Garber, 2004: p. 512).

Malvolio learns at the end that it was Maria, not Countess Olivia, who wrote the letter that encouraged his ridiculous behaviour. The punishment for self-love is deflected onto Malvolio.

The fifth act

In the last act, the plot of this play unravels when Viola, still disguised as Cesario, meets her twin brother Sebastian. The other characters are astounded by the siblings' likeness.

ORSINO: One face, one voice, one habit, and two persons!
          A natural perspective, that is and is not!
          (*Twelfth Night*, V.i.208–209)

Sebastian recognises Antonio, who in turn is also surprised to see Sebastian and Viola together.

ANTONIO: How have you made division of yourself?
           An apple, cleft in two, is not more twin
           Than these two creatures. Which is Sebastian? (V.i.215–217)

In a happy solution Orsino can have Viola and Olivia will have Sebastian. Viola becomes a woman.

VIOLA: If nothing lets to make us happy both
         But this my masculine usurped attire,
         Do not embrace me till each circumstance
         Of place, time, fortune, do cohere and jump
         That I am Viola. (V.i.242–246)
               …
ORSINO: Give me thy hand,
          And let me see thee in thy woman's weeds. (V.i.266–267)
               …
          Here is my hand. You shall from this time be
          Your master's mistress. (V.i.317–318)
          The play proper ends with Orsino's pronouncement:
ORSINO: Cesario, come,

> For so you shall be, while you are a man.
> But when in other habits you are seen,
> Orsino's mistress and his fancy's queen. (V.i.379–381)

It should not escape our attention that Duke Orsino repeats three times, in somewhat different language, that the transition from Cesario to Viola has created no difficulty for him. If anything, the transition from homosexuality to heterosexuality was easy and pleasurable. Based on clinical experiences where such a transition is made either from homosexuality to heterosexuality or in the other direction (the latter often happening after the children leave home), it is never as simple as it appears in this play. Only in a comedy can such a transition be accomplished painlessly and happily. In this play a happy solution was found to a problem that in real life is usually fraught with conflict.

The song of the clown

At the very end of the play the fool, Feste, appears alone and brings the story to an end with a song. The song has often been criticised. I quote from the Variorum edition:

> After Shakespeare had cleared this stage, he should exhibit his clown afresh, and with so poor a recommendation as his song, which is utterly unconnected with the subject of the preceding comedy. (1901: p. 314)

I reached the opposite conclusion: the play and the song are connected, but the connection becomes understandable, only if we see it as an unconscious connection based on the clown representing Shakespeare speaking more directly about his own sexual history. In Shakespearean plays the fool often serves as something like a Greek chorus: he is an actor in the play but he is not as involved in the action and therefore is also an observer and commentator. The full potentiality of the fool will be reached in *King Lear*, but the song in this play provides depth to the otherwise superficial comedy.

FOOL (SINGS):   When that I was and a little tiny boy,
        With hey, ho, the wind and the rain,
        A foolish thing was but a toy,

For the rain it raineth every day.
But when I came to man's estate,
With hey, ho, the wind and the rain,
'Gainst knaves and thieves men shut their gate,
For the rain it raineth every day.
But when I came, alas! to wive,
With hey, ho, the wind and the rain,
By swaggering could I never thrive,
For the rain it raineth every day.
But when I came unto my beds,
With hey, ho, the wind and the rain,
With toss-pots still had drunken heads,
For the rain it raineth every day.
A great while ago the world begun,
With hey, ho, the wind and the rain,
But that's all one, our play is done,
And we'll strive to please you every day.
(*Twelfth Night*, V.i.383–402)

The song is about the penis. "A foolish thing ... but a toy" describes the penis in childhood, which is not yet the sexual organ of adulthood and only a toy, a reference to masturbation. The line "it raineth every day" refers to childhood as an unhappy period, while "when I came to man's estate" is a reference to adolescence. The penis is no longer a toy but a dangerous instrument and men should "shut their gate". This is expressed in "'Gainst knaves and thieves men shut their gate". In the third stanza the poet is an adult, and "when I came ... to wive" means when he reached sexual maturity. "By swaggering could I never thrive", meaning he lacked the capacity to impress women by boasting about his sexual powers. In the fourth stanza the poet is married ("I came unto my beds"). The word "toss-pots", two lines later, refers to empty bottles, implying heavy drinking. The line "it raineth every day" is repeated, meaning the poet was depressed. The song can be read like an autobiographical veiled confession by Shakespeare about why this play was written. The song reveals Shakespeare's belief that there was real sadness all through his life, from infancy onward. It is the sadness that is lurking behind the comedy.

REFERENCES

Adler, A. (1911). The masculine protest is the central problem of neurosis. In: H. Nunberg & E. Federn (Eds.), *Minutes of the Vienna Psychoanalytic Society 1910–1911*, vol. III, 1974. 140–151. New York: International University Press.

Alexander, F. (1933). A note on Falstaff. *Psychoanalytic Quarterly, 2*: 592–606.

Auden, W. H. (2000). *Lectures on Shakespeare*. Princeton: Princeton University Press.

Bak, R. C. (1946). Masochism in paranoia. *Psychoanalytic Quarterly 15*: 285–301.

Bergmann, M. V. (2000). *What I Heard in the Silence: Role Reversal, Trauma, and Creativity in the Lives of Women*. Madison, CT: International Universities Press.

Bergmann, M. S. & Bergman, M. (2008). *What Silent Love Hath Writ: A Psychoanalytic Exploration of Shakespeare's Sonnets*. New York: Gotschna Ventures, Inc.

Bergmann, M. S. (2009). The inability to mourn and the inability to Love in Shakespeare's *Hamlet*. *Psychoanalytic Quarterly 78*: 397–423.

Bergmann, M. S. (2010). The Oedipus complex and psychoanalytic technique. *Psychoanalytic Inquiry 30*: 535–540.

Bloom, H. (1973). *The Anxiety of Influence: A Theory of Poetry*. New York: Oxford University Press.

Bloom, H. (1994). *The Western Canon*. New York: Harcourt Brace.

Bloom, H. (1998). *Shakespeare: The Invention of the Human*. New York: Riverhead Books.

Bradley, A. C. (1904). *Shakespearean Tragedy: Lectures on Hamlet, Othello, King Lear, Macbeth*. New York: St. Martin's Press.

Bradley, A. C. (1969). King Lear. In *Shakespeare: King Lear*. London: Aurora Publishers Incorporated.

Bucknill, J. C. (1867). *The Mad Folk of Shakespeare*. London: Macmillan.

Burrow, C., (Ed.) (2002). *William Shakespeare: The Complete Sonnets and Poems*. Oxford, UK: Oxford University Press.

Cohen, J. M. & Cohen, M. J. (1960). *The Penguin Dictionary of Quotations*. Harmondsworth, New York: Penguin.

Coleridge, S. T. (1811–12). Shakespeare and Milton. In: *Shakespeare: King Lear*. 33–44. London: Aurora Publishers Incorporated.

Coleridge, S. T. (1818). *Lectures and Notes on Shakspeare and Other Poets*. Boston: Adamant Media Corporation.

Devereux, G. (1953). Why Oedipus killed Laius. *International Journal of Psychoanalysis 34*: 132–141.

Eissler, K. M. (1971). *Discourse on Hamlet and HAMLET: a Psychoanalytic Inquiry*. New York: International Universities Press.

Eliot, T. S. (1932). *Selected Essays 1917–1931*. New York: Harcourt Brace.

Faber, M. D. (Ed.), (1970). *The Design Within: Psychoanalytic Approaches to Shakespeare*. New York: Science House.

Ferenczi, S. (1929). The Unwelcome Child and his Death Instinct. In: *Final Contributions to the Theory and Technique of Psycho-Analysis*. 102–107. London: Hogarth.

Freud, S. (1900). *The Interpretation of Dreams. S. E.,* 4–5: 1–632. London: Hogarth.

Freud, S. (1905a). *Three Essays on Sexuality and other Works. S. E.,* 7: 125–245. London: Hogarth.

Freud, S. (1905b). On psychotherapy. *S. E.,* 7: 255–268. London: Hogarth.

Freud, S. (1905c). Psychopathic characters on the stage. *S. E.,* 7: 305–310. London: Hogarth.

Freud, S. (1908). Creative writers and day-dreaming. *S. E.,* 9: 141–153. London: Hogarth.

Freud, S. (1910). A special type of choice of object made by men. *S. E.,* 11: 163–175. London: Hogarth.

Freud, S. (1913a). The theme of the three caskets. *S. E.,* 12: 291–301. London: Hogarth.

Freud, S. (1913b). *Totem and Taboo. S. E.,* 13: 1–162. London: Hogarth.

Freud, S. (1914a). The moses of michelangelo. *S. E., 13*: 211–238. London: Hogarth.

Freud, S. (1914b). *On Narcissism: An introduction. S. E. 14*: 67–102. London: Hogarth.

Freud, S. (1916). *Some Character Types met with in Psycho-analytic Work. S. E., 14*: 311–333. London: Hogarth.

Freud, S. (1917). Mourning and melancholia. *S. E., 14*: 237–260. London: Hogarth.

Freud, S. (1918). The taboo of virginity. *S. E., 11*: 91–208. London: Hogarth.

Freud, S. (1922). Some neurotic mechanisms in jealousy, paranoia and homosexuality. *S. E., 18*: 223–232. London: Hogarth.

Freud, S. (1923). *A Seventeenth Century Demonological Neurosis. S. E., 19*: 72–105. London: Hogarth.

Freud, S. (1923). *The Ego and the Id. S. E., 19*: 3–66. London: Hogarth.

Freud, S. (1924). The Dissolution of the Oedipus Complex. *S. E., 19*: 173–179. London: Hogarth.

Freud, S. (1927). Fetishism. *S. E., 21*: 149–157. London: Hogarth.

Freud, S. (1937). *Construction in Analysis. S. E., 23*: 255–269. London: Hogarth.

Freud, S. (1938). *An Outline of Psycho-Analysis. S. E., 23*: 141–207. London: Hogarth.

Freud, S. (1939). *Moses and Monotheism. S. E., 23*: 3–137. London: Hogarth.

Freud, S. (1942). Psychopathic characters on the stage. *S. E., 7*: 303–310. London: Hogarth.

Furness, H. H., (Ed.) (1892). *The Tempest.* In: The New Variorum Edition of Shakespeare. Philadelphia: J. B. Lippincott Company.

Furness, H. H. (Ed.) (1901). *Twelfth Night.* In: The New Variorum Edition of Shakespeare. Philadelphia: J. B. Lippincott Company.

Furness, H. H., (Ed.) (1963). *Hamlet.* In: The New Variorum Edition of Shakespeare. Vol. One. New York: Dover Publications Inc.

Furness, H. H., (Ed.) (1966). *The Winter's Tale.* In: The New Variorum Edition of Shakespeare. New York: American Scholar Publications Inc.

Garber, M. (2004). *Shakespeare After All.* New York: Pantheon Books.

Gibbons, B. (2006). Introduction. In: *The New Cambridge Shakespeare: Measure for Measure.* Cambridge: Cambridge University Press.

Greenblatt, S. (2004). *Will in the World: How Shakespeare Became Shakespeare.* New York: W. W. Norton & Company.

Hazlitt, W. (1817). *Characters of Shakespear's Plays.* London: C. H. Reynell.

Hofling, C. K. (1957). An interpretation of shakespeare's Coriolanus. *American Imago 14*: 407–435.

Holland, N. N. (1966). *Psychoanalysis and Shakespeare.* New York: McGraw-Hill.

James, D. G. (1937). *Skepticism and Poetry: An Essay on the Poetic Imagination*. London: Allen & Unwin.

Jekels, L. (1943). The riddle of Shakespeare's *Macbeth*. In: *Selected Papers*. New York: International Universities Press. 105–130.

Jones, E. (1910). The Oedipus complex as an explanation of Hamlet's mystery. *American Journal of Psychology 21*: 72–113.

Jones, E. (1931). *On the Nightmare*. London: Hogarth.

Jones, E. (1949). *Hamlet and Oedipus*. New York: W. W. Norton.

Jones, E. (1957). *The Life and Work of Sigmund Freud, Volume III: The Last Phase 1919–1939*. New York: Basic Books.

Kermode, F. (1969). Introduction. In: *Shakespeare: King Lear*. London: Aurora Publishers Incorporated.

Kermode, F. (2000). *Shakespeare's language*. New York: Farrar, Straus and Giroux.

Klein, M. (1935). *Envy and Gratitude: a Study of Unconscious Sources*. New York: Basic Books. (English edition 1957).

Krims, M. B. (2006). *The Mind According to Shakespeare: Psychoanalysis in the Bard's Writing*. Westport, CT: Praeger Publishers.

Kris, E. (1948). Prince Hal's conflict. *Psychoanalytic Quarterly 17*: 487–506.

Lansky, M. (2001). Hidden shame, working through, and the problem of forgiveness in *The Tempest*. *Journal of the American Psychoanalytic Association. 49*: 1005–1033.

Lewin, B. D. (1948). The nature of reality, the meaning of nothing, with an Addendum on concentration. *Psychoanalytic Quarterly, 17*: 524–5.

Mahon, E. (2009). The death of Hamnet: an essay on grief and creativity. *Psychoanalytic Quarterly 78*: 425–444.

Mahoud, M. M. (1987). Introduction. In: *The Merchant of Venice*. Cambridge: Cambridge University Press.

Manheim, L. (1964). The mythical joys of Shakespeare; Or, what you *will*. In: M. D. Farber (Ed.), *The Design Within: Psychoanalytic Approaches to Shakespeare* (pp. 465–478). New York: Science House. 1970.

Masson, J. M., (Ed.) (1985). *The Complete Letters of Sigmund Freud to Wilhelm Fliess 1887–1904*. Cambridge, MA: The Belknap Press of Harvard University Press.

McGinn, C. (2006). *Shakespeare's Philosophy: Discovering the Meaning Behind the Plays*. New York: HarperCollins.

Nunberg, H. & Federn, E. (Eds.) (1974). *Minutes of the Vienna Psychoanalytic Society, vol. III*. New York: International University Press.

Nuttall, A. D. (2007). *Shakespeare the Thinker*. New Haven, CT: Yale University Press.

Oremland, J. (2005). *Death and the Fear of Finiteness in Hamlet*. San Francisco: Lake Street Editions.

Putney, R. (1962). Coriolanus and his mother. *Psychoanalytic Quarterly*. *31*: 364–381.

Rank, O. (1910). Portia's slip as a poetic utilization of a slip of the tongue. *Zentralblatt fur Psychoanalyse*, *1*: 109–116.

Riviere, J. (1932). Jealousy as a mechanism of defense. *International Journal of Psychoanalysis*. *13*: 414–424.

Sachs, H. (1923). The Tempest. *International Journal of Psychoanalysis*. *4*: 43–88.

Sachs, H. (1939). The Measure in *Measure for Measure*. *American Imago* *1*: 60–81, reprinted in: *The Creative Unconscious* (pp. 63–99). Cambridge, MA: Science-Art Publishers, 1942.

Sachs, H. (1943). *The Creative Unconscious. Studies in the Psychoanalysis of Art*. Cambridge, MA: Science-Art Publishers.

Scott-Kilvert, I., (Trans.) (1965). *Makers of Rome: Nine Lives by Plutarch*. Baltimore: Penguin Books.

Sharpe, E. F. (1946). From *King Lear* to *The Tempest*. In: *Collected Papers on Psycho-Analysis*, 1950. London: Hogarth.

Speziale-Bagliacca, R. (1980). Lear, Cordelia, Kent, and the Fool: A psychoanalytical interpretation. *International Review of Psycho-Analysis* *7*: 413–428.

Spitz, R. (1957). *No and Yes: On the Genesis of Human Communication*. New York: International Universities Press.

Spivack, M. (1973). *The Harvard Concordance to Shakespeare*. Cambridge, MA: Harvard University Press.

Spurgeon, C. F. E. (1966). *Shakespeare's Imagery and What It Tells Us*. Boston: Beacon Press Inc.

Taylor, M. P. (1927). A father pleads for the death of his son. *International Journal of Psychoanalysis 8*: 53–55.

Towne, J. E. (1921). A psychoanalytic study of Shakespeare's *Coriolanus*. *Psychoanalytic Review 8*: 84–91.

Volkan, V. D. (2007). Not letting go: From individual perenial mourners to societies with entitlement ideologies. In: L. G. Fiorini, S. Lewkowicz & T. Bokanowski (Eds.), *On Freud's Mourning and Melancholia* (pp. 90–109). London: International Psychoanalytic Association.

Wangh, M. W. (1950). *Othello*: the tragedy of Iago. *Psychoanalytic Quarterly 19*: 202–212.

Wangh, M. W. (1968). A psychoanalytic commentary on Shakespeare's *The Tragedie of King Richard the Second*. *Psychoanalytic Quarterly 37*: 212–238.

INDEX

Detailed coverage of a topic is shown in **bold**. Unattributed texts are written by William Shakespeare